A Comprehensive, Annotated Bibliography of

Selected Psychological Tests:

A Comprehensive, Annotated Bibliography of

Selected Psychological Tests:

Interpersonal Check List

MMPI Short Forms

The Blacky Pictures

by

Earl S. Taulbee

and

Thomas L. Clark

The Whitston Publishing Company
Troy, New York

TABLE OF CONTENTS

Chapter I
Interpersonal Check List

Chapter II
Short Forms of the Minnesota Multiphasic
Personality Inventory
(FAM, Hugo, Mini-Mult, Midi-Mult, Maxi-Mult, and MMPI-168)

Chapter III
The Blacky Pictures

FOREWORD

Everyone interested in the clinical or research use of psychological tests will find the present series an invaluable addition to their libraries. Earl Taulbee and Thomas Clark have made an exhaustive search of the literature and have produced a meaningful and useful annotated bibliography for the three tests in the current volume.

The undersigned is delighted to find a section on the Interpersonal Check List, since this is a theoretically sound and practically useful instrument that has not before been reviewed with this degree of thoroughness. The section on short forms of the MMPI is equally welcome since research in this area proceeds apace and researchers are spending many hours going through many sources. The work of the present authors will save them much time and ensure more complete coverage.

The section on the Blacky Test is interesting by virtue of the fact that the Blacky is one of the few projective tests based on a particular theory of personality and therefore has much theoretical as well as practical significance.

All in all, this kind of work is a tremendous boon to the rest of us, and on behalf of all the future readers of this book, I would like to express my gratitude.

WALTER G. KLOPFER, Ph.D.
Professor of Psychology
Portland State University
and
Editor, Journal of Personality Assessment

This volume is intended to be the first in a series, each of which will include both objective and projective personality tests. Individual intelligence tests will be added in future volumes. The present choice of tests was made primarily for two reasons—our interest in and use of the tests, and the illustration provided by these particular tests of the empirical vs. theoretical approaches to test derivation. The MMPI (short forms) reflects a strict empirical approach and the Blacky Pictures test, an equally strict theoretical approach, with the Interpersonal Check List reflecting a more balanced rational-empirical approach to test construction. This broad-band sampling of test types is done with the conviction that the future growth of personality assessment depends upon a more eclectic, pluralistic approach to theoretical issues and practical, clinical problems. We would not be completely honest in stating the reasons for this choice of tests without pointing out a particular bias in favor of the Interpersonal System of Personality Diagnosis and the feeling that the ICL has tremendous unrealized potential for us in psychological assessment. Further, that we have experienced the most frustration in reviewing the ICL literature and preparing this bibliography, as mentioned below.

Although an effort was made to compile totally comprehensive bibliographies, we faced diminishing returns with more exhaustive searching and, no doubt, have missed a few references. Our apologies are offered to any authors missed and we invite them to provide us with any references omitted in order that they may be included in future volumes. Nevertheless, we are satisfied with the contributions made by the references found. One computer search for ICL references from 1967 to present yielded a meager twelve articles. Sifting through *Psychological Abstracts* under the subject index headings of "Leary" and "Interpersonal Check List" would give the interested reader only three references. By comparison, the present ICL bibliography includes over 140 references from 1967 through 1979, most of which have been annotated.

The major sources of references for the bibliographies were earlier ones compiled by us, our perusal of journals, books, *Psychological Abstracts, Dissertation Abstracts International,* and Buros' *Mental Measurements Yearbook,* and *Tests in Print.*

We are indebted to the American Psychological Association for permission to reproduce from *Psychological Abstracts* those abstracts published prior to 1966, and to University Microfilms International which so graciously granted permission to use titles and abstracts from *Dissertation Abstracts International. PA* references used are followed by a listing of volume, abstract number, and year. The dissertation titles and abstracts are published with permission of University Microfilms International, publishers of *Dissertation Abstracts International* (copyright from 1952 to 1979), and may not be reproduced without their prior permission. Copies of the dissertations may be obtained by addressing requests to: University Microfilms International, 300 North Zeeb Road, Ann Arbor, Michigan 48106, or by telephoning (toll-free) 1-800-521-3042. Thanks are extended to the Editor, *Journal of Personality Assessment,* for permission to revise and republish The Blacky Pictures bibliography by Taulbee and Stenmark (1968).

Special thanks also are due the following individuals who helped to make these bibliographies possible: to Rolfe LaForge, who gave us his hardy approval and more than a handful of obscure ICL references in his manuscript *Using the ICL;* to Walter Klopfer, for his significant contribution to the Interpersonal System through his teaching and his supervision of many theses and doctoral dissertations on the ICL; to David Stenmark, for his approval of updating The Blacky Pictures bibliography and for his inspiration and personal encouragement in many ways; and, to those authors of unpublished articles who provided brief summaries of their own work.

It is hoped that students, teachers, clinicians, researchers, and others using this volume will find it as stimulating and valuable, but not as frustrating, as we have in compiling it.

E.S.T.
T.L.C.

CHAPTER I

INTERPERSONAL CHECK LIST

Introduction

The Interpersonal Check List is a list of 128 adjective phrases used to assess the conscious interpersonal perceptions people have of themselves and of others. It was developed primarily through the efforts of Rolfe LaForge and Robert Suczek (102), as part of Leary's Interpersonal System of Diagnosis. The interpersonal "diagnoses" are actually eight categories of interpersonal behavior arranged in a circular array around the orthogonal axes of Dominance-Submission (DOM) and Love-Hate (LOV). The psychological meaning of each octant in the Leary circle is clearly a function of its position in relation to the two basic axes. For instance, Docile-Dependent behavior is defined by a higher degree of LOV and a lower degree of DOM. The ICL is simply a collection of adjective phrases, drawn from everyday English usage, representing each of these categories of interpersonal behavior. It probably is best viewed as a "structured channel for communication" (99).

Several elegant features of the Interpersonal System contribute to its usefulness in both clinical and research applications. First, the basic axes, Dominance-Submission and Love-Hate, are valid and psychologically meaningful dimensions (78, 99, 103, 109, 111, 113). Independent attempts to develop circular typologies of interpersonal behavior have yielded patterns and dimensions similar to the Leary circle (46, 187, 197).

A second important feature of the Interpersonal System is that the scoring of other psychological tests along the dimensions of DOM and LOV permit direct comparisons between different "levels" of personality within an individual. So, for example, an individual may actually tend to behave in one way in relating with others (Level I-MMPI), yet see himself as relating to others in a very different way (Level II-ICL). This difference, plotted on the Leary circle, would be an index of self-deception. A number of very useful comparisons involve only ICL descriptions, e.g., comparisons between self-descriptions and descriptions of one's parents (identification), between self and ideal-self (self-acceptance) and between spouse and parent (equation), to mention just a few.

Finally, the Interpersonal System allows comparisons, like those mentioned above, between individuals. There is a host of between-person comparisons that are relevant to the interactions of dyads, families and groups, such as the accuracy of interpersonal perceptions, empathy, and complementarity.

The authors hope that this bibliography will make the ICL and the Interpersonal System more accessible and useful to clinicians and researchers. The system has strong theoretical and empirical foundations and deserves continued use and development by psychologists.

Journal and Other References

1. Adams, H. B., M. H. Robertson, and G. D. Cooper. Sensory deprivation and personality change. *J Nerv Ment Dis, 143*(3):256-265, 1966.

   43 white m psych pts were exposed to one of the following treatments: Sensory deprivation plus therapeutic tape recording (Gp I); sensory deprivation only (Gp II); or no treatment (Gp III). All Ss completed the MMPI and the ICL before and after treatment. Gp III changed very little from pre- to post-test. Gps I and II showed sig changes but of a different pattern.

2. Allan, T. K. The California Psychological Inventory and the Interpersonal Check List as predictors of success in student teaching. Master's thesis, University of Maryland, 1964.

3.   —. Personality as a predictor of student teaching success. *SPATE*, 5:12-16, 1966.

4.   Altrocchi, J. Dominance as a factor in interpersonal choice and perception. *J Abnorm Soc Psychol, 59*:303-308, 1959.   (*34*:5595, 1960)

The hypoths tested were that a person chooses to interact with, and tends to perceive other people in terms of the complement of his own degree of dominance. Ss were shown a movie depicting the interaction between 4 people, 2 of whom displayed dominant behavior, 2 submissive. Measures of the Ss own dom were compared with their answers on a sociometric questionnaire which elicited Ss' preference for the actors. The results failed to support the hypoths as stated.

5.   —, O. A. Parsons, and H. Dickoff. Changes in self-ideal discrepancy in repressors and sensitizers. *J Abnorm Soc Psychol, 61*:67-72, 1960.   (*35*:2253, 1961)

Self-ideal discrepancies were measured in "repressors" and "sensitizers." The repressors would manifest smaller self-ideal discrepancies was confirmed; not confirmed was that self-ideal discrepancies would change (repressors increase, sensitizers decrease) in response to therapy.

6.   —, and H. D. Perlitsh. Ego control patterns and attribution of hostility. *Psychol Rep, 12*(3):811-818, 1963.   (*38*:6009, 1964)

From 296 nursing students, 101 were chosen as being either repressors, expressors, expressor-sensitizers, or sensitizers on the basis of the MMPI scores. Love scores from the ICL were used to measure hostility attributed. "Repressors attributed little hostility to themselves and others, and little hostility was attributed to them by others. The degree of hostility attributed by expressors to others and by others to them was sig greater than the degree of hostility they attributed to themselves. Sensitizers were not described as particularly hostile and did not attribute much hostility to others; the degree of hostility attributed to self was slightly more in this group than in the repressors or expressors, but was significantly more for the expressor-sensitizers than for repressors or expressors."

7. Alumbaugh, R. V., and G. D. Brown. A comparison of diagnostic and interpersonal labels as perceived by the "criminally insane" and psychiatric patients. *J Clin Psychol, 25*(4):391-393, 1969.

State hosp criminally insane m inmates and psych pts were admin a series of ICLs to determine how they perceived the Self, Ideal Self, Typical Psychiatric Patient, Typical Criminally Insane Patient, and Typical Convict. The data were factor analyzed. The criminally insane label was associated with dimensions of Dominance and Hate. The psych pt label was related to the Love and Submission dimensions. The study also disclosed a racial factor operating in both groups.

8. Armstrong, R. G. The Leary Interpersonal Check List: A reliability study. *J Clin Psychol, 14*:393-394, 1958.
(*34:2983*, 1960)

Kuder-Richardson estimates of reliability were applied to six ratings obtained from a group of 50 normals and a group of 50 alcoholic males. These r_{tt}'s ranged from .953 to .976, all of them being highly sig, and no sig diffs occurring between any of the 12 reliability coefficients.

9. —, and P. A. Hauck. Sexual identification and the first figure drawn. *J Consult Psychol, 25*(1):51-54, 1961.
(*36*:3HE51A, 1962)

In m and fem coll students sex of the first figure on the DAP is related to ICL for self, parents, and ideal self. There are some diffs between the groups.

10. —, and M. Wertheimer. Personality structure in alcoholism. *Psychol Newsltr, 10*:341-349, 1959. (*34*:3189, 1960)

The ICL was admin to a gp of 50 alcoholics and 50 matched "normals." Findings indicated that the alcoholic tends to use fewer but more intense emotional reaction mechanisms, that the alcoholic perceives his mother as cold and dominant, and his father as warm and passive, that he tends to identify with neither, and that he exhibits a greater self-ideal self, and a greater wife-ideal wife, and a greater ideal self-ideal wife discrepancy than does the "normal."

11. Bain, E. Values and attitudes of militia officer cadets. In H. W. Hendrick (Ed.), *Second Annual Symposium: Psychology in the Air Force.* Colorado Springs: USAF Academy, 1971, pp. 20-22.

12. Barber, T. X., and D. S. Calverley. Hypnotizability, suggestibility, and personality: IV. A study with the Leary Interpersonal Check List. *Br J Soc Clin Psychol, 3*(2): 149-150, 1964.   (*39*:8140, 1965)

   A study of 249 Ss failed to demonstrate that either hypnotizability or suggestibility is related to personality characteritics as measured by the ICL.

13. Baumrind, D. An analysis of some aspects of the "interpersonal system." *Psychiatry, 23*:395-402, 1960.
                                   (*36*:5IF95B, 1962)

   Timothy Leary's "interpersonal system" is evaluated according to logical and methodological criteria in its application to the study of personality change resulting from psychotherapy. While ingeniously conceived, the "system" has not "yet achieved the degree of empirical validation and logical coherence that is required by research aimed at predicting change in interpersonal behavior. . .(but) because of its flexibility and relevant focus, (it) has great promise when used as a clinical instrument or in noninferential research by experts familiar with its special advantages and limitations."

14. Beard, B. H., and V. Pishkin. Self-concept changes in training medical and nursing students. *Dis Nerv Syst, 31*(9): 616-623, 1970.

   Ss were 11 employed nursing assistants (Gp I), 25 psychiatric nursing students (Gp II), 21 public health nursing students (Gp III), and 26 m senior medical students. Each S completed ICL self and ideal-self descriptions before and after a term of study. On the love dimension, there were no diffs between the gps, between the self and ideal-self descriptions and between the first and second testings. On the dom dimension, Gp II scored lower than all the other gps on the first testing, self description, while Gp IV scored lower than all the other gps on the second testing, self description. Between the first and second testing, the medical students dropped in dom attributed to themselves and showed an increase in the self-ideal discrepancy. The nursing students, on the other hand, showed an increase in dom attributed to themselves and a reduction in their self-ideal discrepancy. These changes and gp diffs were related to the training experience encountered by the different students.

15. Bentler, P. M. Interpersonal orientation in relation to hypnotic susceptibility. *J. Consult Psychol,* 27(5):426-431, 1963.   (*38*:4226, 1964)

Two samples of women (N=37, N=47) described themselves on the ICl and were hypnotized according to the Stanford scales, Forms A and C. One sample of 43 men described themselves on the ICL; these men were hypnotized according to procedures of Form A. The Docile-Dependent, Cooperative-Overconventional, and Responsible-Hypernormal octants showed the highest correls with hypnotizability. ICL scores based on factor analyses showed that a "positive" and affiliative interpersonal orientation correl positively with hypnotizability, while the "negative" orientation factor and the dominance-submission factor were unrelated to hypnotizability. A comparison of correls of hypnotic measures with ICL scores indicated that the correls which approached or reached sig for the combined fem samples were almost uniformly smaller for Form C than for Form A.

16. —. The Interpersonal Check List. In O. K. Buros (Ed.), *The sixth mental measurements yearbook.* Highland Park, New Jersey: Gryphon Press, 127-128, 1965.

Discusses strengths and weaknesses of the ICL and makes recommendations for future research. "While this reviewer clearly recommends the use of the ICL in practical situations, he urges focus on further test development research."

17. Bergquist, W. H., and J. E. Crandall. Perceptions of self and group roles as a function of repression-sensitization and

tolerance-intolerance of ambiguity. *J Psychol, 81*(1): 97-103, 1972.

Coll *S*s completed the R-S scale, a tolerance-intolerance of ambiguity scale, and the ICL (for self and 3 gp role targets). Repressors attributed less hostility to themselves than did sensitizers or medium-scoring *S*s. Sensitizers showed greater self-effacement than did the other *S*s. The "task specialist" role was associated with level of intolerance of ambiguity. "Social specialist" and "group dissenter" roles were largely independent of *S*s' own scores on R-S or intolerance.

18. Bieri, J., and R. Lobeck. Self-concept differences in relation to identification, religion and social class. *J Abnorm Soc Psychol, 62*(1):94-98, 1961.
                                        (*36*:3GC94B, 1962)

This study focused on the relationships between. . .3 socialization variables of parental ident, religious affiliation, and social class to 2 aspects of the self-concept, dom and love. . . .No sig diffs in self-concept scores as a function of parental ident were observed. . . .Catholic *S*s have sig higher love scores than do Jewish *S*s, and the former have sig higher love than dom scores. . . Upper class *S*s have sig higher dom scores than lower class *S*s, and upper class *S*s are sig higher on dom than on love.

19. Blank, L. *Psychological evaluation in psychotherapy: Ten case histories.* Chicago: Aldine Publishing Co., 1964.

ICL data are presented in 9 of 10 case histories. Protocols include the Rorschach, TAT, DAP, MMPI, WAIS and a diagnostic interview. In addition to self descriptions, *S*s described how they felt others saw them or how they would like to be.

20. Boe, E. E., E. F. Gocka, and W.S. Kogan. The effect of group psychotherapy on interpersonal perceptions of psychiatric patients. *Newsltr Res Psychol, 7*(4):32, 1965. (Also, *Multivariate Behav Res, 1*:177-187, 1966)

Matched gps of *S*s were randomly assigned to small group psychotherapy and to a *C* condition. The Revised ICL was admin 3 times (0, 3, & 6 weeks) from the time therapy began with 5 instructional sets (I am, Most people are, etc.). Results suggested that group thearpy influenced the interpersonal perceptions of participants in the direction of seeing themselves and others as less assertive and pompous. Seven of the 18 main effects of instructional set were sig and suggested that pts tend to see themselves as unassertive and indulgent of others. Their view of other people was just the opposite.

21. —, and W. S. Kogan. An analysis of various methods for deriving the social desirability score. *Psychol Rep, 14*(1):23-29, 1964. (*39*:1717, 1965)

Seven methods of deriving the SD for the ICL were evaluated by examining their intercorrelations, their correl with 5 MMPI SD measures, and their ability to detect Ss instructed to fake SD responses. The results indicated that SD scores discriminated SD fakers about equally well, that SD scores based only on the tendency to endorse SD items correl least with MMPI SD measures, and various SD scores based upon all the items in the ICL were highly correlated.

22. Boyd, H. S., and V. V. Sisney. Immediate self-image confrontation and changes in self-concept. *J Consult Psychol, 31*(3):291-294, 1967.

A gp of psych inpts were given the ICL following self-image confrontation via video tape, and then compared with a C gp not experiencing self-image confrontation. The findings revealed that the self-concept of the E Ss shifted in the direction of less pathology; the 3 aspects of the self (self-concept, ideal self-concept, and public self-concept) approached one another more closely after the self-image confrontation; and, the self/self-as-others-see him (public self) distance decreased. It was concluded that after one exposure the pathology level of the E gp became less extreme, and remained the same or became more extreme in the C group. These results remained over a period of at least 2 weeks.

23. Briar, S., and J. Bieri. A factor analytic and trait inference study of the Leary Interpersonal Check List. *J Clin Psychol, 19*:193-198, 1963. (*39*:5040, 1965)

250 Ss were admin the ICL. An intercorrelation matrix was computed from octant scores, which indicated factors of dominance, love, and inferiority feelings. Forty social workers judged Ss and their judgments for dom and love were consistent with the factor loadings of these 2 dimensions. The results support Leary's hypoth that the ICL consists of love and dom dimensions but the findings differ in what octants should be used in computing the dimension scores.

24. Brooks, M., and C. H. Hillman. Parent-daughter relationship as factors in nonmarriage studied in identical twins. *J of Marriage & the Family*, 27(3):383-385, 1965.
                                        (*39*:14605, 1965)

Investigates parent ident and dom patterns of married and never-married twin daughters (N=18 pairs). Strength of the variables was measured by the ICL. The hypoths that married daughters had mother ident and equal parental dom, and that never-married daughters had father ident and maternal dom were not supported. Rather, a tendency was noted that never-married daughters had a closer mother ident. Parents were perceived as equally dominating by both gps. There was an indication that the probability of marriage for one twin is dependent upon that of the twin partner.

25. Cairns, R. B., and M. Lewis. Dependency and the reinforcement value of a verbal stimulus. *J Consult Psychol*, 26(1):1-8, 1962.   (*37*:4976, 1963)

Three measures of dependency—the EPPS, ICL, and a behavioural measure—were moderately related. Ss with low scores on the inventories judged the verbal reinforcement stimulus as negative or neutral. The low gp shows a sig decrement when verbally reinforced for producing aggressive sentences, no diffs for producing dependency words.

26. Cohen, C. P., D. L. Johnson, and P. G. Hanson. Interpersonal changes among psychiatric patients in human relations training. *J Pers Assess*, 35(5):472-479, 1971.

Ss were 85 VAH pts who volunteered for a Patient's Training Laboratory (PTL) program. The MMPI was used to measure Levels I-S and III-MM. The ICL was completed for the self (II-

S) and ideal-self (V). All measures were repeated after a 4-week PTL course. Before the training, the men showed sig variations in both level I-S and Level III-MM summary scores, with more rebellious-distrustful and fewer cooperative-over conventional summary points than expected by chance. For comparison between pre- and post-scores, Ss were assigned to halves of the interpers system; i.e., 2 gps consisting of 4 of the octants. Changes from octants *3, 4, 5, 6* to octants *2, 1, 8, 7* occurred only at the level of Public Behavior. Changes from octants *4, 5, 6, 7* (low dom) to octants *3, 2, 1, 8* (high dom) occurred at the I-S, II-S, and III-MM levels. Changes from octants *2, 3, 4, 5* (oppositional) to *6, 7, 8, 1* (affiliative) did not occur at any level.

27. Collier, B. N., Jr. Comparisons between adolescents with and without diabetes. *Personnel Guid J, 47*(7):679-684, 1969.

    125 adolescent diabetics were matched with non-diabetic gp and comparisons made on the ICL. Analysis indicates that the individual with diabetes presents self-descriptions similar to his non-diabetic counterpart.

28. Cone, J. D. Social desirability, marital satisfaction, and concomitant perceptions of self and spouse. *Psychol Rep, 28*(1):173-174, 1971.

    Data from Luckey's (1964) study of marital satisfaction and self-spouse perceptions were analyzed in terms of SD. Correls were calculated between 64 pairs of ICL adjectives and marital adjustment scores. These adjective-adjustment correls were themselves highly correl with the SD scale values of the adjective pairs, for both self and spouse perceptions. Interpretation depends upon one's general interpretation of SD as either a nuisance or a clinically useful construct.

29. Cooper, G. D., H. B. Adams, and L. D. Cohen. Personality changes after sensory deprivation. *J Nerv Ment Dis, 140*(2):103-118, 1965.   (*39*:13642, 1965)

    40 white m psych inpts served as Ss, ½ receiving 3 hrs of deprivation and ½ serving as *C* Ss. Two hypoths were tested: (1) that psych pts would improve following a brief period of social isola-

tion, and (2) differential responses to such deprivation would be related to personality differences. Both hypoths were supported.

30. Crandall, J. E. Self-perception and interpersonal attraction as related to tolerance-intolerance of ambiguity. *J Pers, 37*(1):127-140, 1969.

Budner's Scale of Tolerance-Intolerance of Ambiguity was admin to about 70 coll *S*s. The upper third of the distribution, which was relatively intolerant of ambiguity (IA) and the more tolerant lower third (TA) then completed the ICL describing themselves and one very good friend of the same sex. In describing themselves, the IA gp endorsed more items in octants *5, 6, 7,* and *8* and fewer items in octants *2* and *3* than did the TA gp. In describing their friends, the IA *S*s endorsed more items overall than did TA *S*s. No individual octants differed sig, though octants *6, 7,* and *8* reflected this main effect most clearly. Both gps described their friends as mostly responsible (*8*) and cooperative (*7*), with very low rebelliousness and self effacement (*4* & *5*). Correls were calculated between each *S*'s self-descriptions and friend-descriptions. For IA *S*s the median correl was .44 whereas for TA *S*s the median correl was .03. In an attempt to assess the possible effects of SD in self- and friend-ratings, the author had 22 advanced psychology students read the moderate ICL items and rank the octants for their desirability in a friend. It is tentatively concluded that TA *S*s are more likely to describe themselves in a socially desirable manner.

31. — Effects of intolerance of ambiguity upon interpersonal attraction. *Psychol Rep, 26*:550, 1971.

In contrast to earlier findings, tolerance for ambiguity was associated with greater likability. Even *S*s who were intolerant of ambiguity preferred others who were more tolerant. ICL correlates of ambiguity tolerance-intolerance were similar to earlier findings (see Ref. No. 30).

32. Curtis, G., M. Fogel, D. McEvoy, and C. Zarate. Urine and plasma corticosteroids. Psychological tests and effectiveness of psychological defenses. *Psychiatr Res, 7*(4): 237-247, 1970.

Used the TMAS, the Nowlis Social Affection Scale and the Leary Hostility Scale to study the psychological correlates of urinary 17-OHCS. The Leary Hostility Scale was positively related to urinary 17-OHCS.

33. Davis, J., R. Morrill, J. Fawcett, V. Upton, P. K. Bondy, and H. M. Spiro. Apprehension and elevated serum cortisol levels. *J Psychosom Res, 6*(2):83-86, 1962.
(*37*:5108, 1963)

Plasma hydrocortisone levels of 15 volunteer Ss were measured in a "first time" situation when the Ss were unfamiliar with the blood drawing situation and C situations where the Ss were accustomed to the blood drawing procedures. There was a sig increase in the blood hydrocortisone levels in the "first time" situation. The ICL indicated that "first time" reactors were low on the following dimensions: managerial-autocratic, competitive-narcissistic, and aggressive-sadistic.

34. DeForest, J. W., T. K. Roberts, and J. R. Hays. Drug abuse: A family affair? *J Drug Issues, 4*(2):130-134, 1974.

The personal and interpers behavior patterns of mothers of adolescent drug clinic pts and a C gp were compared using the ICL and MMPI. The E gp of mothers were sig less identified with their mothers than were the C mothers. A sig number of E mothers described their spouses as hostile, critical, and arrogant, and their children as hostile and resentful. It was concluded that members of drug abuse families may be help-rejecting and that mothers can serve as mediators between hostile fathers and children.

35. DeSoto C. B., and J. L. Kuethe. Perception of mathematical properties of interpersonal relations. *Percept Mot Skills, 8*:279-286, 1958.   (*34*:712, 1960)

Differential perception of the abstract mathematical properties of several interpers relations characterized responses of 60 coll Ss, 12 adults, and 18 9- and 10-year-old children. For example, most Ss perceived the transitive, asymmetrical, and irreflexive properties of an interper relation which objectively was a partial or complete ordering ("makes more money than" or "is older than"). Equivalence relations, weak ordering, and dominance relations were also included. There were diffs among age gps in assignment of properties to affective relationships.

36. Dinitz, S., A. R. Mangus, and B. Pasamanick. Integration and conflict in self-other conceptions as factors in mental illness. *Sociometry, 22*:44-55, 1959.

(*34*:1623, 1960)

The findings from a study of 140 institutionalized mental pts using the ICL include: (1) Patient self-concepts do not in general appreciably differ from the concepts of them held by. . . (sig others). (2) Pts tend to view sig others. . .differently from the way these persons view themselves. (3) Pt self-concepts, past, present, and ideal, and the discrepancies among them are almost wholly unrelated to age, sex, diagnosis, length of hosp stay, case outcome, or any of the many other criteria data. These findings suggest that the problem is the person's inability to perceive others realistically and to play his roles in such a way as to lead to a "changing definition of him by others and by himself."

37. Dizney, H. F., and K. Yamamoto. Graduate education students' preferences among professors. *Psychology in the Schools, 4*(1):33-35, 1967.

54 graduate students preferred the following types of faculty members in ranked order: Teacher, socialite, researcher, administrator. Intercorrelations with the ICL revealed that these preferences were based upon the students' needs to be led, directed, and advised by their professors.

38. Doyle, C. W. The relationship between anxiety and self-ideal discrepancy in delinquent adolescents. Master's thesis.

39. Dupont, R. L., Jr., and H. Grunebaum. Willing victims: The husbands of paranoid women. *Am J Psychiatry, 125*(2):151-159, 1968.

*S*s were 16 married paranoid psychotic women and their husbands. The *S*s were divided into 3 sub-gps based on the wife's diagnosis: Gp I - paranoid state (9 couples); Gp II - paranoid

schizophrenia (4 couples); and Gp III - "other diagnostic categories" (3 couples). Three hour-long interviews were held with
each couple (one with the wife, one with the husband, and one
with both together). The focus was on the marital relationship
and the history of the individual's interpers relationships. A complete psychiatric history was obtained from each husband. The
MMPI and ICL were admin to the Ss. The ICL data confirmed
the clinical impression that Gp I husbands saw their mothers
not only as unusually loving, but more significantly, as unusually
dominant. This was in contrast to Gp II husbands who saw their
mothers as very loving but not particularly dominant.

40. Eberlein, L., and J. Park. Self-concept/ideal self-concept
congruence and rated effectiveness of counselor trainees. *Counselor Educ Supv, 10*(2):126-132, 1971.

Counselor trainees completed the ICL with a "set" for self-
concept and self-ideal at the beginning and end of their training
year. The congruence between self and ideal was tested and related to supervisor ratings and practicum grades. The results suggested the presence of an optimal range of congruence.

41. —, J. Park, and W. Matheson. Self-ideal congruence in five
occupational groups. *Alberta J Educ Res, 17*(2):95-
103, 1971.

Using the ICL, self-concept and ideal self-concept measures were
obtained on samples of counselor trainees, teachers in training,
priests, 10th graders, and army officer cadets. Sig diffs were
found among the 5 gps in self-ideal discrepancy scores. Priests
showed the greatest discrepancy, army officers and counselor
trainees showed the least.

42. Edelson, R. I., and E. Seidman. Use of videotaped feedback
in altering interpersonal perceptions of married couples:
A therapy analogue. *J Consult Clin Psychol, 43*(2):244-
250, 1975.

The interpers perception of married, university students partici-
pating in a therapy analogue study was assessed using a modified
and combined version of the Laing and Leary interpers methods.
Study assessed the effect of focused videotaped and verbal feed-

back as compared with that of just verbal feedback or no feedback in altering interpers perception. The hypoth re effects of the various conditions was strongly supported. The greatest changes occurred with videotaped plus verbal feedback, then with verbal feedback only and then with no feedback. There were no sig diffs between the last 2 conditions. No sig main effect for sex or octants. Changes occurred in perspectives pertaining to the self but not those pertaining to spouse.

43. Edwards, A. L. Social desirability and probability of endorsement of items in the Interpersonal Check List. *J Abnorm Soc Psychol, 55*:394-396, 1957.
                                                    (33:1022, 1959)

It has been possible to predict, with a high degree of accuracy, the probabilities of endorsement of particular statements in (self-description) personality inventory items; probabilities of endorsement are directly related to the SDS values of items. The study endeavored to determine whether the relationship between probability of endorsement and SDS value would be found when Ss assessed themselves anonymously. A correl of .83 was found. The correl obtained "is of sufficient magnitude to indicate that assurance of anonymity does not eliminate nor drastically change the nature of the relationship previously found between probability of endorsement and social desirability scale value."

44. —. Social desirability and the description of others. *J Abnorm Soc Psychol, 59*:434-436, 1959. *(34*:5767, 1960)

Ss were asked to use Leary's ICL to describe people they liked, disliked and knew well but neither liked nor disliked. SDS values had been obtained on each of the 128 items of the ICL in a previous study by Edwards (see Ref. No. 304). The present list selections were evaluated in terms of this dimension. Liked people are characterized by items high in SD; disliking people correlates less, but in the predicted direction. A positive relationship also exists between a S's own SD score and that he attributes to others.

45. Fineberg, B. L., and J. Lowman. Affect and status dimensions of marital adjustment. *J of Marriage & the Family, 37*(1):155-160, 1975.

The ICL and the inventory of Family Feelings were admin to 10 maritally adjusted and 10 maladjusted couples. Data from the self-report measure were consistent with the affective dimension of the ICL.

46. Foa, U. G. Convergences in the analysis of the structure of interpersonal behavior. *Psychol Rev, 68*:341-353, 1961.

A review of the findings of Carter (1954), Borgatta et al. (1958), Schaefer et al. (1959) and Leary (1957) reveals strong convergence toward a circular ordering of categories around orthogonal axes roughly equivalent to Leary's Lov and Dom dimensions. The author presents a facet analysis which yields a similar circumplex structure. Eight profiles are defined by the crossing of 3 dichotomous facets: rejection or acceptance, self or other and emotional or social. These facets are conceptualized as the content, the object and the mode of action, respectively.

47. Frost, R. P. Some personality characteristics of education students. *Alberta J Educ Res, 9*:132-139, 1963.

48. —. A semantic differential analysis of the Leary Adjectival Check List. *J Clin Psychol, 27*(3):372-375, 1971.

The Leary ACL was analyzed for measures of meaning or connotation, using the Semantic Differential technique. Each of the 128 adjectives was judged by 50 students. A principle Components Analysis with Varimax Rotation gave 2 factors, Dynamism and Evaluation. Scores on 2 SDT scales each loading high on one of the 2 factors were used to plot a measuring structure for the adjectives. A revision of the ACL was suggested on the basis of the outcome.

49. Gartner, D., and H. S. Goldstein. Leary's interpersonal diagnosis in mothers of severely disturbed children attending a therapeutic nursery. *Psychol Rep, 32*:693, 1973.

19 mothers of severely disturbed children completed the MMPI and TAT, scored with Leary's System, and ICL descriptions of Self, Ideal-self, Spouse, Father and Mother. Ss were previously found to be chronically depressed, three-fourths of them ex-

periencing serious marital conflict. Mean interpers diagnosis indicated extreme managerial-autocratic characteristics at Level I-Self, II-Self (ICL) and III-Self (TAT). Fathers and spouses were both described as extremely exploitive and aggressive. Mothers also were described as exploitive. The Ss' ideal-self was moderately managerial and competitive.

50. Garvey, W. P. The prediction of sociometric rating of a normal population from the MMPI. Unpublished Master's thesis, University of Portland, 1962.

51. Garwood, D. S. Personality factors related to creativity in young scientists. *J Abnorm Soc Psychol, 68*(4):413-419, 1964.   (*39*:1729, 1965)

Male science majors designated as Higher Creative (HC) or Lower Creative (LC) on the basis of scores on a creativity test battery were given personality tests. The HC gp scored higher than the LC gp on: composite personality originality; cognitive flexibility, time since first interest in science; dom, sociability, social presence, and self-acceptance. The HC gp scored lower on: socialization, self-control, desire to make a good impression, and affection. The HC gp showed greater integration of nonconscious material as pertaining to concepts of self, father, and mother than did the LC gp; the 2 gps differed in degree of conscious ident with mother (HC less than LC).

52. Gibby, R. G., Jr., R. G. Gibby, Sr., and T. P. Hogan. Relationships between dominance needs and decision-making ability. *J Clin Psychol, 23*:450-452, 1967.

The Townsend-Smith DMAT and the ICL Self and Ideal-self ratings were admin to 56 m Ss working in managerial or professional occupations. Perceived dom was greater than ideal dom. Only the discrepancy scores between perceived and ideal dom were correl sig with DMAT scores. Ss were divided into 4 gps according to their rank on both perceived dom and discrepancy scores. The men with high dom and high discrepancy scores scored higher on the DMAT than did the men in the high dom-low discrepancy and the low dom-low discrepancy gps. The managerial advantages of combining high perceived dom with lower desired dom are discussed.

53. Golding, S. L., and R. M. Knudson. Multivariable-multi-method convergence in the domain of interpersonal behavior. *Multivariate Behav Res, 10*(4):425-448, 1975.

    A gp of HS seniors completed a variety of self-report assessment devices, direct self-ratings, and peer ratings. Substantial convergence for 3 dimensions of interpers behavior—aggressive dominance, affiliation-sociability, and autonomy—was obtained across all modes of measurement.

54. Goldstein, G., C. Neuringer, C. Reiff, and C. Shelly. Generalizability of field dependency in alcoholics. *J Consult Clin Psychol, 32*(5):560-564, 1968.

    30 VAH alcoh pts completed the Witkin Rod and Frame Test (RFT), the Revised Army Alpha Examination and a variety of tests presumed to measure psychological and social dependency. Dom and Lov scores from L-I (MMPI) and L-II were 4 such measures among 14. Only 2 of the 14 measures, Level I Dom and the GAMIN Ascendence Scale, correl sig with the RFT. Contrary to the prediction from a generalization hypoth, greater field dependence was associated with lower dom and ascendence scores. Field dependence was also associated with lower IQ scores. L-I Dom correl sig with only the RFT, while L-II Dom correl with the GAMIN Ascendence scale and IQ. Level I Lov was correl with the MMPI *Pd* and *Mf* scales, the Edwards Deference scale and the Crowne and Marlowe SD scale. L-II Lov was sig correl with only the SD scale. A principle components factor analysis with Varimax rotation yielded 6 factors, with no clear-cut "dependency" factor.

55. Guerney, B., Jr., and J. L. Burton. Relationships among anxiety and self, typical peer, and ideal percepts in college women. *J Soc Psychol, 61*(2):335-344, 1963.
                                        (*38*:8601, 1964)

    77 coll women taking the MA scale and the ICL showed their Ideal to be highest on both Dom and Lov, with Self coming closer to the Ideal in Lov, while Typical Peer came closer in Dom. Sig correls with anxiety were found for: (1) Self-Typical Peer discrepancy measured globally, on Dom and on Lov; (2) Self-Ideal discrepancy, globally, and on Dom; (3) Typical Peer-

Ideal discrepancy, on Lov. Two independent relationships seemed to lie at the base of these findings: (1) The less Dom a coll woman saw in herself, and (2) the less Lov she saw in her Typical Peer, the more she tended to be anxious.

56. —, and J. L. Burton. Comparison of typical peer, self and ideal percepts related to college achievement. *J Soc Psychol, 73*:253-259, 1967.

The diffs between high- and low-achieving coeds were tested using the ICL. The 3 discrepancy variables that showed trends involved peer dom. High achiever's self was lower in love, and his typical peer rating was lower in dom. It was concluded that typical peer percept is a worthy variable for research.

57. —, and L. Guerney. Analysis of interpersonal relationships as an aid to understanding family dynamics: A case report. *J Clin Psychol, 17*(3):225-228, 1961.
(*38*:8841, 1964)

A 9-yr-old disturbed girl and her parents were studied at the Rutgers University Psychological Clinic. The traditional psychological approach and techniques showed some shortcomings while Leary's IS appeared to indicate an important capacity for understanding of family dynamics. In addition to these theoretical considerations the article represents a detailed case report.

58. —, S. Meininger, & L. Stover. Normative and validation studies of the Interpersonal Check List for young children as seen by their mothers. *J Clin Psychol, 29*(2): 219-225, 1973.

Purposes of the study were: (1) to determine whether diffs existed on Real and Ideal Dom, Real and Ideal Lov, and between Real vs Ideal Dom and Real vs Ideal Lov, for young children as seen by their mothers, as a function of age, sex or SES; (2) to construct a set of norms for use with children in the frequently diagnosed age range of 7 to 9, with mothers as the informants; and (3) study the concurrent validity of the ICL in terms of its ability to differentiate emotionally disturbed children from a normative gp. Two *S* samples were used: (1) 177 boys and 183 girls (120 7-yr olds, 130 8-yr olds, and 110 9-yr olds), white, predominantly

catholic and predominantly lower-middle class and (2) 65 emotionally disturbed (46 males and 19 females), aged 7 to 9, from
MHCs. There were no sig main effects according to SES, sex or
age with respect to Real Dom, Real and Ideal Lov, and Dissatisfaction. Normative data were compiled. Concurrent validity of
the ICL was demonstrated by a highly sig diff between the
normative gp and clinic children. For the normative sample, Ideal
Dom was sig greater than Real Dom, while Ideal Lov did not differ from Real Lov. Interactions among age, sex, and SES are reported for Real and Ideal Dom and Lov.

59. —, E. B. Shapiro, and L. Stover. Parental perceptions of
     maladjusted children: Agreement between parents and
     relation to mother-child interaction. *J Genet Psychol,
     113*:215-225, 1968.

Ratings of emotionally disturbed children's negative feeling,
leadership, and dependency vis-a-vis the mother, in play sessions,
were correl with parents' ratings of the children on the ICL and a
problem list. Mothers' and fathers' ratings on both the ICL and
the problem list were sig correlated.

60. Gynther, M. D. Degree of agreement among three "inter-
     personal system" measures. *J Consult Psychol, 26*(1):
     107, 1962.   (*37*:4982, 1963)

MMPI and sociometric data show no agreement: self-description
and sociometric rating and MMPI and self-rating, show agreement.
"Our contradictory findings cast doubt on Leary's assertion (see
Ref. No. 111) that these tests measure specified, distinct levels of
behaviour." (Ss were gps of coll students who were tested about
one month after their classes began—authors' note).

61. —. A technique for assessing covert interpersonal percep-
     tions. *Personality, 2*(4):299-304, 1971.

Using the ICL, a method for evaluating interpers preceptions
within a gp in a relatively precise way was developed. Ten graduate students independently rated the entire set of items twice.
100 of the 128 items were satisfactorily categorized. It was concluded that competitive attributes may be overrepresented at the
expense of managerial attributes, but that the method appears

worthy of further evaluation.

62. —, and P. J. Brilliant. Marital status, readmission to hospital and intrapersonal and interpersonal perceptions of alcoholics. *Q J Stud Alcohol, 28*:52-58, 1967.

Ss were 40 married alcohs (2 women) and 40 unmarried alcohs (9 women). The pts completed the MMPI, and the ICL on their Self, Ideal self, Spouse (if married) and Ideal-spouse. The spouses completed the ICL on their Self, Ideal self, Spouse (the pt) and Ideal spouse. Readmission was defined as rehosp within 12 months after discharge. More married Ss (26) were readmitted than unmarried Ss (14). The married and unmarried alcohs did not differ in age, education, estimated verbal IQ or Self and Ideal-self concepts on Dom and Lov. Neither did the readmitted and nonreadmitted alcohs differ on these dimensions. Regardless of readmission and marital status, the alcohs described their spouses as more dominant than their spouses described themselves. The alcohs and their spouses did not differ in describing the spouses' Love or the alcohs' Love and Dom. The pts' spouses described an ideal partner as being more dominant and loving than their actual partner, yet described their ideal self as also being more dominant than their actual self. Readmitted alcohs and their spouses tended to attribute more dom to each other than did nonreadmitted alcohs. Readmitted pts also tended to describe their spouses as lower on Love and their spouses tended to describe them as higher on Love than the nonreadmitted pts. Finally, unmarried alcohs who had not participated in AA yielded a greater discrepancy between L-II (ICL) and L-I (MMPI).

63. —, and J. O. Kempson. Seminarians and clinical pastoral training: A follow-up study. *J Soc Psychol, 56*:9-14, 1962. *(36*:5GD09G, 1962)

MMPIs and Self- and Other-ratings were obtained from 6 seminarians and a chaplain supervisor at the beginning and end of a 3-month pastoral training period. Results supported earlier findings that such Ss do not demonstrate personality changes or changes in self-perception as a result of this training.

64. —, and R. L. McDonald. Personality characteristics of prisoners, psychiatric patients, and student nurses as de-

picted by the Leary System. *J Gen Psychol, 64*:387-395, 1961.   (*36*:1HF87G, 1962)

MMPIs obtained from 413 m psych pts, 356 m prisoners, 251 student nurses, and 131 fem psych pts were analyzed by IS techniques. Student nurses, m pts, prisoners, and fem pts displayed "strong, healthy" facades in 87.7%, 60.5%, 59%, and 29% of the cases, respectively. Underlying narcissim, hostility, or distrust was found in 83.5% of the prisoners, 80.6% of the m pts, 39.6% of the fem pts, and 25.9% of the student nurses. Definite systematic relationships between scores at the facade and underlying levels were found. Prediction of a *S*'s gp classification by means of scores at both levels is highly discriminating.

65. —, F. T. Miller, and H. T. Davis. Relations between needs and behavior as measured by the Edwards PPS and Interpersonal Check List. *J Soc Psychol, 57*(2):445-451, 1962.   (*37*:5063, 1963)

This study was designed to investigate the relations between scores on the EPPS and the ICL, tests which are purported to measure needs and behavior, respectively. 95 undergraduate m students served as *S*s. Sig systematic relationships were found between scores on the 2 tests, suggesting that the relations between them are direct and to some extent, predicatble. For example, it was predicted and confirmed that the ICL Love variable is positively associated with EPPS needs Affiliation and Nurturance and negatively associated with needs Autonomy and Aggression. Extrapolation of these results to statements about the relations between needs and behavior may not be warranted due to the relative lack of objective support for such interpretation of the tests. The possibilities that the tests measure very nearly the same level of behavior or are both influenced by the SD factor were presented as alternative explanations of the results.

66. —, C. H. Presher, and R. L. McDonald. Personal and interpersonal factors associated with alcoholism. *Q J Stud Alcohol, 20*:321-333, 1959.   (*34*:6241, 1960)

Analyzed by the Leary IS 50 excessive drinkers had the healthy, facade scores of "help-rejectors" but at underlying levels showed narcissistic, hostile, or indecisive feelings.

67. Hamilton, D. L. Measures of self-esteem, dominance and dogmatism: Convergent and discriminant validity. *Proc 77th Annu Conv Am Psychol Assoc,* 4(1):127-128, 1969. (Abstract)

> *Ss* were 70 coll fraternity members. True-false inventory scales, Likert-type self-rating scales, checklist measures, and peer ratings were used to assess self-esteem, dominance, and dogmatism. Convergent validity among the 3 measures was generally adequate, but they did not correl highly with peer ratings. With all assessment methods, measures of self-esteem and dom were highly correl but these variables were not sig related to dogmatism.

68. —. Responses to cognitive inconsistencies: Personality, discrepancy level, and response stability. *J Pers Soc Psychol,* 11(4):351-362, 1969.

> *Ss* were 243 coll students who were in 3 *E* treatments based on diff in amount of discrepancy between their own self-ratings and bogus ratings presented to them. They responded differently on conformity, rejection, devaluation, and underrecall. Diffs in love-hostility scores were related to different response preferences; dogmatism, repression-sensitization, and dominance-submission were not related to the response variables. Stability of response was examined after a week interval.

69. —. Personality attributes related to response preferences in resolving inconsistency. *J Pers,* 38(1):134-145, 1970.

> Four gps of *Ss* were defined in terms of their response to experimentally induced inconsistency. Personality data on the 4 types —conformers, rejectors-devaluators, underrecallers, and neutrals— were submitted to a discriminant analysis. The gps were sig differentiated, with the R-S Scale of the MMPI and the submissive and cooperative octants of the ICL being the most important discriminating variables.

70. —. A comparative study of five methods of assessing self-esteem, dominance and dogmatism. *Educ Psychol Measmt,* 31:441-452, 1971.

> *Ss* were 70 undergraduate fraternity members. A multitrait-

multimethod matrix was formed using the following 5 methods: the CPI, ICL, simple self ratings, peer ratings, and the combined use of Rokeach's Dogmatism scale and the Janis-Field Feelings of Inadequacy scale. The ICL Dom score was used as a measure of dom, and a discrepancy score between the Self and the Ideal-Self ratings, as a measure of self-esteem. The Dom score was sig correl with CPI Dom, self ratings and peer ratings of dom. Dom scores also correl with self-esteem measures: the CPI, the Janis-Field, self-ratings, peer ratings, and the Self-Ideal Self distance. The Self-Ideal Self was sig correl with only the CPI Self-Esteem, the CPI Dom and the ICL Dom scores. Neither of the 2 ICL indices was correl with any of the measures of dogmatism. The Dom score gained convergent validation as a measure of dom and discriminant validation in relation to dogmatism. As was the case for all the tests in matrix, the Dom score could not discriminate between the concepts of self-esteem and dominance.

71. Heiss, J. S., and M. Gordon. Need patterns and the mutual satisfaction of dating and engaged couples. *J of Marriage and the Family, 26*(3):337-338, 1964.
(*39*:4798, 1965)

Since it has not been demonstrated that specific need patterns are associated with interpers satisfaction, it is argued that previous tests of Winch's hypoth of complementary needs are ambiguous. Using the EPPS and the Leary ICL, an attempt was made to discover those need patterns associated with mutual satisfaction. The results are essentially negative in that it was not found that variation in need patterns is associated with variations in satisfaction. If further research substantiates these findings, it must be concluded that Winch's hypoth is based upon an erroneous assumption.

72. Heller, K., R. A. Myers, and L. V. Kline. Interviewer behavior as a function of standardized client roles. *J Consult Psychol, 27*(2):117-122, 1963.   (*37*:8065, 1963)

In a study of interviewer behavior as a function of client stimulus input it was hypoth that interviewers confronted with client friendliness would respond with likeable, agreeable behavior while interviewers confronted with client hostility would respond with subtle counter hostility and anxiety. Also, it was hypoth that client dom would evoke passive interviewer behavior and client dependence would evoke interviewer activity and hyperresponsibility. To control client input, 4 actors were trained as clients and were presented in counter balanced order to 34 therapist-in-training for ½ hour interviews. On the basis of observer ratings, all hypoths, except for interviewer anxiety, were confirmed.

73. Hoskovec, J., G. Knobloch, and P. Rican. Leary's method of interpersonal diagnosis. *Ceskosl Psychiatrie, 59*(5): 304-310, 1963. *(39*:1891, 1965)

The application of Leary's method (or a checking list) to Czech language and environment was on the whole successful. Restandardization and empirical validation would be of a certain practical value. ***

74. Hume, N., and G. Goldstein. Is there an association between astrological data and personality? *J Clin Psychol, 33*(3):711-713, 1977.

A gp of general psychology students and a gp of coll-age university psychological clinic clients were admin the MMPI and ICL. Leary scores for both Levels I and II, and scores for MMPI scales *Hy, D, Pt, Sc, Ma*, were obtained. An astrological chart was prepared for each *S*. *S*s were divided into those who had extreme scores on any of the 13 measures and those who did not. 632 chi-square tests were performed to test whether the degree of association between the astrological and personality variables exceeded chance and only 23 were sig—less than would be expected by chance alone.

75. Hurwitz, J. I., and D. K. Daya. Non-help-seeking wives of employed alcoholics. *J Stud Alcohol, 38*:1730-1739, 1977.

23 blue-collar employees and their wives evaluated at Levels I (MMPI), II (ICL), and III (TAT) of Leary's IS. The results indicated that most of these non-help-seeking wives behave publicly in a dominant fashion and perceive themselves in the same manner. This dom tended to be friendly and affiliative rather than hostile. They perceived most men as sadistic and some women demonstrated preconscious hostility themselves. In their ideal

self-image, most of the wives consciously idealize a dependent interpers role.

76. Klopfer, W. G. Review of *Interpersonal Diagnosis of Personality* by T. F. Leary. *J Proj Tech, 21*(3):323-324, 1957.

The reviser presents a fairly detailed discussion of Leary's book by sections and Levels of personality. With reference to Levels, the reviewer concluded that the discussion of the level of public communication (L-I) is excellent; level of conscious communication (L-II) is quite good; that his presentation of the level of private perception (L-III) shows less stength and less sophistication; that the level of the unexpressed (L-IV) is presented in a rather muddled theoretical way; and, that the level of values (L-V) seems to dangle in this system without any particularly convincing reason being offered for its inclusion. It was concluded that every clinical psychologist, regardless of his level of sophistication, will find his thinking stimulated and his assess ment program broadened by perusal of this volume.

77. —. A cross-validation of Leary's "public" communication level. *J Clin Psychol, 17*(3):321-322, 1961.
                                           (*38*:8426, 1964)

The question being attacked in this study is whether the predictions based upon the MMPI can be cross-validated by using an independent predictor of "public" interpersonal behavior along the dimensions specified in Leary's system. 31 outpts from a university clinic were given a complete battery of tests. The psychologist evaluated all the material (except for the MMPI) and filled out a copy of the ICL on how the pt was likely to be perceived by people in general. Correl between the MMPI and ICL in terms of Leary's 2 dimensions was sig on the Love-Hate dimension but not sig on the Dominance-Submission dimension.

78. Knudson, R. M., and S. L. Golding. Comparative validity of traditional versus S-R format inventories of interpersonal behavior. *J Res Pers, 8*(2):111-127, 1974.

Using HS seniors, 2 S-R inventories (Schedule of Interpersonal Response and a new Rational S-R Inventory) and 2 "traditional" inventories (Personality Research Form and ICL) were compared on 14 self-report and peer rating criteria. The traditional inventories substantially outperformed the S-R inventories in predicting the criterion variables. Wiggins' "substantive or construct point of view" in personality assessment was supported by the result. It was suggested that the item pool for the S-R inventories may not adequately sample the domain of interpers behavior. The authors emphasized the need for a broad band coverage of interpers dimensions which also takes into account situational parameters.

79. Kogan, K. L. Endorsement of social desirability as a meaningful dimension of response. *J Clin Psychol, 18*(3): 348-349, 1962.

The LaForge and Suczek ICL was used to define 2 types of self-concept—"Denyers" and "Detractors." Denyers have high correls between their self descriptions and socially desirable descriptions, their ideal self descriptions and the descriptions most people give of themselves and they endorse more personal competence items and fewer self-depreciating items. Detractors have the opposite pattern. 36 Ss were Denyers and 39 Detractors. Each S rated the ICL items on a 9-point scale of favorable-unfavorable. Intercorrels were calculated between self-ratings, personal SD ratings and the median SD ratings for all Ss. Denyers yielded higher Self-median SD correls and Self-personal SD correls than Detractors. However, Denyers and Detractors do not differ in the deviations of their personal SD from the median SD. Endorsement of SD items in describing oneself appears to be independent of the deviation of one's personal values (SD) from gp values (median SD) for these alcoholics.

80. —, and J. K. Jackson. Attitudes toward self and others in the sanatarium. *Am Rev Respir Dis, 82*:542-550, 1960.

Ss were 35 TB, alcoh pts; 32 TB, non-alcoh pts; and 32 C pts. Ss completed the CMI and ICL ratings of Self and "Most people." ICL items were also rated on a 9-point scale of favorability. Non-alcoh TB pts described themselves as different from most others, isolated, and dissatisfied with themselves. The alcoh pts denied any diffs between themselves and others, yet tended to see their own traits as less desirable than others'. These patterns were highly sig as gp diffs, but could correctly identify only 62% of the individual cases.

81. —, and J. K. Jackson. Self-concept patterns in tuberculous and non-tuberculous alcoholics. *Am Rev Respir Dis, 83*:407-413, 1961.

> 35 m TB alcohs were differentiated from 29 m non-TB alcohs by each of 3 ICL octant rank order correls and 2-item clusters. The TB alcohs had sig more high correls between Self and SD, Self and "most people," and Self and Ideal ICL ratings. They also endorsed sig more competency items from a 5-item cluster and fewer self-deprecation items from a 12-item cluster. Dividing the self-concept patterns into 2 types, characterized by either denial and claims to desirability or feelings of being different and lacking competence, differentiated these 2 gps and 2 replication gps. The TB alcohs present the denial pattern, while the non-TB alcohs present the self-detracting pattern.

82. —, and J. K. Jackson. Some role perceptions of wives of alcoholics. *Psychol Rep, 9*:119-124, 1961.

> 40 fem Alanon family gp members completed ICL descriptions of "most husbands," "when my husband is sober" and "when my husband is drunk." 20 had husbands who had been abstinent for 12 months or more (AA gp). 20 had husbands who were still active alcohs. The AA and A gps did not differ on any octant score for any of the 3 roles described. All 40 Ss agreed more on the roles of "most husbands" and "my husband drunk" than on "my husband sober." Three subgroups were identified within the total sample on the basis of perceptions of sober husbands. Ss in each of these 3 gps were shown to be like each other and unlike other gps in other aspects of their perceptions of the husband's role.

83. —, and J. K. Jackson. Role perception in hospital interaction. *Nurs Res, 10*:75-78, 1961.

> 11 staff physicians, 14 ward nurses and 16 TB pts completed ICL descriptions of the ideal doctor, nurse and pt roles. Coefficients of concordance were calculated within and between gps for the 3 role descriptions. Pts showed the highest within-gp

agreement in their concepts of all 3 roles. However, the role of the pt elicited the least agreement within each of the 3 gps. Doctor ratings of pts showed the very least agreement. Subsequent exploration revealed that the doctors' discharging of pts AMA tended to be related to opposing concepts of ideal pts. Nurses agreed with the pts' role concepts much more than did the doctors. The role of the ideal nurse elicited the greatest between-gps agreement.

84. —, and J. K. Jackson. Role perceptions in wives of alcoholic and of non-alcoholics. *Q J Stud Alcohol, 24*:627-639, 1963.

40 wives of alcohs and 40 wives of non-alcohs, in separate experimental and replication samples, were compared on their ICL descriptions of 3 wife roles and 3 husband roles. Wives of alcohs more frequently described their own husbands as being socially undesirable, distrustful, lacking in emotional warmth, bitter, and resentful. Their self-descriptions, on the other hand, emphasized greater passivity, submissiveness and adherence to the stereotyped feminine and wifely roles. These diffs were sig in both the experimental and replication samples.

85. —, and J. K. Jackson. Relation between content and response style in ICL femininity scores. *Psychol Rep, 13*: 437-438, 1963.   (*38*:8497, 1964)

ICL responses of 40 Ss were divided into high and normal range Femininity Scores. Hyper-feminine scores were shown to be associated with, but not an artifact of, greater tendency to agree. There was no sig relationship between Femininity and SD.

86. —, and J. K.Jackson. Conventional sex role stereotypes and actual perceptions. *Psychol Rep, 13*(1):27-30, 1963.   (*38*:5865, 1964)

ICL Femininity Scores from 40 wives of non-alcohs failed to show a sig sex-role differentiation between the wife's perception of herself and her husband, while 40 wives of alcohs tended to view themselves as more feminine than their husbands. "The data were construed as lending support to the view that in the 'normal' family of today the role of husband and wife are more likely to be analogous than they are to be differentiated."

87. —, and J. K. Jackson. Perceptions of self and spouse: Some contaminating factors. *J of Marriage and the Family,* *26*(1):60-64, 1964.   (*38*:8125, 1964)

Spouse similarity or complementarity has customarily been studied via spouses' perceptions of their mates. Since perception of others is only a special instance of perception, characteristics of the measuring instrument and of the perceiver must be considered as well as the stimulus perceived. Spouse perceptions of 24 women revealed a wide range in the amount of similarity attributed to self and husband. Further analysis revealed that favorability of the self-perception was closely related to the perceived similarity of self and spouse, and suggested that diffs in endorsement of SD have contaminated efforts to study similarity vs complementarity.

88. Kogan, W. S., and E. E. Boe. Differential responding to items with high and low social desirability scale values. *Psychol Rep, 15*(2):586, 1964.   (*39*:5157, 1965)

Results of several studies reporting correls between SD scales keyed true and SD scales keyed false are cited in support of the hypoth that endorsing SD items is somewhat different than rejecting socially undesirable (SUD) items. The following paradigm is suggested for classifying responses to personality items, with one possible interpretation: (a) endorse SD—bragging, (b) reject SUD—denial, (c) reject SD—modesty, and endorse SUD—self-depreciation.

89. —, E. E. Boe, and E. F. Gocka. Personality changes in unwed mothers following parturition. *J Clin Psychol,* *24*(1):3-11, 1968.

The ICL for 6 instructional sets was admin to unwed mothers at the beginning of the 3rd trimester and shortly after parturition. Staff members also described the *S*s using the ICL. *S*s saw themselves as becoming more self-reliant, warmer, and less indulgent. In general, huge changes in interpers perceptions following parturition were not evidenced.

90. —, E. E. Boe, E. F. Gocka, and M. H. Johnson. Personality changes in psychiatric residents during training. *Newsltr Res Psychol,* 7(4):33, 1965. (Also, *J Psychol, 62*:229-240, 1966)

   The revised ICL was admin to 17 psych residents on 5 occasions (0, .5, 1, 2, & 3 yrs from the beginning of the residency) with 8 instructional sets (I am, Most people are, etc.). Data were analyzed using factor analysis and ANOVA. Three of 18 main effects of occasion were sig and suggested the residents' perceptions of themselves and others change in the direction of less resentment of supervision, less self-sacrificing and supporting of others, and more self-aggrandizing over the course of residency. 12 of the 18 main effects of instructional set were sig and suggested that the residents see themselves as lacking in self reliance and being too indulgent in contrast with what they consider desirable.

91. —, E. E. Boe, and B. L. Valentine. Changes in the self-concept of unwed mothers. *J Psychol, 59*:3-10, 1965. (*39*:7598, 1965)

   Changes in the self-concept of 25 institutionalized unwed mothers during the 3rd trimester were assessed by the ICL. The results indicated that, upon admission to the home, the *S*s viewed themselves as differing greatly from their conception of what they and their parents would like them to be and especially different than their conception of most other teen-age girls. A week after parturition, however, the *S*s saw themselves as being sig more like other teen-age girls and more like what they and their parents would like them to be.

92. —, and W. E. Fordyce. The control of social desirability: A comparison of three different Q-sorts and a check list, all composed of the same items. *J Consul Psychol, 26*(1):26-30, 1962. (*37*:4985, 1963)

   A theoretical discussion of SD and personality inventories. Three variations of Q-sort and a check list, show practical equivalence in variable scores and in control of SD. The check list is somewhat more susceptible to variations.

93. —, C. B. Schultz, and M. H. Johnson. Role perception in

individual psychotherapy. *Percept Mot Skills, 18*(1):81-82, 1964.

Employing a 64-item adjective and phrase check list (ICL modified) with 3 instructional sets (Ideal, I am, Doctor is), a gp of first year psych residents were found to differ sig on patient-therapist role perceptions from a gp of hosp psych pts on 14 of 24 comparisons.

94. Kotlar, S. L.   Instrumental and expressive marital roles. *Sociol Soc Res, 46*:186-194, 1962.

100 middle-class married couples completed the Wallace Adjustment Scale and ICL descriptions of Self, Spouse, Ideal husband and Ideal wife.   ICL adjectives were rated by 14 judges as pertaining to either expressive, instrumental or neutral roles.   Both adjusted wives and adjusted husbands scored higher on expressive role attitudes in their self-descriptions than did unadjusted wives and husbands.   For both husbands and wives, marital adjustment was associated with higher expressive role scores in the mate descriptions.   Adjusted wives described the Ideal husband as higher on expressive role attitudes than did unadjusted wives.   Adjusted and unadjusted husbands and wives described the Ideal husband as having sig more instrumental attitudes.   Only the wives described the Ideal wife as more expressive, although the husbands tended to ascribe more expressive qualities to the Ideal wife.   Reversal of role attitudes was associated with marital maladjustment for expressive but not for instrumental attitudes.

95. —.   Role theory in marriage counseling. *Sociol Soc Res, 52*: 50-62, 1967.

Discusses the role theory approach in marriage counseling and the measurement of 2 important dimensions of marital roles—the hostility-affectional and dominance-submission (using the ICL).

96. Kronenberger, E. J.   Interpersonal aspects of industrial accident and non-accident employees. *Engng Industr Psychol, 2*:57-62, 1960.   (*37*:2168, 1963)

Leary's ICL was admin to 18 *S*s who had accidents and 35 *S*s who had not.   There was some tendency for the accident gp to express more hostility toward themselves than did the non-accident gp, but no sig diffs at the .05 level or better were found.

97. Krus, P. H., and D. J. Krus. *Program for administering and interpretation of the Interpersonal Checklist.* (University Testing Service Tech Rep No. 6). Tempe, Arizona: Arizona State University, 1976.

98. LaForge, R. *Research use of the ICL.* (Oregon Research Institute Tech Rep, 3(4):iii-49, 1963). Eugene, Oregon: Oregon Research Institute.

(see Ref. No. 99)

99. —. *Using the ICL.* Unpublished manuscript, 1976. (Available from the author, 83 Homestead Blvd., Mill Valley, California).

A very useful guide to the ICL. Presents information on administration, scoring, response sets, underlying rationale, interpretive hints, data from non-clinical samples, evidence relating to reliability and validity, the use of individual items, and some suggested statistical methods. Tables present means, standard deviations, intercorrelation matrices, factor analytic results, and correlations with the 16PF and the MMPI. Appendices present computer programs for using the ICL.

100. —. Interpersonal Checklist. In J. E. Jones and J. W. Pfeiffer (Eds.), *The 1977 annual handbook for group facilitators.* La Jolla, California: University Associates, 1977.

Summarizes the development and rationale of the LaForge-Suczek ICL. Sample forms and brief interpretation guidelines are also presented. This is a very good, brief introduction to the ICL.

101. —, T. F. Leary, H. Naboisek, H. S. Coffey, and M. B. Freedman. The interpersonal dimension of personality: II. An objective study of repression. *J Pers, 23*: 129-153, 1954. (*29*:5313, 1955)

The present study is concerned with those aspects of repression producing discrepancies between the conscious level and the private or fantasy level (Level II-Level III discrepency). Repression in two different gps was measured by (1) MMPI profiles, and (2) the individual's self-description as obtained from an adjective list, and (3) a discrepancy between this self-description and coordinate rating of TAT scores. The 2 latter measures together yielded multiple correls of .54 and .46 with the MMPI ratings in the 2 samples. It is judged that the results indicate the importance of conscious self-perception in forming clinical judgments of amounts of repressive tendency present.

102.   —, and R. F. Suczek. The interpersonal dimension of personality: III. An interpersonal check list. *J Pers, 24*: 94-112, 1955.   (*30*:5990, 1956)

An interpersonal check list to instrument an interpersonal personality system is presented. . . . Guiding principles and 2 problems arising in the development of ICL are described. . . . Sample statistics and tentative norms are reproduced. Clinical and research applications are indicated.

103.   Lange, D. E. Validation of the orthogonal dimensions underlying the ICL and the octant constellations assumed to be their measure. *J Proj Tech Pers Assess, 34*(6):519-527, 1970.

Two general hypoths were tested: (1) That ICL profiles from 4 gps of *S*s correspond to the ICL's bipolar dimensions (LaForge, 1963); and (2) the profiles of the gps will not be on the same level. Coll *S*s were randomly assigned to 1 of 4 treatment conditions designed to be illustrative of the bipolar nature of the 2 dimensions, Dominance-Submission and Love-Hostility. After viewing interpers situations, *S*s were instructed to describe the interpers behavior of the main character. The results support original formulations of LaForge & Suczek (1955) that 2 bipolar dimensions underlie the ICL.

104.   —. An EDP system package for scoring the Interpersonal Check List. *Educ Psychol Measmt, 31*:775-776, 1971.

An EDP system package which aids in keying and scoring the

ICL form IV is reported and is offered free of charge to interested researchers. The computer program is written in basic FORTRAN IV and is available for a variety of computer systems.

105. Lantz, D. L. Changes in student teachers' concepts of self and others. *J Teacher Educ, June*:200-203, 1964.

36 fem elementary educ majors were evaluated before and after their teaching experience. They rated themselves, most other elementary teachers and the ideal elementary teacher on a modified ICL, on which Ss indicated how often each item characterized the rated object. On self ratings, the Ss decreased sig on octants *4, 5,* and *7,* from pre- to posttest. Rating other elementary teachers, Ss decreased on octants *3, 4,* and *5.* Rating the ideal elementary teacher, Ss decreased on octants *4, 7,* and *8.*

106. —. Relationship between classroom emotional climate and concepts of self, others, and ideal among elementary student teachers. *J Educ Res, 59*(2):80-83, 1965.

Independent ratings of classroom emotional climate were related to female elementary school teachers' ratings of themselves and others using a modified ICL. The study was an initial attempt to predict classroom emotional climate from teacher self-reports.

107. Lawton, M. P. Correlates of the Opinions about Mental Illness Scale. *J Consult Psychol, 28*(1):94, 1964.

Using 72 psych aides, scores on OMI scale were correl with several other measures, including the ICL. ICL Dom scores were not related to OMI scores, but 4 of the 25 correls on Lov were sig (Authoritarianism to Lov on Ideal aide, Benevolence to Lov on Average Patient and Social Restrictiveness to Self and Average aide ratings on Lov). The correl coefficients were low.

108. —. Personality and attitudinal correlates of psychiatric aid performance. *J Soc Psychol, 66*(2):215-226, 1965.
(*39*:15809, 1965)

A gp of 72 psych aides were rated with varying reliability for

adequacy of job performance by ward physicians and nurses.
The aides completed the OMI, the EPPS and the ICL. Estimates
of therapeutic-role conception were available for 32 aides. All
possible relationships between test scores and criteria were computed, though a limited number of specific relationships between tests and criteria were found, suggesting that the criterion
for adequate performance needs to be defined to fit various situational demands. There were enough sig and predicted relationships to suggest that aides considered more adequate are less
authoritarian, more benevolent, less dominant, and less likely
to see wide diffs between pts and others.

109. Leary, T. F. The theory and measurement methodology
of interpersonal communication. *Psychiatry, 18*:147-
161, 1955.   (*30*:2694, 1956)

Methods for isolating and defining human interactions have
been evolved at the Kaiser Foundation since 1949. This article,
concerned with interpers communication, describes a measurement methodology and a theoretical context for dealing with
overt, public behavior. The empirical unit by which social
interactions are categorized is called the interpersonal reflex.
The system of multilevel measurement of social interaction by
interpers reflexes is illustrated from a group-psychotherapy situation. The hypothetical concepts of "self-determination" and
of "reciprocal interpersonal relations" are discussed. A classification of interpers behavior into 16 reflexes is charted.

110. —. A theory and methodology for measuring fantasy and
imaginative expression. *J Pers, 25*:159-175, 1956.
                              (*32*:257, 1958)

This paper has presented a theory of and measurement method
for dealing with imaginative, preconscious behavior. *** The
implication of the theory is that imaginative productions can
be used by the psychologist to determine the amount and interpers sources of anxiety and to predict future behavior.

111. —. *Interpersonal diagnosis of personality: A functional
theory and methodology for personality evaluation.*
New York: Ronald Press, 1957.   (*31*:2556, 1957)

The book is concerned with intpers behavior as observed in the psychotherapeutic setting. The approach might be called dynamic behaviorism, which has 2 attributes: The impact one person has in interaction with others and the interaction of psychological pressures among different levels of personality. ***

Reviews: In O. K. Buros (Ed.). *The fifth mental measurements yearbook.* Highland Park, New Jersey: The Gryphon Press, 1957.

111a.   Gorlow, L. *J Counsel Psychol,* 4:259-260, 1957.
111b.   Sargent, H. D. *Bull Meninger Clinic,* 21:269, 1957.
111c.   Schutz, W. C. *Contemp Psychol,* 2:227-229, 1957.
111d.   Siegel, L. *J Counsel Psychol,* 4:168-169, 1957.
111e.   Thorpe, L. P. *Educ Psychol Measmt,* 17:639-640, 1957.
111f.   Watson, J. *Am J Sociol,* 63:244-245, 1957.

112. —, and H. S. Coffey. The prediction of interpersonal behavior in group psychotherapy. *Gp Psychother,* 7:7-51, 1954.

Describes research carried out at the Kaiser Foundation with the aim of predicting interpers behavior in group therapy. An exploratory study comparing sociometric ICL data with MMPI scale scores yielded formulas for the measurement of Public Communications (Level I) using 9 of the MMPI scales. The results of 4 validation studies are then presented, in which intake MMPI scores were compared with sociometric ICLs following 6 to 8 sessions of group psychotherapy. The MMPI formulas predicted subsequent sociometric ICL diagnoses better for pt gps than for normal gps, and among normals, the LOV dimension appeared to be predicted more reliably than the DOM dimension. It was concluded that the MMPI predictions are more reliable when they are further away from the center of the circle and that for Level I-MMPI diagnoses close to the center of the circle the interpersonal diagnosis based upon the octant placement is "probably meaningless." The Level I-MMPI diagnosis "will work fairly well for maladjusted, neurotic Ss who manifest intense or extreme security operations, but cannot be depended on too precisely for well-balanced, adaptive (i.e., non-clinical) individuals."

113. —, and H. S. Coffey. Interpersonal diagnosis: Some problems of methodology and validation. *J Abnorm Soc
Psychol, 50*:110-124, 1955.

Seven issues are discussed in this paper. They are: (1) selection
of concepts for functional diagnostic research, (2) methods for
classifying personality data, (3) the organization of the levels of
personality, (4) the level on locus of diagnosis, (5) the purpose
of personality diagnosis, (6) the development of an interpersonal diagnostic system, and (7) the problems of validating
multidimensional personality patterns.

114. —, and J. S. Harvey. A methodology for measuring personality changes in psychotherapy. *J Clin Psychol, 12*:
123-132, 1956.   (*31*:4750, 1957)

This article describes a method for measuring change in personality based on diffs between a test battery given before and. . .
after a time interval. *** The method involves the use of the
interpers system of diagnosis which employs 16 interpers variables at 4 levels of personality. ***

115. —, H. Lane, A. Apfelbaum, M. D. Croppa, and C. Kauf-
mann. *Multilevel measurement of interpersonal behavior: A manual for the use of the interpersonal system of personality.* Psychol Consult Service, 1956.

Introduces the Interpersonal System of Personality and presents the use of it in the diagnostic work with individuals and
groups, in the analysis of family dynamics and in research.

116. Lester, D., and L. F. Orloff. Personality correlates of the
duration of menses. *Psychol Rep, 26*:650, 1970.

Coll fem *S*s completed the Level II ICL, the Maslow test of
dominance-feeling and a questionnaire about menstrual functioning. The duration of menses was sig correl with only octant
6 of the ICL. Duration of menses was not related to the dominance-feeling test, to the number of items checked on the ICL,
or to either the DOM or LOV scores. *S*s with the 12 shortest
menses and the 10 longest menses were compared and showed
a pattern of diffs similar to the correls. These 2 gps were also

compared on each item of the ICL. Women with shorter menses endorsed the item "self confident" (octant 2) more often and endorsed "acts important" (octant 1), "easily embarrassed," "self-punishing" (octant 5), and "often helped by others" (octant 6), less often than women with longer menses.

117. Lewinsohn, P. M. Psychological correlates of overall quality of figure drawings. *J Consult Psychol, 29*:504-512, 1965.

Investigated the relationships between a wide variety of psychological test scores and the overall quality of figure drawings, using hosp psych pts. As concerns the ICL, the number of sig correls were no greater than chance.

118. Liberman, R. Reinforcement of cohesiveness in group therapy: Behavioral and personality changes. *Arch Gen Psychiatry, 25*(2):168-177, 1971.

Two matched therapy gps were studied for 9 months in terms of process and outcome. In the *E* gp, the therapist used techniques of social reinforcement to facilitate inter-member cohesiveness. In the *C* gp, the therapist, matched by personality with the *E* therapist, used a more conventional, intuitive, group-centered approach. Several measures were used, including the ICL, MMPI, and TAT. Every 3 months each *S* rated himself and every other *S* in his gp on the ICL. From the sociometrically admin ICL, 3 indices of gp dynamics were derived: (1) Self-deception (self ratings vs average rating of others); (2) Conscious disidentification (self ratings vs pooled total of his perceptions of the other gp members); and (3) misperception (comparison of a *S*'s perception of each other member with the pooled total of the perceptions made by the other gp members of each member). The *E* gp showed sig greater reduction in self-deception, conscious disidentification, and misperception. Interlevel discrepancy scores were calculated for the pretreatment and posttreatment multilevel tests. The *E* gp showed less interlevel conflict at termination as compared to pretreatment than did the *C* group.

119. —. Behavioral group therapy: A controlled clinical study. *Br J Psychiatry, 119*(552):535-544, 1971.

In 2 matched outpt gps, one therapist used social reinforcement techniques to develop inter-member cohesiveness while the other therapist used a more psychodynamic, intuitive, group-centered approach. In the former gp, more cohesiveness was found associated with greater personality change and more independence from the therapist was found.

120. Lockwood, D. H., and B. Guerney, Jr. Identification and empathy in relation to self-dissatisfaction and adjustment. *J Abnorm Soc Psychol, 65*:343-347, 1962.

20 m and 20 fem students, ages 13 to 16, completed ICL descriptions of Self and Ideal self and the Bell Adjustment Inventory. The S's same-sex parent completed ICL descriptions of Self and how they thought their child would describe himself. Parental empathy was defined by the similarity between the Ss' Self descriptions and their parents' estimates of their child's Self-description. Among the boys, ident with their fathers was correl positively and sig with emotional, home and total adjustment, and was correl negatively with Self-Ideal descrepancy. Also among the boys, Self-Ideal discrepancy was correl negatively with emotional, home and total adjustment. The lack of sig correls with the empathy measure lead to an investigation of assumed similarity, i.e., the similarity between parents' self-descriptions and their estimates of their child's self-description. Assumed similarity by the fathers was positively correl with the sons' ident, home adjustment and total adjustment. The data from the fem Ss yielded no sig correls.

121. Lomont, J. F. Repressors and sensitizers as described by themselves and their peers. *J Pers, 34*:224-240, 1966.

Members of coll fraternities and sororities were admin the MMPI R-S scale and the ICL Self and Ideal ratings. In addition, Ss completed the ICL describing 4 other members in their own house. Self-rating DOM scores were inversely related to the tendency to sensitization. Peer rating DOM scores were likewise inversely related to sensitization, but only for males. For females only, increases in sensitization were associated with self-rated dom becoming increasingly small relative to peer-rated dom. Correls between self ratings and peer ratings were not sig related to R-S scores. With increasing repressive tendencies, self-rating DOM scores increased and more closely approximated the same person's Ideal-self DOM score.

122. —, F. H. Gilner, N. J. Spector, and K. K. Skinner. Group assertion training and group insight therapies. *Psychol Rep, 25*(2):463-470, 1969.

Compared an assertion therapy gp and an insight therapy gp, using pts free from psychotic thought disorder, concurrently over a 6-wk period. The assertion gp showed sig decreases on the *D* and *Pt* scales of the MMPI, nearly sig decreases on the *Pd, Pa,* and *Sc* scales and a nearly sig increase on the dominance-submission dimension of the ICL. The insight gp showed no test change that approached significance.

123. Longabaugh, R. *An analysis of the cross-cultural study of children's social behavior.* (Final Report, Research Project No. S-106). Ithaca, New York: Cornell University, 1966.

124. —. The structure of interpersonal behavior. *Sociometry, 29*:441-460, 1966.

The cross-cultural replicability of factor structures obtained from small gp and personality research was tested using children from 6 diverse societies. Two factor structures show cross-cultural generality: the Carter 3-factor structure of individual prominence, aiding group attainment and sociability; and Leary 2-factor formulation of power and affiliation.

125. Lorr, M., D. M. McNair, W. W. Michaux, and A. Raskin. Frequency of treatment and change in psychotherapy. *J Abnorm Soc Psychol, 64*(4):281-292, 1962.

133 m psych outpts were assigned to 1 of 3 treatment schedules —twice weekly, once weekly, or once biweekly. Assessments were completed before treatment, after 16 wks and after 32 wks. 75 therapists participated in the study, all regarded as competent to conduct intensive psychotherapy. Assessment included 10 pt measures, 4 of which came from the ICL; 4 therapist measures, 1 of which was patient-therapist similarity on ICL ratings of pt; and various social worker measures. After 4

months, there were no relationships between any of the measures and treatment frequency, and no sig changes in the pt measures. The patient-therapist ICL concomitance index increased sig, but this was not due to changes in the pts' self-descriptions. After 8 months, the patient-therapist concomitance index was the only measure to approach a sig relationship with treatment frequency. Two pt measures changed sig over the 8 months, Ego strength and a 30-adjective Dependent-Docile scale derived from the ICL. Among pts still in treatment after one year, higher treatment frequency was associated with lower scores on a 12-adjective ICL Cooperative-Responsibility scale. Among pts out of therapy at 12 months, higher treatment frequency was associated with fewer Cooperative-Responsible and Dependent-Docile adjectives endorsed in ICL self-descriptions. Overall, treatment duration appeared to be more influential than treatment frequency.

126. Luckey, E. B. Marital satisfaction and congruent self-spouse concepts. *Social Forces, 39*:153-157, 1960.
(*35*:3680, 1961)

Within the limits of this study which include samples which were selected, and evaluative instruments which are paper-and-pencil, it can be safely concluded that the congruence of the wives' perceptions of their husbands and their husbands' own self concept is sig related to satisfaction in marriage. It was not found true of concepts of wives held by their husbands. The meaning of this diff can be clarified only by further investigation both into perception and factors within the marital relationship.

127. —. Marital satisfaction and its association with congruence of perception. *Marriage and Family Living, 22*:49-54, 1960.
(*36*:2IQ49L, 1962)

Selecting persons who scored in the upper and lower quartiles of the Locke Modified MAS and Terman's Seven Point Self-Rating Happiness Scale as samples of satisfied and less satisfied couples, the ICL was used to measure Self-Other concepts. The satisfied couples reported greater agreement of perception of Self and of Self by other, of Self and parent of same sex, of Spouse and parent of opposite sex, and of one's Ideal-self and one's Spouse. No sig diffs were found regarding congruence of Self and Ideal-self perceptions.

128. —. Implications for marriage counseling of self percep- tions and spouse perceptions. *J Counsel Psychol, 7*:3- 9, 1960. (*35*:2440, 1961)

The concepts of Self, Ideal-self, and Spouse were evaluated by means of the ICL in a gp of *S*s determined to be satisfactorily married and in a gp classified as less satisfactorily married. The interrelationships of these measures were then established. "Generally, the findings support the theory that perception of (a) self and ideal-self, and (b) ideal-self and spouse are signifi- cantly related to marital satisfaction." The implications of these findings for marital counseling are considered.

129. —. Marital satisfaction and parent concepts. *J Consult Psychol, 24*(3):195-204, 1960.

A gp of "satisfactorily" (S) and a gp of "less satisfactorily" (U) married couples completed the ICL Self, Spouse, Parent of the same sex, and Parent of the opposite sex. Discrepancy scores were determined between Self and same sex parent, Spouse and opposite sex parent. Some very interesting findings were reported, including the following: S men, compared to U men, identified more with their fathers, saw their mothers and wives as being less skeptical and distrustful; S women compared to U women, perceived their husbands as being more similar to their fathers; comparing both S men and women with U men and women, there was a greater degree of congruence between ratings of spouse and parent of the opposite sex for women but the findings were not clear for men; S women compared to U women, perceived their husbands as being more similar to their fathers. Marital satisfaction in men was associated with greater congruence in perception of self and same sex parent. For women, equation of spouse and opposite sex parent was related to marital satisfaction; the findings for men were not conclusive.

130. —. Perceptual congruence of self and family concepts as related to marital interaction. *Sociometry, 24*:234- 250, 1961. (*36*:3IQ34L, 1962)

The 2 samples investigated were designated as "satisfactorily" (N=41) and "less satisfactorily" (N=40) married on the basis of the highest and lowest couple scores on items from the Locke and Terman scales. The 2 samples were found to be homogeneous in regard to 26 items of descriptive personal information, such as age, number of years married, number of children, and income. Ss completed the ICL for Self, Spouse, Mother, Father, and Ideal-self. "These findings suggest that certain perceptual congruencies and dimensions on which the perceptions are congruent are related to the degree of satisfaction the Ss find in marriage. The importance of perceptual congruence and marital satisfaction seems related in some cases to the sex of the S."

131. —. Marital satisfaction and personality correlates of spouse. *J Marriage & the Family, 26*:217-220, 1964.

80 married couples completed the LMAS and ICL descriptions of their spouse. Marital satisfaction correl positively with at least one item pair of low intensity in each octant, except octant 4, and correl positively with none of the more intense item pairs. Marital satisfaction correl negatively with item pairs of higher intensity in each octant, except octants 7 and 8, and correl negatively with low intensity item pairs only in octant 4.

132. —. Marital satisfaction and its concomitant perceptions of self and spouse. *J Counsel Psychol, 11*(2):136-145, 1964. (*39*:5527, 1965)

The relationship of marriage satisfaction to personality variables used in describing self and spouse was investigated by correlating scores of the LMAS and items marked in each of the 8 octants of the ICL. Phrases in the categories of "Skeptical-Distrustful" and "Blunt-Aggressive" were most often associated with lack of satisfaction in marriage; this was true when they were used to describe self as well as to describe spouse. Phrases denoting warmth, generosity, cooperativeness when perceived in self and in spouse were reliably associated with satisfaction. Although the data do not demonstrate a causal relationship between marital satisfaction and self and spouse perception, they are consistent with such an interpretation. The implication for marriage counseling as person-centered rather than problem-centered is discussed.

133. —. Number of years married as related to personality perception and marital satisfaction. *J Marriage & the Family, 28*(1):44-48, 1966.

80 couples, married from 2 to 21 years, completed the LMAS and ICL ratings of self and spouse. Regardless of marital satisfaction, more time in a marriage was associated with the perception of less favorable personality qualities in their mates. Overall marital satisfaction was directly related to the number of years of schooling and inversely related to the number of years of marriage.

134. Lupton, D. E. A preliminary investigation of the personality of female temporomandibular joint dysfunction patients. *Psychother Psychosom, 14*(3):199-216, 1966.

Studied the interpers diagnosis of pts who manifested craniofacial pain, limitation of jaw movement, or one in combination with crepitation or clicking of the joint, using the MMPI, TAT, and ICL. A sig number manifested a common and distinctive personality pattern when compared with other dental pts, medical pts, psych pts, and a gp of apparently healthy females.

135. Mahoney, J., and J. Hartnett. Self-actualization and self-ideal discrepancy. *J Psychol, 85*:37-42, 1973.

28 m and 47 fem coll *S*s completed the Time Competence Scale (TCS) from the POI and ICL descriptions of their real and ideal selves. Self-actualizing *S*s, as determined by TCS scores, showed greater congruence between their Self and Ideal-self descriptions than did non-actualizing *S*s. Compared with self-actualizing *S*s, the non-actualizing *S*s also manifested a greater Self-Ideal discrepancy on the Dom dimension, tending to idealize dom more.

136. McDavid, J. W., and F. Sistrunk. Personality correlates to two kinds of conforming behavior. *J Pers, 32*:420-435, 1964.

43 m and 43 fem coll Ss completed the experimental protocol. Testing included the EPPS, Gordon Survey of Interpersonal Values, G-Z Temperament Survey, Social Reinforcement Scale and ICL Self rating. Conforming behavior was observed within a contrived laboratory situation, on "soluble" and "insoluble" tasks. Among males, conforming behavior correl positively with ICL octants *6, 7,* and *8* and negatively with octant *3.* Among females, conforming behavior correl negatively with octant *4* scores. These sig correls were found only on the "insoluble" tasks.

137. McDonald, R. L. Personality characteristics of freshman medical students as depicted by the Leary system. *J Genet Psychol, 100*(2):313-323, 1962.

(*37*:3838, 1963)

The Leary IS was used to analyze MMPIs and ICLs obtained from 64 freshmen medical students. These results were compared with other normative data for the public interpersonal level (I-S) and the level of the underlying character structure (III-MM). 91% of the medical students presented healthy symptomatic behavior and 81% described themselves as responsible, generous, managerial persons in interpers situations. Characterologically, 85% had underlying managerial, competitive, responsible feelings. In spite of the large percentages of "healthy" behavior at this level and the "facade" level, the most frequent Ideal of these Ss was to be a critical-sadistic person. These interlevel conflicts point to the possibility of future poor adjustment on the part of many of the students.

138. —. Intrafamilial conflict and emotional disturbance. *J Genet Psychol, 101*(2):201-208, 1962.

(*37*:6492, 1963)

The purpose of this study was to assess the diffs between parents of emotionally disturbed children and the parents of normal children with respect to self-descriptions, attitudes toward each other, and attitudes toward their children by means of the Leary ICL. The parents of 10 emotionally disturbed children free of organic damage, of at least normal intelligence, and of elementary school age, rated Self, Spouse, Child and Ideal as did the parents of 10 normal children who were matched with the disturbed children according to sex, age, and intelligence. To insure matched gps, the educational status of the parents and socioeconomic status of the fathers were also controlled. The results indicated that the parents of the disturbed children (a) rejected their own behavior more often than did parents of normal children; (b) described their children as distrustful, self-effacing, and dependent more frequently than parents of normal children; (c) devaluated the personalities of their spouses and children more frequently than parents of normal children; and (d) were more frequently disidentified with their children than were parents of normal children. The parents of disturbed children also tended to disidentify with each other more than did parents of normal children.

139. —. Ego-control patterns and attribution of hostility to self and others. *J Pers Soc Psychol, 2*(2):273-277, 1965.
(*39*:15438, 1965)

To determine if Ss who use different types of ego controls in response to threatening situations would differ in their attribution of hostility to themselves or others. Four ego control patterns—expressors, repressors, sensitizers, and expressor-sensitizers—were derived by combinations of scores on the MMPI-based repressor-sensitizer and expressor scales. The ICL was admin to 177 white single pregnant females at the 7th month of pregnancy to obtain ratings of self and parents. Reliable diffs in the predicted direction were found between the 4 subgroups with regards to attribution of hostility to self and parents. Attribution of hostility to others (parents) was also found to be related to the S's parental identification.

140. —. The effects of stress on self-attribution of hostility among ego control patterns. *J Pers, 35*(2):234-245, 1967.

182 single pregnant females were identified as expressors, sensitizers, repressors or neutrals using the MMPI R-S and Expressor scales. Self-attribution of hostility, as revealed on the ICL, proceeded in the following rank order: expressors greater than sensitizers, sensitizers greater than repressors.

141. —. Leary's overt interpersonal behavior: A validation at-

tempt. *J Soc Psychol,* 74:259-264, 1968.

MMPI protocols were obtained from 102 single pregnant females who had been living together in a dormitory for at least 2 to 3 months. Ss were divided into gps of 5 to obtain sociometric ratings using the ICL. The MMPI and sociometric diagnoses were defined by the quadrant receiving the heaviest loadings. The quadrants were: dominant (octants 1 and 2), hostile (octants *3* and *4*), submissive (octants 5 and *6*), and warm, friendly behavior (octants 7 and *8*). The percentage of agreement differed sig for the 4 quadrants, as follows: dominant, 76.3%; hostile, 30%; submissive, 0%; and warm, friendly behavior, 72.2%. Agreement was greater for the love dimension than for the dom scores.

142.   —. Effects of sex, race, and class on self, ideal-self, and parental ratings in southern adolescents. *Percept Mot Skills,* 27:15-25, 1968.

Ss were both black and white students from 2 totally segregated southern rural HSs. Perceived congruence between self and parental ratings was defined by the absolute distance between the summary points. The findings of McDonald and Gynther (1965) with regard to sex and race diffs were replicated. However, with this rural population social class was sig related to the ICL descriptions. Regarding congruency, both sexes described themselves as being more similar to their father than their mother.

143.   —, and A. C. Christakos. Relationship of emotional adjustment during pregnancy to obstetric complications. *Am J Obstet Gynecol,* 86:341-348, 1963.

Ss were 86 white pts from a very low socioeconomic grouping. During pregnancy, Ss were admin the MMPI, MAS, Kent EGY tests and ICL ratings of Self, Husband, Ideal-self and both parents or surrogate parents. Following delivery, medical records were used to categorize Ss as either normal or abnormal, regarding gestation, fetus development and delivery irregularities. These 2 gps were similar in age, I. Q., labor time, gravidity and infant birth weight. The abnormals scored sig higher on the MAS and MMPI scales *F, Hs, D, Hy, Pa, Pt, Sc,* and *Ma,* and lower on scales *K, Pgb* and *Hyd*. Of the ICL indices, only Ideal Dom scores differentiated the gps, abnormals scoring higher than normals.

144. —, and M. D. Gynther. Nonintellectual factors associated with performance in medical school. *J Genet Psychol, 103*:185-194, 1963.

EPPS scores, Self- and Ideal-ratings, admission test scores, and cumulative grade averages of 66 junior medical students were compared. Abilities to accept routine, to function independently, a need for achievement, and perceptions of self as friendly and responsible were associated with above-average academic performance.

145. —, and M. D. Gynther. Relationship of self and ideal-self descriptions with sex, race, and class in southern adolescents. *J Pers Soc Psychol, 1*(1):85-88, 1965.
(*39*:7700, 1965)

This study evaluated the effects of sex, race, and social class on the Self- and Ideal-self-concepts of adolescent *S*s. ICL data were obtained from 261 Negro and 211 white HS seniors from urban segregated schools whose social class was determined on the basis of parental occupations as reported by the *S*s. Sex and race markedly influenced the results, but class was not found to have any effect. Negro *S*s obtained higher dom and love scores than the white *S*s for self-ratings, but lower scores on ideal descriptions. Males' Self- and Ideal-self-ratings yielded higher scores on dom while females' ratings yielded higher scores on the love variable. There was less discrepancy between Ideal- and Self-ratings of: (a) Negroes compared with whites, (b) males compared with females on dom, and (c) females compared with males on love.

146. —, and M. D. Gynther. Relations between self and parental perceptions of unwed mothers and obstetric complications. *Psychosom Med, 27*(1):31-38, 1965.
(*39*:12240, 1965)

The study was designed to determine whether there are diffs in self-concepts, descriptions of parents, or perceived similarity to parents prior or after delivery between women with obstetric complications and those with uneventful parturitions. The ICL was admin to 177 white single females at the 7th month of gestation and 2nd week postpartum. No reliable diffs were found in the pretest. On the posttest both gps shifted toward strong self descriptions. The abnormal gp emphasized power and aggression while the normal gp was more nurturant. The abnormal gp avoided extreme intensity check list items.

147. McGreevey, J. C. Interlevel disparity and predictive efficiency. *J Proj Tech, 26*(1):80-87, 1962.

Gps of student nurses were used to investigate the accuracy of self-rating questionnaires and projective tests (TAT & SCT) for predicting Level I (peer-rated) and L-II behavior, and the effect on these predictions expected by the presence or absence of ego-threat. L-II behavior can be predicted more accurately from questionnaire tests for non-ego-threatened traits than for ego-threatened traits. L-I behavior can be predicted with equal accuracy from questionnaire tests for ego-threatened traits and for non-ego-threatened traits. Clinicians' judgments from projective tests agree more closely with Level II behavior for non-ego-threatened traits than for ego-threatened traits. For ego-threatened traits, the clinicians' judgments underrated the desirable traits and overrated the undesirable traits relative to the *S*s' own self-concepts. Clinicians' judgments agree with peer-ratings equally for the ego-threatened and non-ego-threatened traits.

148. McKegney, F. P. Psychological correlates of behavior in seriously delinquent juveniles. *Br J Psychiatry, 113*: 781-792, 1967.

While study of 200 admissions to the National Training School for Boys failed to discover relationships between single behaviors and single background events, 5 clusters of traits were designated and related to personality test scores.

149. McKenna-Hartung, S., J. R. Hartung, and J. C. Baxter. Self and ideal self-concept in a drug using subculture. *J Pers Assess, 35*(5):463-471, 1971.

*S*s were 26 males and 17 females who had taken LSD twice or more (median of 10) and had taken at least one semester of coll work. A *C* gap of 39 *S*s were matched for sex, age, and coll experience. All *S*s rated their Self and their Ideal-self. For both gps, the Ideal-self was more Managerial-Autocratic and Responsible-Hypernormal and less Aggressive-Sadistic, Rebellious-Distrustful, Self-effacing-Masochistic, and Docile-Dependent. Females were less Competitive-Narcissistic than males in their Self rating but not in their Ideal-self rating. The drug-users endorsed fewer Managerial-Autocratic and more Rebellious-Distrustful characteristics than non-drug-users in both their Self and Ideal-self descriptions. Drug-users also presented sig smaller discrepancies between their Self and their Ideal-self summary scores.

150. Mebane, D. F., and J. G. Die. A scoring system for human figure drawings as a measure of personality at Level III of the Leary Interpersonal Diagnostic System. *Percept Mot Skills*, 30(2):385-386, 1970.

   *S*s were m coll students. DAP, ICL, and TAT were admin. Results revealed only gross discrimination of *S*s having loving or hating, dominant or passive interpers attitudes.

151. Meers, M. The emergence of dependency as a function of the degree of congruency between Level I (public communication) and Level II (self concept) of the Leary Interpersonal Check List. Master's thesis, University of Kansas, 1966.

152. —, and C. Neuringer. A validation of self-concept measures of the Leary Interpersonal Check List. *J Gen Psychol*, 77:237-242, 1967.

   80 m coll *S*s were admin 8 measures of social adherence and dependence (EPPS). Congruence or noncongruence between Level I and Level II ICL summary points was also determined for each *S* (though the Level I measure is not clarified). Congruence was defined as a *S* obtaining Level I and Level II summary points both within either the latter half of octant *6, 7,* and *8,* or in the first half of octant *1.* Noncongruence was defined as a Level I summary point in the octant sections delineated above

with a Level II summary point in octant 2. The congruent Ss, therefore, showed leanings toward socially sanctioned behavior on both Level I and Level II, whereas noncongruent Ss demonstrated this bias only on Level I. The congruent Ss scored sig higher on 7 of the 8 measures of social adherence. Only the SD scale failed to reach significance.

153. Mellan, J. Interpersonal relationships of female patients with sexual disorders as assessed by Leary's test. *Arch Sex Behav, 1*:263, 1971.

267 women with complaints of functional sexual disturbances or disharmony in a heterosexual relationship were compared with 137 *C* Ss on ICL descriptions of Self, Partner, Mother, Father, Ideal-self and Ideal-partner. The *E* Ss gave sig more neurotic self-descriptions (ICL diagnosis in octants *3, 4, 5,* or *6*) than did the *C* Ss. Women with diagnoses of anesthetic-frigid syndrome, primary and secondary orgasmic deficiency, dysparenuria, vaginismus, aversion to partner or sex, and hypereroticism yielded some sig diffs in their interpersonal diagnoses.

154. Murstein, B. I., and V. Glaudin. The relationship of marital adjustment to personality; A factor analysis of the Interpersonal Check List. *J Marriage & the Family, 28*:37-43, 1966.

ICL was admin under 6 different "sets" (Self, Ideal-self, Spouse, Ideal-spouse, Mother, and Father) to 26 couples initiating marriage counseling and 24 *C* couples. The experimental-control dichotomy served as an indicator of marital adjustment (MA). Data were factor analyzed by sex. For men, ICL factors were not related to MA, but unhappy husbands described their Ideal-spouse as competitive-narcissistic. For women there were 3 factors which had moderate loadings for MA—Spouse-dominant, Spouse-good, and Ideals and Self not rebellious distrustful.

155. Owens, A. G. *The assessment of individual performance in small Antarctic groups. Part II. Ratings on the Leary Interpersonal Check List.* (Psychological Research Unit Report 6/67, Australian Military Forces).

Leaders of Antarctic expeditions rated their men on the ICL

and performance scales with dimensions of task, intra- and interpersonal performance. LOV scores were related to inter- personal performance; DOM scores were related to task and intrapersonal performance. Octant *8* was related to task and interpersonal performance, while octant *4* was related to intra- and interpersonal performance.

156. —. *The assessment of performance in small Antarctic groups. Part III. Factor Analysis of Leary Interper- sonal Check List Items.* (Psychological Research Unit Report 10/67, Australian Military Forces).

Reports a factor analysis on ICL descriptions of the Antarctic gp members by the leaders. Four major factors—agreeableness, leadership, rigid defensiveness and group cooperation—and 5 minor factors were identified. All the major factors and 2 of the minor factors were related to overall performance in the groups.

157. Palmer, J., and D. Byrne. Attraction toward dominant and submissive strangers: Similarity versus complementari ty. *J Exper Res Pers,* 4:108-115, 1970.

Study investigated the similarity and complementarity hypoths of personality and attraction using coll Ss and the ICL to mea- sure dominance-submissiveness. Attraction was influenced by an interaction between dominance-submissiveness of S and stranger, with the direction supporting the similarity hypoth. There was an overall preference across Ss for the dominant over the submissive stranger.

158. Park, J., and L. Eberlein. Self-ideal congruence and flexi- bility in counseling. *West Psychol,* 1(1):39-45, 1969.

Using the ICL and the Counselor Rating Scale, the study ex- amined relationship between Self-Ideal (S-I) congruence and supervisor ratings of counselor trainee performance on a cogni- tive flexibility scale. Ss were 69 counselor trainees. Results failed to support a linear relationship, but 8 of the 11 sub- scales were sig related to S-I values under a curvilinear analysis. These findings suggest the presence of an optimal range of S-I congruence: i.e., those trainees with moderate S-I discrepancies generally received higher supervisor ratings.

159. Parsons, O. A., J. Altrocchi, and F. E. Spring. Discrepancies in interpersonal perception, adjustment and therapeutic skill. *Percept Mot Skills, 18*(3):697-702, 1964.
(*39*:5239, 1965)

> From interpersonal theories of Sullivan, Leary, and Rogers, it was predicted that discrepancy between self-description and others' description of *S*, disagreement among others in describing *S* and maladjustment would be positively interrelated and negatively related to skill in psycho-therapeutically oriented psychiatric nursing. These predictions were tested in 2 gps of student nurses from successive years. Adjustment was rated from the MMPI. The discrepancy and disagreement measures were derived from ICL self and peer ratings. Psychotherapeutic skillfulness was rated by 2 psych supervisors on a specially devised scale. Results from Gp I (N=64) provided some support for the major predictions but were not cross-validated in Gp II (N=74). Reasons for lack of replication were discussed.

160. Perr, H. M. Criteria distinguishing parents of schizophrenic and normal children: An initial study with the interpersonal diagnostic sytem. *Arch Neurol Psychiatry, 79*:217-224, 1958.
(*33*:6274, 1959)

> 5 couples, 10 parents of autistic children, were compared with 6 couples, 12 parents of normal children, by use of the Leary method of Interpersonal Diagnosis and by admin of the MMPI, as well as of 10 cards from the TAT. Results indicated that personality and characterological traits might well differentially exist, but that additional study was needed to isolate these. Parents of schizophrenic children tended to exhibit more rigidity and stereotypy in perception, and to show greater self-deception. "Patient-parents consciously identified their mothers and their spouses."

161. Peskin, H. The duration of normal menses as a psychosomatic phenomenon. *Psychosom Med, 30*(4):378-389, 1968.

> Adult *S*s with long (6 days or more), short (4 days or less)

and 5-day menstrual periods were compared on the basis of a pool of adolescent and adult behavioral dimensions reflecting masculinity-femininity and general ego functioning. Measuring instruments included the California Q-sort, CPI, and the ICL. An M-F index had been derived previously from the ICLs of a sample of 65 m and 82 fem Ss. A high score for a S indicating femininity was computed by adding the number of items differentially checked by the females, minus the number of items differentially checked by the males. Female-descriptive adjectives state interpers behaviors of dependency, responsibility, modesty, and cooperativeness; male-descriptive adjectives concern the managerial, competitive, aggressive, and skeptical. On the ICL M-F and CPI Fe scales, the short and long menstruation gps occupy positions at opposite extremes, falling respectively below and above the mean of the 5-day gp. The ICL sector-scores can be used to determine the most differentiating components of the M-F scale. Then best sectors refer to the greater docility and dependency of the long-menstruation Ss and to the greater competitiveness of the short-menstruation gp.

162. Posavac, E. J., and H. C. Triandis. Personality characteristics, race, and grades as determinants of interpersonal attitudes. *J Soc Psychol*, 76:227-242, 1968.

White m coll Ss completed Triandis' Behavioral Differential (BD) questionnaire on "stimulus persons," described as either Negro or white, extraverted or introverted, agreeable or nasty and an "A" student or a "C" student. Complete crossing of these 4 descriptors yielded 16 different stimulus persons. The ICL self-description (II-S) was also obtained for each S. Factor analysis of the BD resulted in 5 distinct factors: instrumental friendship, expressive friendship, evaluation, social distance, and dominance. A two-mode factor analysis was then used to develop a typology of Ss. Four types of students, or subject factors, emerged. S's loadings on these 4 factors were combined with the 8 ICL scores in a subsequent factor analysis. This analysis yielded 5 factors, with none of the ICL scores loading on the same factor with any of the 4 subject type scores. Rather, 3 of the factors were defined exclusively by ICL octant scores; factor alpha, factor beta, and factor gamma. The composition of these 3 factors were similar in Wiggins' (1961) factor analysis of the ICL. These ICL factors and the individual

ICL octant scores were independent of the personality types derived by the BD.

163. Powell, L.   The effect of self esteem on perceiving self and others.   Master's thesis, University of Chicago, 1969.

164. Preston, C. E.   Traits endorsed by older non-retired and retired subjects. *J Gerontol, 21*(2):261-264, 1966.

The Kogan modification of the ICL was admin to a gp of retired older *S*s and a gp of older *S*s still currently employed and their spouses.   No quantitative diffs in the endorsement of traits were found to be systematically associated with retirement compared with non-retirement, with age, sex, and other psychosocial parameters.

165. —, and K. S. Gudiksen.   A measure of self-perception among older people. *J Gerontol, 21*:63-71, 1966.

*S*s were 120 males and females over 65 years of age, from 4 different retirement conditions: Affluent retirement homes, modest retirement homes, participants in a recreational activity club, and indigents seeking outpt medical care at a county hosp. They completed a special 110 item questionnaire and the Kogan and Fordyce (1962) modification of the LaForge-Suczek ICL, first for themselves and then again for "most people my age." In this modified form each ICL item is given either a true or false rating.   These ICL forms were analyzed only for the number of SD items answered true and the number of socially undesirable items answered false.   Apparently, SD norms were taken from Edwards (1957) or Kogan and Fordyce.   The indigent older people endorsed fewer positive items and more negative items than the other gps in both their self-ratings and their ratings of "most people my age."   No such diffs were found among the other 3 groups.

166. Rawlinson, M. E.   A study of projection in relation to interpersonal perception.   Master's thesis, University of Portland, 1964.

(see Ref. No. 167)

167. —. Projection in relation to interpersonal perception.
Nurs Res, 14:114-118, 1965.

> 92 fem sophomore nursing students were divided into 8 gps and
> completed ICL descriptions of self, ideal nurse, how others see
> them, and how they see each person in their gps. Contrary to
> expectations, Ss who were seen by others as more hostile de-
> scribed others as higher on Lov than did a gp described as high
> on Lov. A subsequent analysis revealed that this diff applied
> only to Ss defined as low on insight. Insight was defined as
> agreement on the Lov dimension between rating of self and the
> mean rating of that person by others. Among Ss with insight,
> Ss described by others as high on Lov saw their ideal nurse as
> more loving, while Ss described as hostile saw their ideal nurse
> as being more hostile. Regardless of insight, Ss who described
> themselves as hostile and Ss who thought others saw them as
> hostile also described their ideal nurse as more hostile.

168. Rein, I. Medical and nursing students: Concepts of self
and ideal self, typical and ideal work partner. *J Pers
Assess, 41*(4):368-374, 1977.

> Several comparisons of mean scores were done. Comparing the
> Ideal-self (IS) and Self (S) scores for medical students (MS)
> and nursing students (NS) reveals: (1) IS >S scores on Dom for
> both gps; (2) IS >S on Love for MS but not NS; (3) IS scores
> for NS on Dom score > Dom score for the ideal nurse as de-
> scribed by MS gp, but not on Lov; (4) IS scores on MS gp on
> Dom score < Dom score for the ideal physician as described
> by the NS gp, but not on Lov; (5) MS described the typical
> nurse as less dominant than the ideal nurse; (6) NS see the typi-
> cal physician as more dominant and less loving than the ideal
> physician. Further comparisons were made to determine
> whether sex and year in school made a diff in the Ss' responses.
> Fewer sig findings were reported.

169. Romano, R. L. The use of the interpersonal system of
diagnosis in marital counseling. *J Counsel Psychol,
7*(1):10-18, 1960.

> Interpers diagnoses from 3 cases of marital counseling are de-
> picted graphically and interpreted in relation to the presenting

complaints of each couple. The interpers system is presented as a useful tool for the assessment of marital conflicts and for the evaluation of marital counseling.

170. Salas, R. G., and P. R. Jones. A balanced version of the Leary Interpersonal Check List. *Aust Psychol, 3*(3): 181-185, 1969. (Also, *Aust Mil Forces Res Rep,* No. 2-68, 1968)

Reports on the development of an apparently improved ICL, constructed to correct the original item order which as suggested by the constructors of the checklist results in an uneven distribution of items representing the various ICL octants.

171. Sands, P. M., P. Rothaus, and H. G. Osburn. Application of the Interpersonal Problems Attitude Survey. *Newsltr Res Psychol, 9*(3):19-21, 1967.

Ss were 59 psych pts admitted to the Patients' Training Laboratory. IPAS, MMPI, Rotter ISB, AGCT, and an estimate of general intelligence were admin. Three rating scales were used: (1) the ICL, (2) Group Member Evaluation—composed of 13 items about gp behavior—Ss are rated on these 13 items by fellow participants during laboratory training, and (3) the Shaver Rating Scale composed of 28 questions about psych symptoms such as anxiety, depression and withdrawal. Sig changes were found for 6 self-rating items of the ICL after laboratory training. Ss rated themselves as: (a) less resentful of others; (b) less passive and more confident; (c) less self-sacrificing and over-helpful to others; (d) less over-compliant; (e) less idealistic and more realistic in their own view of themselves; and (f) more satisfied with themselves. Improvements were shown on the other measures. It was concluded that the changes reflected are reasonable and should be expected from the particular kind of training received.

172. Savage, C., J. Fadiman, R. Mogar, and M. H. Allen. The effects of psychedelic (LSD) therapy on values, personality and behavior. *Int J Neuropsychiatry, 2*:241-254, 1966.

Ss were 47 males and 30 females who passed a thorough medical and psychological screening process. Treatment was a single, day-long psychedelic session in the company of a male and female therapist who provided companionship but not interpretation. Assessment included the MMPI and ICL at admission, 2 month and 6 month followup, a Value-Belief Q-sort, independent behavior change interviews and clinical evaluations. As a whole, the sample showed spectacular personality changes at 2 months followup. After this, different MMPI sub-types showed different patterns of change. Psychotic and borderline profiles were associated with regression to original levels of adjustment after 6 months, although mood and sense of well-being remained elevated. Hysterical personality types regressed also, but retained some degree of improvement at 6 months. All other sub-types demonstrated positive changes which continued through the 6 month followup. The ICL revealed sig increases in Dom scores at 2 and 6 months for each sub-type and without a sex difference. Love scores did not change, except for the psychotic gp. This gp had lower initial Lov scores, which increased at 2 months and decreased again at 6 months. Sig changes were also evidenced in the clinical evaluations, global staff ratings, Behavior Change Interviews and the Value-Belief Q-Sort.

173. Scapinello, K. F., and C. P. Sibbald. Structured group interaction: An evaluation of Bales' and Leary's methods of scoring interactions of first incarcerates. *Ontario Psychol*, 8(1):22-25, 1976.

    20 gps of 4 first incarcerates were asked to assume they had crash-landed on the moon and then individually and as a group rank-ordered the survival items necessary for returning to the mother ship. The IPA and ICL were used to measure interaction. Both methods classified the majority of Ss as active-rejecting. The ICL classified more as resentful, distrustful, and self-effacing.

174. Schoolar, J. C., E. H. White, and C. P. Cohen. Drug abusers and their clinic-patient counterparts: A comparison of personality dimensions. *J Consult Clin Psychol*, 39(1):9-14, 1972.

    80 multi-drug-habituated pts and 80 C outpts were compared.

The MMPI was used to diagnose L-I S and L-IIIMM. ICL ratings were obtained for self (II-S), Father (II-F), Mother (II-M); and Ideal-self (L-V). At L-I S, the drug-abusers were sig more hostile and critical. Both gps manifested sig self-deception. Drug abusers failed to perceive their strong, competitive, critical and distrustful public behaviors and exaggerated their perceptions of submissive and dependent behaviors. The outpts likewise did not perceive as much strength and autocratic behavior as others would see in them, and they exaggerated their perceptions of dependent behavior. The drug abusers idealized distrust and dependency more than the outpts, the outpts idealized competitive and overconventional behavior more than the drug abusers. Compared with the outpts, the drug abusers saw their mothers as more autocratic and less cooperative and their fathers as more distrustful and less competitive. Diffs in Level III-MM diagnoses were highly sig. Drug abusers manifested a basic intentionality characterized as skeptical-distrustful, self-effacing, docile-dependent and critical-sadistic. The basic intentionality (III-MM) of outpts was more cooperative overconventional, responsible-overgenerous, managerial-autocratic and competitive.

175. Seegars, J. E., Jr., and R. L. McDonald. The role of interaction groups in counselor education. *J Counsel Psychol, 10*(2):156-162, 1963.   (*38*:10303, 1964)

This study was designed to assess the effectiveness of an interaction gp in fostering emotional growth and self-knowledge in the graduate counseling student. ICL pre- and postgroup ratings of Self, Ideal, and Other gp members obtained from each student served as measures of detecting changes in characteristic modes of reaction in interpers situations. Open-ended questionnaires evaluating gp members' feelings toward the gp process were also admin. Postgroup self-descriptive behavioral changes revealed shifts from managerial to competitive modes of interaction. The most sig changes were obtained on the Ideal ratings, where a shift from aggressive, distrustful, self-effacing behavior toward more dominant, competitive interpers behaviour occurred. Pooled ratings demonstrated a perceptiveness by participants of other gp members' changing stimulus values. Subjective evaluations of the interaction gp as a method of achieving greater clinical skills were unanimously favorable.

176. Sheehan, P. W. Countering preconceptions about hypnosis: An objective index of involvement with the hypnotist. *J Abnorm Psychol, 78*(3):299-322, 1971.

> The results of 5 studies investigating the real-simulating model of hypnosis testing the basic hypoth that hypnotic *Ss* will stop responding when they perceive that the hypnotist is about to remove a suggestion while simulators will not. One study reported on personality factors as the causal determinants of hypnotic response, using undergraduate psychology students and the ICL. Results indicated virtually no association at all between *Ss'* interpersonal orientation and their response to the hypnotist's casual test for arm compulsion suggestion. There was no association between the hypnotist's rating of *S*'s ICL identity and *S*'s actual score classification as submissive or assertive.

177. Shry, S. A. Relative size of same and opposite sex drawings on the DAP as an index of dominance-submissiveness. *J Consult Psychol, 30*(6):568, 1966.

> Coll fraternity and sorority members were admin the DAP, 16PF, and ICL. The relationships between size of figures drawn and ICL and 16PF scores were studied. Results did not support the hypoth that relative size of the same and opposite sex drawings is related to the personality trait of dominance-submissiveness.

178. Silver, A. W., and D. W. Mood. Group homogeneity, conformity, and flexibility of interpersonal perceptions. *Comparative Group Studies, 2*(1):25-35, 1971.

> 17 m and 17 fem graduate students completed the ICL before and after participation in an experientially oriented workshop on group therapy. No overall diffs on Lov and Dom occurred for the combined gps. Sig changes indicating greater conformity occurred within gps more homogeneous on the ICL. More heterogeneous gps yielded changes over time suggestive of increased convergence between self- and peer-rankings of effectiveness (insight).

179. Simmons, D. D. Self-concept, occupational stereotype, and engineering career plans. *Psychol Rep, 20*:514, 1967.

*S*s were 149 HS juniors and seniors who were attending a summer institute. They were admin the ICL to obtain self-concept and stereotype scores of 3 gps: No career choice of engineering, 1 of 3 career choices was engineering, and all 3 career choices were engineering. Choice gps did not differ in the similarity of their self-concepts to their own or to the gp stereotype of engineers. There was a sig diff between similarity of self-concept to one's own engineer stereotype and similarity of self-concept to the group's engineer stereotype. The correl between the 2 similarity scores suggests that self-concepts are related to one's own stereotype and to a gp stereotype.

180. Simon, W. B. A comparison between free and forced responding to check lists: Assessment of the social desirability of stereotypes. *J Clin Psychol, 23*:475-479, 1967.

100 state hosp attendants completed the ICL in describing the typical mental pt (PT) and the typical person (PR). Each description was completed in halves, Forms A and B, with the 2 forms equated for SD values and for weights assigned to them by LaForge and Suczek (1955). *S*s also completed a 32-item chek list prepared to tap psychopathological tendencies (Form P). *S*s described each type of person (PT and PR) twice: Once they were to check a fixed number of items (FX) and once they were free to check any number of items (FR). The order of admin for PT and PR ratings and for FX and FR ratings were counter-balanced. Finally, each check list item was rated as either favorable (F) or unfavorable (U). The *S*'s PT ratings included more items which they also characterized as unfavorable. Fewer items were checked under the FR admin than the FX admin (forced choice of 42 of the 128 ICL items). The additional items checked in the FX admin tended to be favorable items. For the PR ratings, *S*s who received FX before FR endorsed more F items over both administrations than *S*s who received FR before FX. The 2 matched halves of the ICL did not diff sig in the proportion of F to U item ratings.

181. Smelser, W. T. Dominance as a factor in achievement and perception in cooperative problem solving interactions. *J Abnorm Soc Psychol, 62*(3):535-542, 1961.
(36:4CN35S, 1962)

Sullivanian theory was quoted as assuming that a person's mode of relating himself to others enables him to minimize the experience of anxiety in these interpers relations. On the basis that some people are primarily dominant (D) and others submissive (S) in interpers relationships, an experimental design was constructed so as to test the hypoth that the most propitious pairing of these was D with S and each playing their habitual role. The measure of successful integration was a problem solving situation. Ss were assigned to role congruent and dissonant with their habitual modes and paired with naturally and experimentally similar and dissimilar Ss. The results confirmed the hypoth that "congruence of role and habitual pattern within the S and complementarity of patterns as between Ss were major determining variables in cooperative achievement."

182. Sperber, Z., and M. Spanner. Social desirability, psychopathology, and item endorsement. *J Gen Psychol, 67*: 105-112, 1962. (*37*:3238, 1963)

The prediction was made that the self-descriptive response to a personality inventory by Ss suffering from some degree of psychopathology would be sig less related to the SD values of the items than was the case for a gp of normal Ss. The prediction was verified. Ss' responses to the items in high and low SD quartiles also supported the conclusion that the use of self-descriptive personality assessment procedures is not necessarily invalidated because of the operation of the SD variable.

183. Spilka, B., and M. Lewis. Empathy, assimilative projection, and disowning projection. *Psychol Rec, 9*:99-102, 1959. (*34*:2615, 1960)

A method of defining empathy, assimilative projection, disowning projection, and a general error term was investigated. The Leary ICL was given to 54 boys who responded for themselves and another person. The other persons then responded for themselves. The similarities and discrepancies between the 3 sets of scores were used to define the components of interpers judgments. The 2 projection measures were negatively correl as were empathy and disowning projection.

184. Stabenau, J. R., and W. Pollin. Comparative life history differences of families of schizophrenics, delinquents, and "normals."   *Am J Psychiatry,* *124*(11):1526-1534, 1968.

> 24 families completed an extensive battery of gp and individual psych interviews and psychological tests, including ICL ratings of self, each other family member, and the "ideal" person. In 11 families, the index child was schizophrenic (S) in 8 the index was delinquent (D), and in 5 the index was a nonschizophrenic, nondelinquent "normal" (N). Each family unit included an index child, a nonschizophrenic, nondelinquent sibling of the same sex, a mother, and a father. A correl matrix between the view of Self, Ideal, and the other 3 family members for 16 check list variables was derived for each individual. These correls indicated that the S parents described their index child as unlike themselves and their Ideal-self and described their control child as being relatively similar to themselves and their Ideal-self. The D parents showed less discrimination between their children in this regard, while the N parents described both index and control children as equally similar to their Self and Ideal-self. Although the S children were described as remembered prior to illness, these data are consistent with the hypoth that projective identification by the parents discriminates schizophrenic children from their normal siblings. The clinical data further supported this hypothesis.

185. —, and W. Pollin. Experiential differences for schizophrenics as compared with their non-schizophrenic siblings: Twin and family studies. In M. Roff and D. F. Ricks (Eds.), *Life history research in psychopathology.* Minneapolis: University of Minnesota Press, 1970.

> Presents an NIMH study of monozygotic twins discordant for schizophrenia and their families. The ICL was used to test hypoths regarding projective ident which emerged from the clinical material.

186. Stanik, J. M. (The problem of interpersonal functioning of personality). *Przeglad Psychologiczny, 20*(2):259-280, 1977.

The research data from several studies of personality carried out within the framework of several theories were analyzed from the point of view of Leary's IS. Leary's classification system is discussed.

187. Stern, G. G. *People in context: Measuring person-environment congruence in education and industry.* New York: Wiley, 1970.

   Compares three circular typologies of personality, including the ICL.

188. Stewart, R. H. Birth order and dependency. *J Pers Soc Psychol, 6*(2):192-194, 1967.

   Five gps of 20 Ss each were selected from a larger sampling of male students. Birth order (oldest and youngest) and the sex of the other siblings were crossed to form 4 gps. The 5th gp included Ss selected at random. Ss were admin the Barron Stems and the Embedded Figures Test (EFT). In addition, each S completed the ICL twice—once to describe Self (II-S) and once to describe themselves as they think other people see them (Estimated L-I). The diff between Lov and Dom scores was taken as a measure of dependency. The 5 gps did not differ in Lov or Dom at either Level II-S or the Estimated Level I.

189. Suczck, R. F. Psychological aspects of weight reduction. *Weight Control*, 147-159, 1955.   (*30*:7588, 1956)

   A sample of 100 overweight women who volunteered for a gp weight reduction program was examined in reference to (1) the fat person's personality and (2) any changes associated with the participation in the program. The women stressed strength, responsibility and generosity as the major traits. The facade of power and independence was interpreted by the author as a denial of underlying fears of weakness, helplessness and passivity. The women presented themselves as free of conflict, not ready to admit or recognize ambivalence about themselves and, consequently, like to resist change in behavior and self-appraisal. This is what was actually found on comparing the results obtained before and at the end of the 16-week period.

190. Teasdale, J. D., and J. Hinkson. Stimulant drugs: Perceived effect on the interpersonal behavior of dependent patients. *Int J Addict,* 6(3):407-417, 1971.

> Stimulant-drug-dependent pts completed the ICL to describe their Normal-self-concept, their Ideal-self-concept, and their concept of themselves under the influence of stimulant drugs. Both their Ideal-self descriptions, and their descriptions of themselves under the effects of stimulant drugs were sig higher on dom than their Normal-self-descriptions, but not sig diff from each other. It is suggested that the results support the hypoth that a proportion of such drug users suffer from lack of self-confidence and/or social anxiety, and that drug use serves an adaptive function in improving their interpers behavior.

191. Valek, J., and E. Kuhn. Stress-induced changes in carbohydrate and lipid metabolism in coronary heart disease (CHD). *Psychother Psychosom,* 18:275-280, 1970.

> Assessed the role of stress in the metabolism of CHD pts. No diffs in the strength of emotion and personality traits were found. Higher levels of cholesterol or its increments were ascertained in CHD Ss with dominant or aggressive traits.

192. Walhood, D. S., and W. G. Klopfer. Congruence between self-concept and public image. *J Consult Clin Psychol,* 37:148-150, 1971.

> 13 graduate students in psychology completed the ICL and a sociometric ranking of Dom and Lov on themselves (Level II), and on each other (Level I), and on how they predicted others would see them (Level I-P). For both methods of measurement and for both Dom and Lov, the highest correl between any 2 levels was between the self-concept (Level II) and the predicted image (Level I-P). The correls among the 3 levels were higher for Dom ratings than for Lov ratings. On the Lov dimension, only the Level II—Level I-P correls were sig. Checklist ratings of Dom and Lov were negatively correl at Levels I and II, while sociometric rankings of Dom and Lov were positively correl at Level I-P. Finally, the correls between the scores obtained by the 2 methods, checklist and sociometric ranking, were higher for Dom ratings than for Lov ratings (only public image was sig).

193. Weinberg, N., M. Mendelson, and A. Stunkard. A failure to find distinctive personality features in a group of obese men. *Am J Psychiatry, 117*:1035-1037, 1961.

Ss were 18 obese men and a C gp. Test battery included 4 WAIS subtests, the CPI, TMAS, TAT, Draw-A-Man test and the ICL. The gps did not differ in their Dom scores, in their ICL descriptions of their parents, or any of the other comparisons tested.

194. Weiss, W. U., and A. W. McFarland. Comparison of methadone clinic patients and methadone clinic drop-outs using the Leary Interpersonal Check List. *Proc 81st Annu Conv Am Psychol Assoc, 8*:401-402, 1973.

Using the ICL, raters compared active and inactive methadone clinic pts. An ICL self-rating was obtained on each pt. No sig diffs were obtained on the love-hate dimension but highly sig diffs were obtained between gps on dominance-submission. The inactive gp was more passive. The Self-Other discrepancy was sig for both gps, with the discrepancy being sig larger for the inactive gp.

195. Wiener, D. J. Failure of personality variables to mediate interpersonal attraction. *Psychol Rep, 26*(3):784-786, 1970.

A consistent finding reported by D. Byrne has been that attraction toward a stranger is a direct linear function of the proportion of attitudes S and the stranger share. However, considerable individual diffs in attraction responses toward strangers evincing equal-attitude similarity suggest the existence of mediating personality variables. Attraction scores derived from the standard Byrne paradigm were correl with several diff personality measures for coll Ss. Only the Dominence-Submission measure of the ICL correl sig with attraction and only for high similarity Ss.

196. Wiggins, J. S. Test battery for the multilevel measurement of interpersonal behavior. In O. K. Buros (Ed.), *The sixth mental measurements yearbook.* Highland Park, New Jersey: Gryphon Press, 1965.

197. —. *Personality and predictions: Principles of personality assessment.* Reading, Massachusetts: Addison-Wesley Publishers, 1973.

> The section on the interpers model presents a succinct overview of Sullivanian constructs and their bearing on assessment models. It includes a good introduction to the circumplex model, Leary's Interpersonal System of Personality Diagnosis, and the ICL.

198. Wiggins, N. A. Structural aspects of the interpersonal system of personality diagnosis Level II. Master's thesis, Stanford University, 1961.

199. Zimfer, D. G. Interpersonal attitudes of employment service supervisory personnel. *Counselor Educ Supv, 7*: 267-272, 1968.

> 21 counselors and supervisors at an employment service for youth presented similar Self and Ideal-self ICL descriptions. Ideal-self descriptions clustered in the Blunt-Aggressive octant. Both descriptions, Self and Ideal-self, represented primarily the Dominant and Hate octants.

200. Zuckerman, M., E. E. Levitt, and B. Lubin. Concurrent and construct validity of direct and indirect measures of dependency. *J Consult Psychol, 25*:316-323, 1961.

> The validity of a wide range of direct and indirect tests against a peer rating criterion and the factors derived from a factor analysis of all measures was studied, using a gp of student nurses. Ss did ICL ratings for self and peers. Specific ICL findings were not reported.

Doctoral Dissertation References

201. Arffa, M. S. An investigation of some criteria of adjustive behavior among chronic female psychiatric patients in

a state mental hospital. *D A, 26:*5544, 1966.

Three gps of *Ss*—20 pts in remission, 20 not in remission, and 20 nonhosp—were admin the ICL and TAT. Using the ICL, Public-self was measured by others' ratings, Perceived-self was measured by Self-ratings, ideal self was measured by Ideal-self ratings; and Projected-self was measured by the TAT. Results indicated that the nonhosp *Ss* showed sig more independent-dominant behaviors than the other 2 gps, also, showed more rebellious-aggressive behavior than patients-in-remission.

202. Armstrong, R. G. Personality structure in alcoholics. *D A, 18:*1851, 1958.

Ss were 50 non-psychotic alcoh state hosp pts and 50 exhibiting non-alcoh "normal" adjustment. Each *S* rated himself, his mother, father, wife, ideal wife, and ideal self. Hypoths generally corroborated were that the alcoh (1) has more intense, but fewer emotional reactions, and that passivity and aggression are stronger; (2) has a greater Self-Ideal-self discrepancy; (3) has a greater Wife-Ideal-wife discrepancy; and (4) has a greater Ideal-self-Ideal-wife discrepancy. Hypoths *not* corroborated were that the alcoholic (1) would identify with his mother; (2) would describe his mother as over-protective and over-indulgent and his father as severe and autocratic (the alcoh actually described his mother as dominant and aggressive and his father as affectionate and submissive); (3) would identify his ideal self and his father (neither did the "normal" reveal a hypothesized ideal-self identification with the father); and (4) would describe his ideal wife as resembling his mother. Based on these findings, the author offered a revision of the Neo-Freudian theoretical framework which emphasized perception of the mother as a cold, dominant person and of the father as a warm, but ineffectual person, thus leading to difficulties in emotional development and in ident as well as to tendencies to regress in the oral level.

203. Bednar, M. A. Changes in social perception in adolescents during group psychotherapy. *D A, 26:*1166, 1965.

Six psychotherapy and 4 social interacting *C* gps were evaluated 4 times over a 9 month period. *Ss*, adolescent boys and girls, completed ICL descriptions of themselves and other gp members, an anxiety test and Loevinger's Sentence Completion (LSC). Over the duration of their gp experience, both therapy and *C* Ss attributed increasingly more dom to themselves and to other gp members, with *C* gps actually changing more in their perceptions of dom in others. For both therapy and *C* gps, there were no changes in congruency of self or gp perceptions. An association between anxiety and incongruity of self and other perception was found, but only in the *C* gps. Ego development, measured with the LSC, increased more in the therapy than the *C* gps.

204. Belair, R. R. Selected developmental correlates of hypnotic susceptibility. *D A, 29*:765B, 1968.

65 m coll Ss completed the Biographical Inventory for Students, the Family Relations Inventory, a modified ICL, and the criterion measure, the Harvard Group Scale of Hypnotic Susceptibility. A number of hypoths were supported, although the relationships were of low magnitude. Partial confirmation of Hilgard's developmental-interactive theory of hypnosis was indicated.

205. Bobgan, M. A comparison of variability in identification and self-acceptance of male delinquents and male socially acceptable school students. *D A, 21*:3355, 1961.

A gp of m incarcerated delinquents and a gp of socially acceptable HS students were admin the ICL, describing Self, Mother, Father, and Ideal-self. The 2 gps were compared. The results revealed that the socially acceptable students, compared to the delinquents; (1) identified sig more with parental figures; (2) demonstrated a much greater degree of ident with the mother figure; (3) demonstrated a greater degree of ident with the father figure; and (4) indicated a much greater degree of self-acceptance. The degree of variability in maternal ident was especially sig in the octants or directions indicating Rebellious-Distrustful, Cooperative-Over-conventional, and Responsible-Hypernormal behaviors. The degree of variability in paternal ident was especially sig in the octant indicating Rebellious-Distrustful behavior. The degree of variability in self-acceptance was especially sig in octants indicating Aggressive-Sadistic, Rebellious-Distrustful, and Cooperative-Over-conventional behaviors.

206. Brown, E. J. Some psychological differences between neglected and delinquent adolescent girls. *D A, 29:* 1503B, 1968.

Hypoths were based primarily on Ausubel's theoretical formulations of satellizers (controls) and non-satellizers (neglected and delinquent). Levels I and III in the Leary IS were computed from the MMPI, and Level II from the ICL. Neglected girls were singularly positive toward others at L-II and negative at L-III, supporting Ausubel's conceptualization of the rejected non-satellizer. At L-III, the delinquent girls were more directly vengeful than the neglected girls, though both of these gps were apparently less able to depend on others than their "normal" counterparts. The L-III aggression and narcissism which characterized the neglected and delinquent girls were viewed as defenses against satellization.

207. Brown, J. B. Some factors in response to criticism in group therapy. *D A I, 30:*376B, 1969.

The degree to which an individual in a psychotherapy gp responds to criticism from other gp members was explored using the Behind-the-Back technique. 52 m VA psych pts in a Human Relations Training Laboratory comprised 7 self-directed (no therapist) gps. Each *S* was admin the ICL, AGCT, I-E Scale, and FIRO-B. All criticism feedback was taped and judged by 3 people. The results indicate that attraction to the gp was not related to response-to-criticism. *S*s with high Self-Ideal discrepancies were more able to retain the criticism they received over time than low-discrepancy *S*s. Also, contrary to the prediction, they were less pleased with their feedback. *S*s with low discrepancies remember more self-evaluation segments at first, however, over time, they do not diff sig from the high-discrepancy *S*s. If *S*s saw themselves as similar to others, they were more impressed by the criticism than those seen as dissimilar. Finally, *S*s retained more feedback over time from those they saw as dissimilar than from those seen as similar. This finding was contrary to prediction.

208. Bruno, M. *Similarity-Dissimilarity of married couples' personality characteristics.* Unpublished doctoral dissertation, University of Portland, 1961.

209. Bulatao, J. C. The direction of aggression in clinically depressed women. *D A, 22*:1249, 1962.

> Attempted to apply experimental methodology to test the observation that in mental pts suffering from depression there is an underlying turning of aggression against the self. 40 hosp women judged to be depressed were tested before a series of electroshock and again after the depression had lifted. A C gp was also tested twice with the interval between testing approximately the same as the E gp. Tests used were the Semantic Differential Test (SDT), the SDT in combination with the DAP, the ICL (the "Lov" dimension was scored for the Self and the Other), and SD Scale (sum of weights attached to the items on the ICL) and the P-F Study. The writer concluded that the results seemed to have confirmed the main hypoths, namely that, with the lifting of depression by ECT, intro-punitiveness would decrease and extro-punitiveness would increase.

210. Christopher, S. A. Perceived strength of interpersonal relationships and parental value orientations as factors related to academic achievement. *D A, 27*:666A, 1966.

> Certain aspects of the parent-child relationship as possible antecedents for achievement motivation, using 384 10th and 11th grade HS students, were examined. Data were gathered by using the ICL and an Academic Attitude Scale developed for this study. The criterion data, measures of achievement, and the intelligence data were gathered from the students' records. Among the major conclusions were: Partial support for the relationship between perceived strength of parent-child relationship and academic achievement, and between perceived parental valuing of achievement and the fact of achievement, was observed; and expected sex diffs were obtained.

211. Collier, H. L. *An attempt to extend Festinger's Dissonance Reduction Theory to situations involving inaccurate social perceptions.* Doctoral dissertation, Uni-

versity of Portland, 1962. (see *J Proj Tech Pers Assess,*
28:20-30, 1964)

In Phase I, a gp of coll *S*s was admin the ICL twice in order to
provide a pool of ego-syntonic and ego-alien personality characteristics for each *S*. The *S*s evaluated each adjective checked
along a five-point rating scale, from highly undesirable to highly
desirable. On the second admin they were required to evaluate
their worst enemy and again rate each adjective checked along
the same rating scale. In Phase II, 100 m *S*s were randomly
drawn and assigned to 1 of 4 sub-groups, each of which received different instructions designed to test the "attractive
partner" and "relevant experiment" variables singly and in
interaction. Hypoth 1, which predicted that there would be a
sig greater mean number of words produced by *S*s to influence
their S-P (stooge partner) to change their opinions in the socially dissonant situation than in the cognitively dissonant situation
was not upheld. Hypoth 2, that there will be sig greater magnitude of dissonance aroused in the socially dissonant situation
than in a cognitively dissonant situation when the S-P is described as attractive, as opposed to when he is described as non-
attractive; and hypoth 3, that there will be a sig greater amount
of dissonance produced in a setting described as relevant as opposed to one nonrelevant, were confirmed. Hypoth 4, which
predicted that *S*s would produce sig greater mean number of
words when commenting on ego-alien adjectives assigned them
by S-P as opposed to when they commented upon ego-syntonic
adjectives, was upheld. Hypoth 5, which predicted that *S*s
would assign their S-P sig fewer mean number of ego-syntonic
adjectives following a socially dissonant situation compared to
a cognitively dissonant situation, was upheld.

212. Conley, S. J. Strategies of maneuvers during the acquain-
tance process. *D A I, 30*:378B, 1969.

Coll *S*s were randomly assigned to male-female dyads and instructed to obtain 1 of 3 types of relationships; to get acquaint-
ed, to be friends, or to really get to know one another. Their
9, ½-hr sessions, were rated for genuineness, warmth, and empathy, and frequency of moving toward, moving away, and
moving against maneuvers. After the 9 sessions, *S*s rated themselves and the others on the ICL. The ICL data were unrelated

to the aforementioned observer ratings. The levels of genuineness, warmth and empathy were directly related to each other but were unrelated to the assigned relationship types and the movement maneuvers.

213.   Cooper, B.   Parents of schizophrenic children compared with the parents of non-psychotic emotionally disturbed and well children: A discriminant function analysis. *D A, 24*:1694, 1963.

This study sought to demonstrate that the parents of schizophrenic children differ from the parents of neurotic and impulsive children and from parents of well children in ways suggested by the clinical literature. Diffs among the parents were studied using the MMPI, ICL, Becker Parent Attitude Schedule, Locke MAS, and Wallace MSS. The results suggest that parents of schizophrenic children display a lack of dom (emotional non-involvement) which is different from the instability of parents of non-psychotic emotionally disturbed children. The variables of mother's warmth as measured by the ICL and mother's dom as measured by the BPAS contributed most to the discrimination (in a negative direction). The variables which contributed most to the second discrimination were spouse ratings of instability in relationship to the child and mother's hostility with the ICL warmth variables (mother's and father's) having negative weight. Parental instability in the context of mother's hostility was interpreted as an emotional instability factor.

214.   Cottingham, A. L.   Defensive organization of personality and its relation to the prediction of progress in therapy. *D A, 25*:1332, 1964.

To evaluate short term, individual, psychoanalytically oriented psychotherapy in 39 pts, ICL descriptions of the *S*s were obtained from the therapist at the onset and termination of therapy. From the interpersonal system, preconscious variability indices and discrepancies between diagnositc levels differentiated the least and marginally improved gps of *S*s. Improvement in therapy was related to the preferred defenses of the *S*s and to their predisposition to reorganize their defenses.

215. Counselman, E. F. A comparison of the self-concept, self-acceptance, ideal self-concepts, and career women stereotypes of career- and non-career-oriented college senior women. *D A I, 32*:1996A, 1971.

> Career-oriented and non-career-oriented fem coll Ss completed ICL descriptions of Self, Ideal-self, and career women stereotype. Self-acceptance was measured using Bills' IAV. Career-oriented Ss described themselves as more responsible-over-generous and their Ideal-self as more skeptical and distrustful than did the non-career-oriented Ss. The non-career-oriented Ss described themselves as more competitive-exploitative than they would like to be. The 2 gps differed sig in Self-concept, Ideal-self-concept, and Self-Ideal discrepancy. The Ss were asked to indicate the specific home-work balance they planned and subdivided into 3 gps. The home-work balance gps differed sig in Self-concept and career woman stereotype in one of the colleges sampled. On the other college sampled, the 3 gps differed in Ideal self-concept and in Self-Ideal discrepancy. Vocational development appeared to involve a self-actualizing aspect.

216. Crites, K. R. Interpersonal concerns as a function of perceived parental identification and influence. *D A, 29*: 4842B, 1969.

> 36 coll m freshmen were selected on the basis of their ident with their parents, as measued by the ICL, and their scores on the Perceived Parental Influence Inventory of Steimel and Suziedelis. Four gps were defined by high versus low ident and high versus low perceived parental influence. These gps were then compared on the Schedule of Interpersonal Concerns, L-I (MMPI) Lov score and on a concensus of opinion about efficiency in the performance of a gp task. Compared with high influence disidentifiers, the low influence identifiers showed less interpers concern with responsibility and higher L-I Lov scores. The high influence identifiers scored higher on the L-I Lov scale than did the low influence disidentifiers. The concensus measure of efficiency in gp performance yielded no sig gp diffs.

217. Cumming, G. H. A study of adjustment to a family crisis in the form of a disability to the male wage earner.

D A I, 31:3667A, 1970.

The reactions and adjustment of 72 couples to the disability of the male head of the family were studied using the ICL, MMPI, Human Relations Inventory, and the Terman Marital Happiness Scale. The husband's perception of self and the wife's perception of her mate were modified as a result of the husband's disability. Scales *Hs, D,* and *Hy* from the MMPI predicted successful return of the male to the labor market.

218. David, C. G. *Interpersonal patterns of two occupational interest groups.* Unpublished doctoral dissertation, University of Portland, 1960.

219. DeLange, W. H. Conceptions of patient role by patients and staff in a state mental hospital. *D A, 22*:2461, 1962.

Investigated selected aspects of the role of the patient in the mental hosp. It was predicted that pts who are high on dimensions of role conflict (patient-patient, patient-staff, and self-role) are less satisfied with hosp and are less well adjusted to the hosp than pts who are low on these dimensions. *S*s were state hosp pts and staff members. ICL and interviews were used. ICL was used to assess dimensions of the patient role and role conflict variable. It was concluded that the results added confirmation to many of the more informal observations of the pt role reported in the literature, and the findings were viewed as demonstrating the utility of investigation of mental pts within the framework of role theory.

220. Doherty, A. The relationship of dependency and perception of parents to the development of feminine sex role and conscience. *D A I, 30*:2415B, 1969.

*S*s were 736 fem volunteers from 6 colleges and 2 schools of nursing. The ICL was used to measure ident, the EPPS n-succorance scale to measure dependency, Schaefer's Parental Behavior Inventory to estimate parental nurturance and control, Gough's Femininity Scale to measure standards of *S*s and their parents, and a 7-point scale to measure guilt. Ident with the father was associated with *S*s' perceptions of maternal control and dependency on their fathers. Paternal ident was not associated with closer agreement with the father's standards of morality and femininity or with guilt about objective rather than interpers issues. Ss who identified with their fathers were more independent of their parents' standards and became more independent with age.

221. Drudge, W. J. The relationship between self-spouse perceptions and marital satisfaction. *D A, 29*:4558A, 1969.

It was hypoth that husband-wife agreement in trait perceptions would be directly related to marital satisfaction and that increases in agreement would be associated with increases in marital satisfaction. 54 couples seeking outpt treatment for marital disturbances completed the Locke Modified MAS and ICL Self and Spouse descriptions both before and after 4½ months of treatment. The hypoth involving between couples comparisons found partial support. The hypoth involving changes within couples over time was not supported. As a gp, the couples did not increase in either agreement of trait perceptions or marital satisfaction.

222. Edmunds, P. K., Jr. Committee chairmen and doctoral candidates: Their expectations and perceptions of the role of each. *D A I, 31*:2043A, 1970.

32 College of Education doctoral committee chairmen and 97 doctoral candidates each completed 4 ICL descriptions—perceived and expected roles for chairmen and candidates. Chairmen both perceived and expected a role for themselves which favors dominant over affiliative behavior. Chairmen perceived candidates as possessing less dom and more affiliation than the candidates perceived in themselves. The candidates expected more dom than they perceived in their own role, and perceived more dom in the chairmen's role than did the chairmen. The chairmen's perceptions and expectations of dom in their own role were positively correl with the dom they expected from the candidate. The candidates' expectations of dom in their own role was positively correl with their expectations for chairman dom. For both chairmen and candidates, the affiliation expected in themselves was directly related to the affiliation

they expected from the other.

223. Edquist, M. H. Interpersonal choice and social attraction among four interpersonal types. *D A I, 34*:1722B, 1973.

The major hypoth was that a person with a consistent interpers style, as measured by the Personality Research Form (PRF), would prefer to interact with others whose interpers behavior is "complementary" to their own. Categorizing interpers behavior into Friendly-Dominant (FD), Friendly-Submissive (FS), Hostile-Dominant (HD), and Hostile-Submissive (HS), 2 pairs were defined as complementary, FD with FS and HD with HS. 144 fem coll Ss were assigned to 1 of these 4 categories, according to their ICL summary scores. They were then presented with information and tape recordings representative of the same 4 interpers behavior categories. The Ss were to decide which of the 4 persons they would like to be paired with for dyadic interaction. The "Complementarity" hypoth was not supported by the results. Friendly Ss did prefer a friendly partner while hostile Ss showed a stronger preference for hostile partners. However, Dominant Ss preferred Dominant partners and Submissive Ss preferred Submissive partners. In other words, similarity, rather than the above-defined complementarity, was associated with expressed preference for future interaction.

224. Fehr, D. H. Perceptual field dependence and inconsistency of interpersonal perceptions in alcoholics. *D A I, 32*: 4209B, 1972.

Field-dependent and field-independent alcohs and non-alcohs were evaluated using the ICL. Discrepancy scores were obtained between Levels I and II, Levels II and III, and Levels II and V. Alcoholism was associated with greater discrepancy scores, but only in field-dependent alcohs. Field-independent alcohs and controls manifested similar degrees of consistency in their interpers diagnoses. Field-dependent non-alcohs showed the least inconsistency in interpers diagnoses.

225. Fisher, D. *Anomia, self-concept, and need achievement values of "Failure."* Unpublished doctoral dissertation, University of Portland, 1962.

226. Forsleff, L. P. A study of counselor supervisor and counselor-client dyadic relationships. *D A, 28*:1677A, 1967.

Tested the major hypoth that there is consistency of feeling-verbalization made by a counselor in counselor-client and counselor-supervisor relationships. Transcripts from an entire summer institute on counseling were rated by 3 judges for the feeling versus cognitive responses of the counselor. A sig correl was found between the proportions of feeling verbalizations expressed by counselors in their counseling and supervisory sessions. In addition, supervisors rated self and counselors, counselor rated self, supervisors, and clients, and clients rated self and counselor on the ICL. Sig diffs were found between clients' self descriptions and descriptions of them by their counselors.

227. Friedman, A. L. The effect of personality and interest variables on learning by linear and scrambled methods of programmed instructions. *D A, 27*:390A, 1966.

Purpose of this study was to determine whether diffs in achievement were the function of personality and/or interest variables. *S*s from a State University and a State Agricultural and Technical Institute were divided into 2 gps and given 2 methods of programmed instruction. All *S*s were given the MMPI, ICL, TAT, and 2 interest measures. Pre- and Post-achievement tests were admin. Results: (1) No relationship was noted between multi-level submissive personality variables to achievement by the linear method; (2) Only a bi-level relationship between the submissive personality variables and achievement by the scrambled method was noted; (3) The effect of variability between levels as stated in the hypoth was not confirmed; (4) A relationship between personality and interest variables to each other and to achievement by the linear and scrambled methods of programmed instruction was noted.

228. Fullilove, E. S. Patients' views of actual and ideal characteristics of the psychiatric clinical nurse specialist as depicted by the LaForge and Suczek Interpersonal Check List. *D A I, 34*:6496-6497A, 1974.

160 m and fem psych outpts who were either newly admitted or admitted for a longer period of time, were compared on their ICL descriptions of actual and ideal psych clinical nurse specialist. Perceptions of ideal and actual nurse characteristics showed very few diffs between m and fem Ss or between newly admitted and long-term patients.

229. Galligan, C. W. Personality correlates of varying degrees of adherence to an orthodox structure. *D A, 24*:3835, 1964.

Study examined the personality correlates of some varying degrees of adherence to the Roman Catholicism orthodox structure, using 4 diff gps of practicing Catholic coll Ss. Instruments used were a Catholic Belief and Behavior Questionnaire, the ICL, the Interpersonal Fantasy Test in conjunction with the TAT, and Optimism Sheet and the Rokeach Narrow-mindedness Scale. Personality correlates under investigation were arranged in 3 general questions. The findings for the 3 questions were principally negative.

230. Garner, G. F. Patterns of communication in training school for adolescent girls. *D A I, 30*:3866B, 1970.

The adolescent girls and the staff at a training school rated themselves and each other on the ICL. The institution was going through rapid changes, and episodes of disturbance were frequent. Ss were divided into 4 gps, acting-out and non-acting-out girls in either quiet or disturbed cottages, on the basis of 3 judges' ratings. As predicted, during quiet times the acting-out girls and the staff indicated complementary relationships along the dimension of dom. The non-acting-out girls reported a complementary relationship with the staff along the love dimension, rather than the predicted dom dimension. In disturbed times, the predicted symmetrical relationship on the dom dimension was indicated by the girls, but not by the staff. Exploratory findings indicated that distinct gp of girls emerged during quiet and disturbed times, which reflected the prevailing mood of the time.

231. Garvey, W. P. *Role discrepancies and marital adjustment.* Unpublished doctoral dissertation, Univeristy of Port-

land, 1966.

232. Garwood, D. S. Some personality factors related to creativity in young scientists. *D A, 22*:3273, 1962.

(see Ref. No. 51)

233. Gilbert, W. M. Toward the development of an animal analog of the Leary test. *D A, 29*:2632B, 1969.

The goal of the study was to develop an "Animal Analog Leary" test which would be more economical in approximating the locations of the summary points and which perhaps would extend the Leary test procedures to the younger age levels. The "Animal Analog Leary" test, as derived in the study, was unable to predict any of the conventional Leary summary point locations under any of the groupings tested.

234. Goldstein, L. Empathy and its relationship to personality factors and personality organization. *D A, 22*:4402, 1962.

51 graduate students were used to determine the relationship of empathy to personality factors and to personality organization. Three random gps of Ss were admin the MMPI, ICL, and TAT. Each S rated himself on the ICL and predicted the self-ratings of 3 other members of his gp. Empathy score was measured by the average validity of each predictor. It was hypoth that empathy would be directly related to Love and inversely related to Dom, Repression and Self-Deception. Results tended to support only the one relating empathy and Repression. The further expectation that these findings would be more sig at L-III (private self), than at L-I (public self) or L-II (conscious self) was not confirmed.

235. Gottuso, J. B. An interpersonal approach to female adolescent delinquency. *D A I, 34*:5191B, 1974.

100 delinquent and non-delinquent adolescent females completed the ICL descriptions of Self, Ideal-self, both parents and significant peers. The delinquents were perceived by themselves and others as relatively aggressive, hostile towards

authority, power-oriented and without regard for warm, loving relationships. Their Ideal-self images were more dominant and loving than their self-concepts. Delinquency was associated with relationships lacking in strength, authoritativeness, warmth, love and responsiveness. A number of hypoths were confirmed with sig statistical results, but the specific hypoths and results were not stated in the DAI abstracts.

236.   Graff, R. L. Identification as related to perceived parental attitudes and powerlessness in delinquents and normals. *D A, 29*:369B, 1968.

60 delinquent and 60 nondelinquent boys completed ICL descriptions for their self, mother and father. Perceived parental nurturance and punitiveness were assessed with the Parental Attitude Measure and powerlessness was measured using a modified version of the I-E Scale. Ident with a parental figure was directly related to perceived nurturance of that parent, while ident was unrelated to either perceived punitiveness or sense of powerlessness. Delinquents and nondelinquents did not differ in degree of ident with parents but did differ in a number of respects. Compared with the nondelinquents, the delinquents indicated a greater sense of powerlessness, described their fathers as more punitive and less nurturant and loving, and described their mothers as less dominant.

237.   Graham, J. A. The effect of the use of counselor positive responses to positive perceptions of mate in marriage counseling. *D A, 28*:3504A, 1968.

Purpose to (1) investigate the effect of using positive responses by the counselor to positive statements regarding perception of mate which occurred in a joint counseling setting, and (2) compare the effect of using positive responses in joint counseling settings with a problem-centered counseling approach without positive responses by counselor. All sessions were taped and positive references to mate tallied. Dom and affiliation scores on the ICL; the positive reference to mate and the number of reconciliations within 3 weeks after counseling were analyzed, using ANOVA and exact probabilities. Ss were 36 couples applying for marriage counseling. 12 couples were randomly assigned to experimental Gp-I, which was exposed to 4, 50-

minute joint counseling sessions; Gp-II was exposed to 2 individual 50-minute and 1, 100-minute joint counseling session; and the *C* Gp was not counseled during the experimental treatment. The sessions for Gp-I were structured around issues as they arose during the sessions; and for Gp-II, around problems previously checked on a prepared list. *S*s exposed to 4, 50-minute joint counseling sessions with positive responses from the counselors developed greater positive reference to mate than did *S*s each of whom was exposed to 1, 50-minute, problem-oriented counseling session and both of whom were exposed to 1, 100-minute joint counseling session. Respondents developed greater positive reference to mate than did petitioners regardless of exposure to marital counseling. *S*s who eventually became reconciled were those who made the most positive reference to mate during the counseling sessions. *S*s exposed to 4, 50-minute, joint counseling sessions with positive responses from the counselor were reconciled more frequently than *S*s exposed to 2, individual, 50-minute counseling sessions and 1, 100-minute joint counseling session. *S*s who had a divorce pending perceived their mates as more dom than *S*s who did not have a divorce pending. *S*s who had a divorce pending and who were exposed to 4, 50-minute joint counseling sessions, with positive responses from the counselor, perceived their mates as less dom than did the *S*s exposed to the 2 individual 50-minute and 1, 100-minute, joint counseling session. *S*s who had a divorce pending perceived their mates as less dom than *S*s who did not have a divorce pending if they were not exposed to counseling. Male *S*s perceived their mates as possessing greater affiliation than did fem *S*s regardless of exposure to marital counseling.

238. Gravatt, A. E. Perception as a factor in mate selection. *D A, 25*:684, 1964.

80 pinned, fem coll students were admin an Engagement Success Inventory, a measure of "basic understanding," and ICL descriptions of Self, Partner, Ideal-self and Parents. This battery was completed again after 3 months. Engagement success was related to agreement between Self and Ideal-self, between Self and same-sex parent, and between Ideal-self and Partner. Lov scores for Self and Partner were positively correl with basic understanding. Changes in self-rated dom were inversely related

to changes in partner-rated dom. Finally, changes in the ratings
of Self and Partner along the Lov dimension were associated
with changes in basic understanding and courtship success.

239. Griffin, C. L. Dominance in marriage and the post-hospital
      adjustment of male psychiatric patients. *D A, 28*:
      2136B, 1968.

      40 white, married m pts and their wives completed the ICL
      Self description. 20 pts had remained out in the community for
      at least 2 years after their hosp discharge, while 20 pts had re-
      turned to the hosp. The non-returners showed greater Self-
      Spouse discrepancy in dom scores than did the returning pts.

240. Hall, A. J. *Prediction of interpersonal behavior by Berne's
      Ego State Psychology.* Unpublished doctoral disserta-
      tion, University of Portland, 1963.

241. Hamilton, D. L. A multivariate analysis of personological
      differences in response to unfavorable evaluation of
      one's self. *D A I, 30*:388A, 1969.

      Ss were given contrived feedback on psychological tests which
      varied in its degree of inconsistency with prior self-ratings. A
      C gp received no feedback. Four responses to inconsistency
      were measured: changes in self-ratings (conformity), change
      in evaluation of the source of the ratings (rejection); change
      in evaluation of the tests (devaluation) and Ss recall of the
      ratings he received. The battery of tests which presumably pro-
      vided the basis for the feedback ratings included the ICL. Con-
      formity, rejection and devaluation increased linearly with in-
      creasing discrepancy of feedback. All 3 feedback gps recalled
      less than the C gp. High Lov socres were associated with less
      recall of ratings, whereas low Lov scores were associated with
      higher conformity and rejection scores. Dom scores were un-
      related to the 4 response measures. In view of the Lov-recall
      relationship, it is interesting to note that Repressors recalled
      less than did Sensitizers.

242. Hatfield, F. C. Effects of self-perception, interpersonal
      attraction and tolerance-intolerance of ambiguity on
      athletic team productivity. *D A I, 34*:4910A, 1974.

Various athletic teams were created experimentally, such that they were composed of athletes either high or low in tolerance of ambiguity. The athletes' perceptions of their teammates and of themselves did not differ between the tolerant and intolerant gps. The absence of sig diffs was attributed to a stereotyped "athlete" response bias. In sports requiring less interpersonal cooperation, tolerance for ambiguity was associated with successful performance as reflected in win-loss percentages. In sports requiring more interpersonal cooperation, the teams comprised of athletes intolerant of ambiguity were more successful.

243. Hattem, J. V. The precipitating role of discordant interpersonal relationships in suicidal behavior. *D A, 25*: 1335, 1964.

The ICL, the G-ZTS and the TAT were admin to 20 couples in which one of the partners was suicidal and to 3 couples in which both of the partners were suicidal. In addition, a structured evaluation was completed independently by 3 staff for each suicidal *S*. The suicidal *S*s were less well educated and worked in positions of less prestige than their spouses. On the ICL, the suicidal *S*s characterized themselves as submissive, dependent and self-effacing and showed considerable discrepancies between their Self and Ideal-self descriptions. The nonsuicidal partners were described as competitive and exploitative, both by themselves and by their suicidal partners. Their Ideal-self descriptions were similar to their Self descriptions on dom, but were higher on the dimension of love. High and low risk suicidal gps did not appear to differ in their ICL descriptions.

244. Hewitt, J. L. A communications approach to the prediction and alteration of hypnotic susceptibility. *D A, 26*:4075, 1966.

61 m coll *S*s completed the MMPI (L-I) and ICL ratings for Self and Parents and the Stanford Hypnotic Susceptibility Scale. No sig relationships were found between hypnotic susceptibility and any of the ICL variables, including discrepancy scores. There was a nonsignificant tendency for *S*s with cooperative and responsible L-I behavior to score higher on hypnotic susceptibility.

245. Hill, F. E. The attraction of upper-class and under-class vocationally undecided male students towards a counseling relationship. *D A, 29*:122A, 1968.

Ss were 100 under- and upper-class m coll Ss who had requested vocational counseling. Each S completed the Picture Impressions, the EPPS and ICL descriptions of Self and their expectations of a counselor and a friend. Upperclassmen were more attracted to an interpersonal counseling relationship than were the underclassmen. Underclassmen perceived a counselor to be more dominant and themselves to be relatively submissive. Such diffs on the affiliative dimension were not observed. Among upperclassmen, vocational commitment was associated with perceived personal adequacy.

246. Hull, J. S., III. An investigation of identification of male college students with their fathers as a variable influencing vocational interests and vocational counseling. *D A I, 30*:4775A, 1970.

28 coll m Ss completed ICL ratings of Self and Father and the SVIB. In addition, tape recordings of vocational counseling sessions were rated on the Relationship Scale of Gendlin. High and low father identifiers did not differ in the intensity, type, or range of their vocational interests, or in their manner of relating to their counselors. There was a marked trend for Ss in the technical and skilled trades area to be highly identified with their fathers and for Ss with interests in the social services to be less identified with their fathers.

247. Josse, J. Z. An analysis of the interpersonal check list responses of college students. *D A, 24*:5195, 1964.

45 m coll Ss were selected on the basis of their predicted and actual GPA. Ss were divided into 4 gps, crossing high and low ability (predicted GPA) with high and low achievement (actual GPA). Ss completed ICL descriptions of Self, Ideal-self, Underachiever, and Overachiever. Across all gps and all descriptions, Dom scores were sig higher than Lov scores, suggesting a need for coll norms. Self and Overachiever descriptions were more dominant than Ideal-self and Underachiever descriptions. Underachiever and Overachiever descriptions were similar to all

gps, suggesting a stereotyped image of over- and under-achieving students. The ICL diagnostic categories indicated a high degree of homogeneity in the total sample.

248. Kamerschen, K. S. Multiple therapy: Variables relating to co-therapist satisfaction. *D A I, 31*:915B, 1970.

The relationship between male-female therapist pairs who were simultaneously doing psychotherapy with an individual or couple was explored and elucidated. Variables of Selection of Co-therapist, Self-disclosure, Flexibility, and Attitudes toward the Opposite Sex, were related to the central variable of satisfaction in the multiple therapy relationship. 23 non-independent current multiple therapist pairs were chosen from the University Counseling Center being comparable with respect to age and experience level. The 9 females and 18 males were admin the ICL (under Self, Ideal Co-therapist, and Actual Co-therapist(s) instructional sets), the Co-therapist Inventory (CI), Jourard's SDQ, and an Attitudes toward the Opposite Sex (AOS) questionnaire conceived of by the researcher. Two satisfaction measures were derived: (1) a D-score by comparing each therapist's ICL scores for his/her Ideal Co-therapist with scores for his/her Actual Co-therapist(s); and (2) a measure from the CI. The findings of this study were that the ICL and CI satisfaction measures were positively and sig correl with each other for both the individual co-therapist's evaluation and his/her multiple therapy satisfaction and for the multiple therapist pair's combined evaluation. Also, the ICL was not sig related to amount of therapist Self-Disclosure, Personal acknowledgement, Impersonal message, or pair Flexibility. In addition, Attitudes toward the Opposite Sex were not found to be sig related to the ICL. One conclusion was that Self-Disclosure and the Personal/Impersonal dimension of co-therapist selection are relevant variables to satisfaction in a co-therapeutic relationship.

249. Keefe, J. F. A study of two seminary and two non-seminary high school groups on selected aspects of maturity. *D A, 26*:4076, 1965.

Compared 140 catholic seminary students with 140 catholic HS students on factors related to maturity. Included in the battery were the ICL, the TAT (L-III), and the integration index, which is the ICL-TAT discrepancy score. ICL and TAT scores did not differentiate the gps. Seminarians who manifested conflict between L-II and L-III presented a facade of passivity or docility with underlying dom, whereas non-seminarians showed the reverse pattern, a facade of dom with underlying passivity.

250. King, E. V. Personality characteristics—ideal and perceived in relation to mate selection. *D A, 21:*3883, *1961.*

Studied the concept of romantic idealization, defined as the tendency of persons in love to become blind to the faults of their future spouses and to overvalue their virtues. 215 couples applying for marriage licenses completed the ICL to describe the partner and the "ideal mate," and a short questionnaire. Results revealed (1) the incidence of romantic idealization of the prospective mate is higher than expected by chance, (2) women seem more prone toward romantic idealization than men, (3) ethnic membership, SES, marital status, and length of engagement seem to be unrelated to the incidence of unrealistic perceptions of the prospective mate, (4) age does appear to be related to the incidence of idealization—being higher among those age 40 and above compared to younger gps.

251. Kinsinger, J. R. The relationship between lethality of suicidal intentions and assertive, aggressive and hostile traits. *D A I, 31:*7600B, *1971.*

60 white females who had attempted suicide were interviewed and then rated for lethality of suicide intent by 3 judges. The MMPI, ICL and Buss-Durke Hostility Inventory were admin to these Ss and to 3 C gps—nonsuicidal normals, nonsuicidal psych pts, and psych pts who had only threatened suicide. 48 scales from the test battery yielded no relationships to lethality of intent beyond probable chance findings. Ss who had attempted suicide and the nonsuicidal psych controls produced very similar test results. The threat-only Ss had more elevated MMPI profiles and indicated greater submissiveness, dependence and masochism. This attempt to find unique personality characteristics among suicide attempters was unsuccessful.

252. Kobos, J. C. An exploration of aspects of the client-therapist relationship in group psychotherapy. *D A I, 31:*

7601B, 1971.

Study tested the following predictions: (1) those clients are rated as most improved who give the most accurate description of the therapist; (2a) therapists rate as improved those clients whom they perceive as similar to themselves; or (2b) therapists rate as most improved those clients whom they perceive as similar to their ideal; (3) clients who are rated as improved at the conclusion of gp therapy will have more congruent Self and Ideal-self concepts; and (4) A congruent therapist is more likely to be rated as effective, where congruent is defined as the lack of discrepancy between Self and Ideal-self concept. The ICL was used to obtain description of Self, Ideal-self, and other members in the therapy gp. Clients ascribed sig higher Dom scores to the therapists at both pre- and post-testing. Therapists described clients accurately at the first testing, but ascribed sig higher Lov scores to the clients at the second testing. Co-therapists agreed highly in rating the improvement of individual clients though clients and peers do not agree with the therapists. Therapists and clients consistently agreed that one therapist in each co-therapy pair was more effective.

253. Kotlar, S. L. Middle-class marital roles—ideal and perceived in relation to adjustment in marriage. *D A, 22*: 1734, 1962.

The Wallace MSS was used to select 50 adjusted and 50 matched maladjusted marital couples. Ss completed ICL descriptions of Self, Spouse, Ideal Husband, Ideal Wife and a role attitude survey. Adjusted wives were described by themselves and their husbands as more dominant and affectionate than were the unadjusted wives. The unadjusted husbands were seen by themselves and their wives as more hostile than were the adjusted husbands. Self-perceptions and perceptions by spouse were more disparate for the unadjusted than the adjusted couples. Regardless of marital adjustment, the ideal marital roles emphasized affectionate-dominant roles, conventionality, independence, self-confidence, competence, and drive for status. The unadjusted couples deviated from these ideal role qualities more than did adjusted couples in both self and spouse perceptions. Regardless of marital adjustment, the role attitude survey reflected a more instrumental husband role, a more expressive wife role, and over-all equalitarian role expectations. Marital adjustment scores were negatively correl with length of marriage and number of children.

254. Lafferty, J. C. A study of changes in self-concepts of teachers following participation in a consulting mental health program. *D A, 22*:489, 1961.

This study evaluated the effectiveness of 5 mental health consultants who worked with 121 teachers and administrators during one academic year. *E* and *C* gps were compared in a pre-post-test design. In the *E* gp, *S*s felt more self-respect, friendliness, independence, and self-confidence, less easily embarrassed, less apologetic and less self-effacing. Consultation participants also showed a reduction in strongly managerial and controlling ideal-self qualities, a reduction in Self-Ideal discrepancy and a positive relationship between reduction in Self-Ideal discrepancy and expressed satisfaction with the mental health consultation program. The *C S*s actually showed sig declines in self-confidence and friendliness over the same period of time. Consultation participants described themselves as being more similar to the consultants than did the non-participants and, among the participants, perceived similarity with the consultant was related to continuation in the consultation project.

255. Lantz, D. L. The relationships between self concepts and teaching behavior among elementary student teachers. *D A, 22*:1510, 1962.

This study explored the predictive relationship of self reports to classroom behavior, using 36 senior women who were making normal progress in a University Elementary Education Program. The "Integrative Verbal Behavior" scores derived from Flander's Categories for Indirect Teacher Control, were found unrelated to the 8 dimensions of self-concept. The "Classroom-Emotional Climate (CEC) scores derived from the OScAR were sig related to a combination of certain self-related variables. Students whose self-concept scores were higher on the Skeptical-Distrustful dimension of interpersonal behavior than their concept of other elementary teachers received higher CEC scores. Self-concept variables were unrelated to Miller Analogies, MTAT, and "Women's Role" of the SVIB. Self-concept scores were related to the *Hy, Sc, K,* and *F* scales of the MMPI. During the 6 months of student teaching experience, the means of scores on self-concept changed to a sig lower status on the Skeptical-Distrustful, Modest-Self-effacing, and Cooperative-Over-conventional dimensions of interpers behavior. At the end of this period the means of scores on concept of other elementary teachers were sig lower on the Blunt-Aggressive, Skeptical-Distrustful, and Modest-Self-effacing dimensions of interpers behavior. Also, the later means of scores on their concept of an ideal elementary teacher were sig lower on the Skeptical-Distrustful, Cooperative-Over-conventional, and Responsible-Over-generous dimensions of interpers behavior.

256. Lee, R. E. An investigation of relationships between patient self perception and hospital ward behavior. *D A, 25*:2051, 1964.

69 locked ward and 90 open ward pts were described, using the ICL, by themselves and by 2 nursing assistants. In addition, 2 trained observers completed the Psychotic Reaction Profile (PRP). This battery was completed a second time after a 3-month interval. "Insight" was defined as the discrepancy between self-descriptions and the average description of the 2 assistants. The initial battery revealed sig relationships between "insight" and the observed behavioral measures (PRP), whereas, self-descriptions were unrelated to the PRP scores. On follow-up, the self-descriptions showed a trend toward stronger relationships with the PRP. Extremely submissive self-ratings were associated with average or better observed behavior. Open ward Ss were similar to closed ward Ss except that the former were sig less hostile and depressed than the latter. Interestingly, those who saw themselves as friendly did, over time, become more friendly. (Nietzche was right!)

257. Leisinger, M. R. Interpersonal perception in families with monozygotic twins discordant for schizophrenia. *D A I, 33*:3949B, 1973.

The Leary IS was used to diagnose 16 pairs of monozygotic twins discordant for schizophrenia, both biological parents and 14 matched normal families. Confirmation was apparently defined as agreement between self-perception and perception of self by others. The schizophrenic Ss received less confirmation than their co-twin and normal twins, even though they all confirmed other family members equally. The disconfirmation is related to parental repression. Highly repressed parents emphasize the submissiveness of the schizoprenic twin and the dom of the normal co-twin. The families with a schizophrenic twin were more similar in their self-perceptions. The fathers in the schizophrenic families assumed a personality style more similar to the mothers. Normal and experimental mothers did not appear to differ. The schizophrenic co-twins did not have aberrant perceptions of their family members. Family process theories of schizophrenia were supported.

258. Levinson, A. A comparison of concepts of self and parental figures in selected groups of under-, average, and high-achieving high school boys: A comparison of a group of under-achievers with groups of average and above average achievers selected for intelligence, age, and grade. *D A, 25*:1320, 1964.

The relationship between level of achievement and concepts of the self and the parental figures was investigated through the use of the Leary IS of Diagnosis. The MMPI, the ICL, and the TAT were employed. Level of achievement was statistically determined by the standard error of diff between actual and predicted reading achievement scores. While the major hypoths of the research were not confirmed, 2 hypoths were partially confirmed. It was found that a high achiever, overtly, is very likely to be highly identified with the father figure, but the ident might not be maintained at the covert level of personality. In contrast, an under-achiever's image of himself and of his father may be similar, but he is not at all likely to maintain this harmony at the covert level of personality.

259. Luckey, E. B. An investigation of the concepts of the self, mate, parents, and ideal in relation to degree of marital satisfaction. *D A, 20*:396, 1960.

Tested 5 hypoths suggested by and common to the 3 major orientations which have dealt specifically with marriage counseling—the psychoanalytic, the sociopsychiatric, and the role and self theory. It was hypoth that there is no diff in population means between 2 gps defined as satisfactorily and less satisfactorily married (based on the Locke and Terman marital scales) in regard to: (1) the degree of congruence between the concept each spouse holds of himself and the concept of him held by his marital partner; (2) the degree of congruence between one's self-concept and the concept of his ideal; (3) the degree of congruence between the *S*'s self-concept and his concept of the parent of the same sex; (4) the degree of congruence of the concepts the *S* holds of his spouse and of his parent of the opposite sex; (5) the degree of congruence of the concept the *S* holds of his ideal self and the concept he holds of his spouse. The 2 samples were homogeneous in regard to 26 items of descriptive personal information. The ICL was used to measure concepts of Self, Spouse, Mother, Father and Ideal-self. Results revealed that: (1) satisfaction in marriage was related sig to the congruency of the husband's Self-concept and that held of him by his wife but was found unrelated to the agreement of the concepts the wife holds of herself and that which her husband holds of her; (2) marital satisfaction was sig associated with congruence of the husband's concepts of Self and Ideal-self, but the results were not clear when congruence of wife's Self and Ideal-self were tested; (3) husbands in satisfactory marriages identified themselves with their fathers to a sig greater degree than did the less satisfied (this was not true of wives identifying with their mothers); (4) associated positively with marital satisfaction was congruence of wives' concepts of their husbands and fathers; (5) both husbands and wives in the satisfactory gp saw their spouse as being like their own Self ideals to a sig degree than did those in the unsatisfactory group.

260. Meredith, J. C. Comparative life styles of women: Secretarial career vs. career and marriage. *D A, 27:3063B,* 1967.

The study focused on the developmental background of single and married women secretaries. Ident was studied as a psychoanalytically derived two-factor theory to reflect diffs in the socialization roles of mother and father. A second goal was to determine how generalization from family interactions influence mate selection. Another purpose was to compare life styles (ongoing life activities) as they may vary for single and married women. Sig diffs between gps existed in mother ident and father ident. Results supported the two-factor theory of ident, with parents assuming diff roles in the socialization process. Married women showed more favorable patterns of ident and reciprocal role relationships with both parents. Generalization from the family reflected more favorable development of the married women in their role interactions with men—freer expression of both angry and affectionate feelings, and more successful interaction on dominant traits. Single women showed stronger patterns of dom, inferiority feelings, and emotional withdrawal. Less positive attitudes of single women toward sex during adolescence and currently greater confusion in regard to sex values were the major findings from the developmental histories. Single women also had more caretaking responsibilities and more often came from fatherless homes. Single women showed considerable conflict in lifestyle, job dissatisfaction and frustration over lack of family life. Married women showed no conflict in their dual role of wife and career woman.

261. Miller, L. I. Familial role typology, accuracy of perception, and mutual needs among pre-nuptual partners. *D A, 27*:265A, 1966.

Winch's theory of need complementarity in mate selection was tested in 210 caucasian, middle-class partners. The Family Typology Scale (FTS) discriminated the couples on traditional versus equalitarian attitudes toward the family. The accuracy of Perception Scale measured each *S*'s ability to predict the mate's FTS responses. The ICL was used as a measure of psychological needs (self-rating only). The only sig finding, a positive correl among partners on dom scores, actually contradicted the theory of need complementarity.

262. Murphy, D. C. Verbal and nonverbal communication in high and low marital adjustment. *D A I, 31*:4919A, 1971.

Study examined the relationship between verbal and nonverbal communication patterns in high and low maritally adjusted couples. It made use of the observational method as a tool for understanding marital communication, and compared this method with self-report data.   Inter-rater agreement of the couples' interactions, where raters were employing the ICL categories, was greater for audio-videotape than for transcripts. There were sig correls between the researchers' observations and the self-reports of the couples regarding their own communication.

263. Maksimczyk, W. *Multiple concepts of delinquency.* Unpublished doctoral dissertation, University of Portland, 1960.

100 delinquents and 100 nondelinquents completed ICL description of Self, Ideal-self, both parents, typical delinquent and typical adolescent.   The 2 gps differed sig on each of these descriptions.   The delinquents were less identified with their mothers on Dom and Lov, and less identified with their fathers on the Lov dimension.   Compared with nondelinquents, the delinquents described their fathers more often as octants *4, 5, 6,* and *7* and less often as octants *1, 2,* and *3;* their mothers more often as octants *1, 2,* and *3;* their mothers more often as octant *1* and less often as octant *2;* their Self more often as octants *3* and *4,* and less often as octants *5* and *8;* their Ideal-self more often as octant *3* and less often as octant *2.*

264. Olsson, J. E. The influence of the personality of the perceiver upon perception of hostility in other persons. *D A, 28:*2629B, 1968.

Sociometric ICL ratings were used to identify 4 gps of *S*s: hostile, non-hostile, moderately-friendly, and overly-friendly. *S*s viewed films of persons categorized by psychologists as friendly, neutral, and hostile types, and rated them on a hostility scale. Total perceived hostility did not differentiate the hostile and non-hostile gps, the moderately-friendly and overly-friendly gps, or the dominant and submissive subgroups.   Compared with moderately-friendly gp, overly-friendly *S*s perceived less hostility in hostile persons.   These 2 gps did not differ in their hostility ratings for neutral and friendly persons.   Comparing dominant-hostile *S*s with submissive-hostile *S*s, the former attributed more hostility to the hostile type persons, while the latter attributed more hostility to the neutral and friendly types.

265. Padover, A. F.   Impact on attitudes, personality factors and behavior of an N.D.E.A. summer institute for teachers and other professional school personnel of disadvantaged youth. *D A I, 30*:4780B, 1970.

> This study evaluated the effects of an N.D.E.A. Summer Institue on the participants' attitudes towards children, self, and teaching.   The teachers and professional school personnel who participated showed no changes over the summer institute on a battery of tests which included the ICL.

266. Paxton, W. W.   *Interpersonal relationships with families of adolescent delinquent and non-delinquent boys.* Unpublished doctoral dissertation, University of Portland, 1962.

267. Peck, M. L.   *The relation of suicidal behavior to characteristics of the significant other.*   Unpublished doctoral dissertation, University of Portland, 1965.

> The spouses of 40 suicidal pts completed the MMPI, Rosenzweig P-F test and ICL descriptions of Self.   The pts completed the MMPI and ICL descriptions of Self and Spouse.   Spouses were categorized as a "double binder" if they endorsed the more intense items of octants 7 and *8* in describing themselves.   The double-binder spouse was extremely defensive (*K* scale), rarely able to express anger and presented a bland exterior which gave the impression of strength.   The spouses of persons who were not double-binders "tended to admit problems, express mild disturbance and in general, not exaggerate their normality or competence."

268. Randers-Pehrson, S. B.   The congruence of spousal perceptions and marital satisfaction: An extrapolation of Leary's theory of interpersonal diagnosis of personality. *D A I, 37*(6-B):3091-3092, 1976.

> The purpose of this study was to examine the congruence of perceptions of Self and Spouse as it was related to marital satisfaction using 59 married couples.   Married partners were asked to rate their perceptions on the ICL under 4 conditions: Self as a marital partner, Spouse as a marital partner, role expectations

of a husband, and role expectations of a wife. The congruence of perceptual ratings were correl with the marital satisfaction criteria to test the various theories and hypoths under consideration. Speilberger's STAI was chosen because it measured 2 types of anxiety, the Burr's version of Bowerman's General Evaluation of Marriage Scale provided a more traditional measure of marital satisfaction. The major finding for the study was the relationship between the congruence of role expectations that both partners had for the wives on the dom dimension with the intraperceptual ratings each had of the wives as marital partners and the marital satisfaction criteria. The husbands' congruence of perceptions of their wives with their role of expectations of dom for wives positively correl with the husbands' ratings on Burr's MSS and negatively related to the husbands' ratings on the STAI. Also, the congruence between the wives' self-perceptions and role expectations of themselves was negatively related to the wives' trait anxiety ratings. The confirming results supported an extrapolation from role theory.

269. Rholl, K. N. A study of relationships between occupational and marital roles and marital adjustment. *D A, 29*:2375A, 1969.

This study investigated the relationship between an individual's own expectation for himself and his actual behavior, as well as between his spouse's expectation and enactment; explored relationships between spouses in their memberships in family and occupational gps; and, was also interested in building interconnections between family and industrial sociology. 50 couples in church gp and 50 couples who were undergoing counseling completed questionnaires, the Wallace MSS, the ICL, and the Occupational Role Inventory. Conclusions: couples who have less disparity in occupational role perceptions and expectations have less difficulty in their marital interrelationship. Occupational and marital role disparity appear to be independently related to lower marital adjustment. The findings suggest the conclusion that occupational and marital role behavior commitment are directly related, but there is no association between occupational and marital role expectation commitment.

270. Rice, P. L. K. The modification of interpersonal roles.

D A I, 30:4797B, 1970.

Three advanced clinical psychology graduate students were trained to assume Managerial, Docile, and Ambiguous interpers roles. 27 veterans who were characterized as "self-effacing" were assigned to interviews in which the therapist assumed 1 of the 3 roles. In the interviews, a baseline of client role behavior was obtained prior to the therapists assuming their trained role. Two trained observers then rated each *S* and therapist on the ICL and on an anxiety rating scale. The clients of the Managerial therapists became more dom and friendly, showed greater flexibility at shifting to the reciprocal role (submissiveness), and were the only gp to experience a reduction in their anxiety level. The clients of Docile therapists became more dominant and more hostile. The *C* gp, clients of ambiguous-role therapists, showed no sig changes in the observer ratings of their interpersonal behavior.

271. Romano, E. The impact of mental retardation upon the self-concept of the mother: A comparative study of the self-regarding attitudes of mothers of trainable retarded children and selected mothers of non-retarded children. *D A, 29*:1510B, 1968.

Study examined the impact of mental retardation in the children upon the Self of the mother. *S*s were 32 mothers whose children were attending public schools for trainable mental retardates and 32 mothers of non-retardates. Six instruments, including the ICL, were admin. As to the ICL, it was hypoth that mothers of retardates would demonstrate greater discrepancies between Self and Ideal in comparison with the *C* gp. No sig diffs between gps were found.

272. Roth, H. S. Personal and demographic characteristics associated with L-I-D response bias of domiciled veterans on an institutional interest inventory. *D A, 28*:1209B, 1967.

This investigation involved response set bias employing the Like, Indifferent, and Dislike dimensions of an instrument other than the SVIB. 164 VA Domiciliary admissions were admin a Leary battery (ICL, MMPI, and TAT), AGCT, CMI and an attitudes and activities questionnaire. Data from VA records and Domiciliary activities were gathered during a 3-year posttesting follow-up. Extreme L-I-D respondents did not differ sig on 3 MMPI and Leary indices of psychological deviance. Intergroup comparisons were performed with all 6 deviant gps and one "normal" gp. The Dislike gp was excluded because of small sample size. Two or more of the gps used in the final analysis differed from each other on 9 of 17 scored MMPI scales. Also, gp diffs were found at all levels of the Leary IS except the pt's conscious descriptions of his mother, father, and spouse. The author presents a "modal model" as a steteotypic caricature of each gp. Each response gp was described in a narrative biographical sketch.

273. Rutan, J. S., Jr. Self-acceptance change as a function of a short term small group experience. *D A I, 32*:2194A, 1971.

This study evaluated the effects of a short term (15-week) small gp on an individual's self-acceptance, defined as the discrepancy between Actual and Ideal-self-concept. 126 *E* and 36 *C S*s completed ICL descriptions of Self and Ideal-self and Bills' IAV. At the end of the gps, *E S*s demonstrated sig more self-acceptance than did the *C S*s, who did not participate in a small gp. Increase in self-acceptance were correl with increases in trust. The amount of change in self-acceptance was not related to gp type (sensitivity, therapy, consultation), sex of *S*s, different leaders or different age gps. Of the ICL variables measured, level of trust changed the most from the small gp experience.

274. Scheiner, S. B. Differential perception of personality characteristics in cross-cultural interaction. *D A I, 30*: 477B, 1969.

It was hypoth that when members of 2 cultures differ in personality characteristics as evidenced in diffs of self-concept they would differ also in their perception of members of a third culture, and that this diff in perception would be related to diffs in both the self-concept and the sociocultural background of the perceivers. It was further hypoth that diffs in perception emerging with affective reaction (like/dislike of stimulus object) held constant would be of a different nature and more directly related to culturally valued personality traits. Ss were 31 Buddhist Japanese and 16 Moslem Middle Eastern students, attending 2 major universities in the Los Angeles area. Ss used the ICL to describe themselves, their culture-ideal and the average American of their experience. Japanese students differentiated themselves from American on the dom vector. When Japanese who liked Americans are compared to those who did not, the contrast between Self and American in the dom vector remains, but a diff becomes apparent in the perceived "loving" characteristics of the Americans: those who liked Americans, in contrast to those who did not, described Americans as very similar to themselves in this quality. Middle Eastern Ss, on the other hand, differentiated themselves most markedly from Americans on the love vector. This diff in the love vector remains constant regardless of affective reaction, but Middle Easterners who liked Americans, in contrast to those who did not, ascribed to them dom qualities similar to their own.

275. Schneider, C. D. *The relationship of patient expected change to patient perceived change and therapist rating of change.* Unpublished doctoral dissertation, University of Portland, 1970.

276. Schopler, J. H. The relation of patient-therapist personality similarity to the outcome of psychotherapy. *D A, 19*:2659, 1959.

58 pts completed the ICL descriptions for themselves, their fathers, and an ideal person. 15 therapists were described by themselves and 5 by other therapists. Therapy outcome was evaluated using therapist ratings of success and the number of interviews attended by the patient. Similarity of client and therapist self-ratings along the Love-Hate dimension showed a nonsig trend in relation to therapist ratings of success. Low similarity was associated with moderate success, whereas high similarity was associated with either high or low success. No relationships were found between therapy outcome and similarity between pt self-rating and the ratings of the therapist by others. The degree to which a therapist differentiated others' affiliative behavior from his own was positively related to the therapist ratings of success and duration of treatment. No such relationship was observed along the dom dimension. These re-

sults were interpreted as suggesting that more successful therapists are less likely to use their own affiliative characteristics as
a frame of reference for reacting to their parents' behavior.

277. Seegars, J. E., Jr. Dogmatism and college achievement.
      D A I, 30:1827A, 1969.

> Study investigated academic success as a function of the stu-
> dent's thinking flexibility or his open-mindedness. The Rok-
> each Dogmatism Scale was used to measure open-mindedness,
> and the ICL determined the degree and direction of parental
> ident. The students completed the ICL and both they and their
> parents completed the Dogmatism Scale. The results reveal that
> open-mindedness in students is correl sig with academic grades;
> open-minded sons come from homes in which both parents are
> open, but the father is more influential; and, closed fathers,
> when paired with open mothers, tend to produce close-minded
> sons.

278. Sellers, D. J. Effect of threat on self-esteem, esteem for
      others and anxiety in well adjusted and poorly ad-
      justed persons. *D A, 24*:5552, 1964.

> 42 normal m hosp employees and 45 nonschizophrenic psych
> pts were presented with either a threatening (experimental) or
> nonthreatening (control) situation. Self-esteem and esteem
> for others was assessed in pretest-posttest fashion using ICL
> ratings of Self and Ideal-self, Izard's Self-Related Positive Af-
> fect Scale (SRPA), and the Izard First Impression Rating Scale
> (FIRS). Anxiety was measured using a 4-item, polar adjective
> test. Pts and normals were differentiated on all self-esteem
> measures, including Self-Ideal-self discrepancy. The experi-
> mental manipulation of threat produced no sig diffs in self-
> esteem change scores. Initial self-esteem and the amount of
> change in self-esteem were correl in the normal *S*s only. Dif-
> ferential availability of defenses and distinct levels of defenses
> against threats to self-esteem were suggested.

279. Sharp, W. H. An investigation of certain aspects of the
      interaction between a group of delinquent boys and
      their mother-figures. *D A, 20*:2391, 1960.

Three gps of delinquent boys were selected on the basis of specific delinquent acts: theft, home incorrigibility, and home truancy. Each boy and his mother described themselves and each other using the ICL. The 3 gps of delinquent boys did not differ sig in the accuracy of perceiving their mothers' self-perceptions. The mothers of thieves were sig more accurate in perceiving their sons' self-perceptions than were the mothers of the other 2 delinquent gps. The delinquent Ss were more accurate in perceiving their mothers' self-perceptions than the mothers were in perceiving their sons' self-perceptions.

280. Sherin, C. R.   Some relationships among popularity, friendship choice and personality variables. *D A, 27:* 1931A, 1966.

144 student nurses in a residential hosp training program completed a battery of tests which included the ICL, the G-ZTS, the EPPS, the TSCS, and some sociometric rating scales designed for this study. Popularity status was not interchangeable with friendship clusterings, the former being more closely related to the selection and perception of friends. Ss tended to see their friends as similar to themselves, although complementarity tended to emerge with increasing similarity of friendship pairs on other variables.

281. Smalley, N. S.   Implicit personality theory in interpersonal perception: A study of married couples. *D A, 29:*762B, 1968.

Ss were described only as being married. Two studies were reported using the Burgess-Wallin General Satisfaction and Marital Consensus Schedules and ICL ratings of Self, Spouse, Ideal-self, Ideal-spouse, and Mirror-self. Self-Spouse intersection was related to agreement between ideal traits and mirror self-ratings. A negative correl between Dom attributed to self and to spouse (complementarity) was found in Study I but not in Study II. In Study II, the similarity between an individual's Self and Spouse ratings was greater than the similarity between that individual's self-rating and his spouse's self-rating (assumed vs. actual similarity). Marital satisfaction was related to the intersection of Mirror-self and Ideal-self. Marital consensus was related to the intersection of Self and Spouse-ratings. The use of "intersections" between ratings appears to be different from the more commonly used similarity or discrepancy scores, but the definition of intersection is not clear.

282. Smith, C. O. Interpersonal responsivity in a free responding verbal conditioning situation as a function of need for approval, expectancy of experimenter congeniality, and evaluation of task performance. *D A, 25*:6067, 1965.

The major purpose of the study was to extend the investigation of responsivity to social reinforcement as a function of "emotional atmosphere" to a verbal conditioning situation requiring the emission of verbal behavior that is free responding, purposeful, and communicative in nature. Several major hypoths were derived and subjected to experimental test. Also, the effects of several variables upon responsivity to social reinforcement were investigated. One of these variables was the 8 interpers traits of the ICL. The results, as pertain to the ICL, were that the ICL interpers traits were unrelated to measures of interpers responsivity.

283. Smith, H. L. Predictive ability of elementary teachers: The relationship between selected personality variables and the ability to judge ratings pupils make of themselves and others. *D A I, 30*:1439A, 1969.

*S*s were 45 teachers of grades 4, 5, and 6, and their pupils. Teachers were admin a battery of attitude and personality tests which included the ICL. Pupils were given the How I See Myself Test and the Granlund sociometric questionnaire. Teachers who were better at predicting their students' self and peer-concepts were sig more other-person-oriented and more responsible than were low predicting teachers. They also tended to be more affiliative than the low predictors. Overall, the teachers achieved an average accuracy level of 53%, only slightly better than chance. Subgroups of high and low predictors averaged 64% and 34% accuracy, respectively.

284. Snyder, J. A. An investigation of certain personality needs and relational patterns in a group of 70 premaritally pregnant girls. *D A, 28*:3043A, 1968.

70 premaritally pregnant girls (ages 16 to 23) were assigned to 4 gps based on their relationships with the putative fathers: Pick-up, Casual Dating, Steady Dating, or Engaged. It was hypoth that there are sig diffs among these gps as measured by the EPPS, the ICL, and perception of the boys' patterns of relationships as measured by the ICL. The Pick-up relationships were more passive, dependent, disappointing, and self-punishing. Casual Dating relationships were similar to Pick-up relationships in their strongly negative views of the putative fathers; but in some other ways were more similar to the girls in the other gps. Girls in Steady Dating relationships were more self-assertive and self-confident; were more straightforward, critical and direct; and were less self-effacing and self-punishing. The girls in Engaged relationships had some different, submissive, and unaggressive characteristics similar to girls in Pick-up and Casual relationships; but were more similar to girls in Steady Dating relationships in their positive views of the putative fathers.

285. Spencer, R. L. The Interpersonal Check List as an instrument in person perception. *D A, 29*:3922-3923B, 1969.

Members of 10 six-person families and 12 gps of 8 males each described themselves and the other family or gp members using the ICL. Of the m gps, 4 were normal, 4 were disturbed men living in the community, and 4 were hosp mental pts. Ss tended to agree in their descriptions of others, and self-ratings agreed well with the ratings of that person by others. Response sets on the dimensions of Dom, Lov, and SD were sig in the m gps only. There was no evidence that some individuals were consistently more or less accurate in describing others, although families were more accurate than the m gps. The 3 classes of m gps differed sig on few ICL measures, one of which involved SD. Normals described themselves and their normal peers as more socially desirable than did the community or hosp pts.

286. Spero, J. R. A study of the relationship between selected functional menstrual disorders and interpersonal conflict. *D A, 29*:2905A, 1969.

From 425 nursing students, 130 with severe functional menstrual disorders and 105 with no functional menstrual disorders were selected for study. Levels I, II, and III of the Leary system were assessed using the MMPI, ICL, and TAT, respectively. Comparisons were made between scores in the "neurotic" octants (*3, 4, 5,* and *6*) and the "idealized" octants (*1, 2, 7,* and *8*) and between the 3 levels of personality, via Leary's Variability Indices. Functional menstrual disorders were sig related to the Level I and Level III "neurotic" traits, the Index of Self-Deception, the Index of Preconscious Maternal Identification, and the MMPI *Hs* scale. The multilevel profile of women with functional menstrual disorders reflected an autocratic-nurturant personality with underlying feelings of narcissism and power. Women without these disorders present an autocratic-managerial personality with underlying feelings of power. The former are characterized by inter-level conflict, the latter with stability and organization.

287. Stanger, W. An investigation of the relationship of test-taking defensiveness to the personality dimension of self-responsibility. *D A, 25*:1346, 1964.

The ICL was used as a test of psychological adjustment, along with the MMPI *MAS* and *Es* scales. Measures of test-taking defensiveness and self-responsibility were also employed. Male coll students were given false feedback about their personality tests and asked to rate their degree of agreement. For *S*s high in adjustment, those high in defensiveness and those high in self-responsibility, agreement with socially undesirable feedback was higher when the instructional set emphasized the integrity of self-reports and lower when truthfulness in self-reporting was minimized.

288. Strahl, G. T. The relationship of centrality of occupational choice to sex, parental identification and socio-economic level in university undergraduate students. *D A, 28*:4917A, 1968.

84 m and 102 fem *S*s described themselves, their parents, their "occupational persona" and their "occupational role expectation" using the ICL. Centrality of occupational choice was defined as the deviations among the occupational and self-descriptions of each person, greater deviations meaning lesser centrali-

ty. Males showed a tendency for greater centrality than females. For males, centrality was greatest in *S*s identified with
both parents; second greatest in *S*s identified with the father;
third, identified with the mother; and last, identified with
neither parent. Males also showed an inverse relationship between socioeconomic level and the degree of centrality. These
relationships did not appear in the female data.

289. Swarr, R. R. An exploratory study of masculinity and the
attribution of dominance and love to parents. *D A,
26*:4818, 1966.

> *S*s were 92 m coll students whose parents were still alive and
> married. *S*s completed ICL descriptions of both parents and the
> first 420 MMPI items, from which the *Mf* scale was scored.
> Contrary to predictions, there was a positive relationship be-
> tween masculinity and mother Dom and no sig relationship be-
> tween masculinity and either father Dom or father Lov. Also,
> there was a sig negative correl between the love and dom at-
> tributed to the parents.

290. Taplin, J. R. Interpersonal expectancies of newly hospitalized psychiatric patients. *D A, 28*:2634B, 1968.

> 63 VAH psych pts completed the ICL under 4 instructional
> sets: self, ideal expectancy of interpersonal climate (IE), their
> real expectancy (RE) and, after a period of hosp, a sig staff per-
> son. Psychotic pts yielded sig greater IE than RE Lov scores,
> while non-psychotic pts showed a trend toward greater IE Dom
> scores. RE and self-description scores were sig and positively
> correl on the Lov dimension but were not statistically correl
> on the Dom dimension. A Maladjustment Index was derived
> from the intense ICL items. *S*s who described sig ward staff as
> being different from their RE demonstrated greater improve-
> ment on the Maladjustment Index than did *S*s with a relatively
> small staff-RE discrepancy.

291. Tarasi, A. R. A sentence completion technique as a measure of Level IV behavior with the interpersonal checklist. *D A I, 34*:1763B, 1973.

> 25 drug abusers, 25 psych pts and 25 normal *C S*s, matched for

age, sex, race, and family income, were admin a complete Leary
test battery and a forced-choice, sentence-completion form as a
measure of avoided behavior (Level IV). The results supported
the utility of the sentence completion form as a measure of
L-IV behavior. In addition, the perception of parents was related to the choice of partners and to the perception of others.

292. Taylor, A. B. Role perception, empathy, and marital adjustment. *D A, 26*:3527, 1966.

50 adjusted couples (in church gps) and 50 unadjusted couples
(entering marital counseling) were compared on the Wallace
MSS and discrepancy scores among various ICL ratings. Discrepancy scores were calculated for each octant in 2 different
ways: using the octant raw scores and using octant scores as a
percentage of the total items checked. Marital adjustment was
inversely related to the discrepancy between self-ratings and
spouse ratings of that same self. This relationship was sig for
the raw score comparisons, but not the percentage score comparisons. Marital adjustment was also related to the similarity
between Ss' self-ratings and their predictions of how their
spouse would rate them, for both raw score and percentage
score comparisons.

293. Terrill, J. M. The relationships between Level II and Level
III in the interpersonal system of personality diagnosis.
D A, 21:3529, 1961.

105 coll Ss were admin 2 8-card TATs, one with standard instructions and one with instructions to assume the identity of
a character in each of the stories (Self-TAT). The standard
TAT was scored for TAT-Hero and TAT-Other. They also completed 2 ICL descriptions, one on themselves and one in which
they were to check SD items. The Self-TAT, TAT-Hero and
TAT-Other all showed an equal lack of correl with the ICL Self,
suggesting that the 3 projective indices (L-III) were of equal
"depth." The ICL Self conformed more closely to each S's
standard of SD, while the L-III measures were all equally unrelated to SD. Discrepancy between ICL Self and TAT-Hero
were positively correl with anxiety (A scale scores), although a
negative correl had been predicted. Intercorrels among variables
within each of the 4 interpers measures revealed that the ICL

conformed to the theoretical predictions, whereas the TAT data did not.

294. Thommes, M. J. Changes in values perceptions and academic performance of college freshmen underachievers in a remedial program. *D A I, 31:*2969B, 1970.

This study evaluated the effectiveness of an Intensive Study Program for coll underachievers, which involved normal freshman courses, encounter gp sessions and long-term counseling. 23 underachieving program participants were compared with a gp of achieving freshmen who received no special treatment. The 2 gps scored similarly on the SAT but differed in their GPA; the underachievers earning a GPA of 1.87, the achievers earning a GPA of 3.14. A variety of measures, including ICL ratings of Self, Parents and Ideal-self, were taken in October and June of the *S*s' freshman year. The underachievers' GPA increased sig to 2.89. They also increased in their value of decisiveness. On the ICL, the underachievers increased sig in perceiving themselves and their fathers as more aggressive. However, the comparison gp of achievers also increased sig in perceiving themselves as more aggressive and rebellious, their fathers as more managerial, and their mothers as more competitive.

295. Truckenmiller, J. L. Equivalence of personality structure in Leary's interpersonal system of diagnosis. *D A I, 32:*6663B, 1972.

Investigated whether Leary's structural model of interpersonal behavior could be demonstrated to hold for 3 levels—ICL I, ICL II, and TAT III. *S*s were 11 university sorority women who rated 5 of their gp members, themselves, and wrote stories for 10 TAT cards. There was a total of 150 *S*s whose data were included in the factor analyses, for a few of the gps lacked one *S*. The data provided partial confirmation of Leary's scheme. Three roughly orthogonal factors, two bipolar and one monopolar, forming a rough hemisphere, emerged in partial approximation of Leary's 2 bipolar orthogonal factor model. (see Ref. No. 319)

296. Turner, L. N. The certainty of belief as a variable of personality. *D A, 24*:5554, 1964.

> 95 adult volunteers from 5 Protestant churches completed a specially developed test measuring certainty of religious beliefs, the MMPI, and ICL ratings of Self, Mother, and Father. The ICL was used as a measure of differentiation. As hypoth, *S*s who were more certain in their religious beliefs were also less differentiated in their self-concepts, described their mothers in a less differentiated manner, and used repression as a defense mechanism to a greater extent. Judgments of certainty on tasks that differed in their verifiability were not sig related to certainty of religious beliefs.

297. Vanderhost, L. L. An investigation of displacement and identification as variables affecting academic achievement. *D A, 27*:971A, 1966.

> 134 tenth grade students completed 2 standardized achievement tests and ICL descriptions of self, both parents, and their teachers. It was hypoth that achievement would be positively related to the degree of dissimilarity perceived by the students between teachers and parents. Using Diagnostic scores, Dom scores, Lov scores, and individual item comparisons, this hypoth found partial support. A negative relationship was hypoth between achievement and the degree of overlap in maladaptive interpers behavior perceived by the students in their parents and teachers. This hypoth was not confirmed. Ident with teachers was not related to achievement.

298. Wharton, M. C. Some personality characteristics of frequent and infrequent visitors to a university infirmary. *D A, 23*:3483, 1963.

> University sophomores representing 3 levels of infirmary use were compared on MMPI scores, the Jourard SDQ, the ICL, academic performance and demographic variables. It was hypoth that higher infirmary use would be associated with restricted ICL self-description. This and other hypoths were not supported by the results of this study.

Addendum

299. Anderson, E. H. A study of the relationship between depression and interpersonal conflict in the postpartum. *D A, 28*:2493B, 1968.

> 38 women with medically uneventful parturition courses were admin the MMPI, ICL Self and Mother ratings and the TAT on 3 consecutive days following childbirth. Structured interviews 6 weeks after birth established the presence of post-partum depression in 21 Ss. The depressed Ss manifested a greater discrepancy between Levels II and III of the Leary IS (Repression) and between Level III and their ICL Mother description (Preconscious Maternal Identification). The depressed and nondepressed gps did not differ in their Level I-Level II discrepancy (Self-Deception) or their Self-Mother discrepancy (Conscious Maternal Ident). The depressed gp was characterized by repressed aggression and by a lack of maternal ident.

300. Angleitner, A. Health, socioeconomic status and self-perception in the elderly: An application of the Interpersonal Checklist. *Int J Aging Human Dev, 8*(4):293-299, 1977-1978.

> As part of the Bonn Longitudinal Study of Aging, 134 m and fem Ss, ages 62 to 81, completed the ICL twice, with a one-year inter-test interval. The study related self-perception to health, sex, SES, and time (first vs. second testing). A multiple analysis of variance revealed 2 interactions and 3 main effects. On octant *4*, "Rebellious-Distrustful," healthy men scored higher than healthy women, while unhealthy men scored lower than unhealthy women. On octant *5*, "Self-effacing-Masochistic," healthy Ss scored higher than unhealthy Ss on the second testing, but not on the first testing. The males scored higher than the females on octant *3*. Lower SES Ss described themselves as more self-effacing (octant *5*) than did the Ss of the higher SES. At the second testing, Ss described themselves as more "Docile-Dependent" (octant *6*) than they did on the first testing.

301. Carson, R. C. *Interaction concepts of personality.* Chicago: Aldine Publishing Company, 1969.

This is an ambitious and impressive attempt to extend and reformulate Sullivan's interpersonal concepts. The author reviews Sullivan's conceptions and discusses the learning of interpersonal behavior; taxonomies of interpersonal behavior; the forces and implicit contracts involved in interpersonal transactions; disordered transactions, persons, and social systems; and finally an interpersonal account of the psychotherapeutic relationship. In the introduction, series editor R. W. Heine says, "In propounding a psychotherapy that avoids the 'disease model' he (Carson) does not adopt a position that rules out, as some radical behaviorists would propose, significant internal processes." The IS of Diagnosis is discussed at length in Chapter 4.

302. Crowder, J. E. Relationship between therapist and client interpersonal behaviors and psychotherapy outcome. *J Counsel Psychol, 19*(1):68-75, 1972.

15 successful and 10 unsuccessful therapy cases were thus categorized according to comparisons of pre- and post-therapy MMPIs. 15 minute segments from early, middle and late therapy sessions were then rated using the interpers diagnosis schema. 9,808 units of interaction between therapist and client were reliably categorized into one of 4 quadrants: hostile-competitive, passive-resistant, support-seeking and supportive-interpretive. Transference behavior by the client was defined as behavior categorized in any but the support-seeking quadrant. Counter-transference behavior by the therapist was defined as behavior categorized in any but the supportive-interpretive quadrant. Successful therapists displayed a lower proportion of counter-transference behaviors only in the later therapy sessions. In the early sessions there was a difference in the types of counter-transference behaviors, the successful therapists showing more hostile-competitive and less passive-resistant behavior. Successful clients showed a lower proportion of transference behavior only in the early and middle stages of therapy. The types of transference reactions also differed. In the early sessions successful clients were more hostile-competitve and less passive-resistant and supportive-interpretive. In the middle sessions, the unsuccessful clients continued to show more passive-resistant behavior.

303. Dietzel, C. S., and N. Abeles. Client-therapist complemen-

tarity and therapeutic outcome. *J Counsel Psychol,
22*(4):264-272, 1975.

> 10 successful and 10 unsuccessful therapy cases were thus classi-
> fied on the basis of pre- and post-therapy MMPIs. For each
> case, 15 minute taped segments from early, middle and late
> therapy sessions were rated using the interpers diagnosis schema.
> Behaviors were categorized into 1 of 4 quadrants: friendly-
> dominant, friendly-submissive, hostile-dominant and hostile-
> submissive. Complementary interactions were defined as fol-
> lows: friendly followed by friendly behavior, hostile followed
> by hostile behavior, dominant followed by submissive behavior
> and submissive followed by dominant behavior. Therapist com-
> plementarity was not different for successful and unsuccessful
> cases when early, middle and late sessions were combined.
> Successful therapists showed somewhat greater complemen-
> tarity early in therapy, sig less complementarity in the middle
> sessions and somewhat less complementarity in the late sessions.
> Behavior ratings of clients in the early sessions were also con-
> verted to T-scores on DOM and LOV. Maladjustment was then
> defined as distance from the center of the interpers circle, which
> would reflect more rigid adherence to a particular response
> pattern. This maladjustment index was sig correl with therapist
> complementarity.

304. Edwards, A. L. *The social desirability variable in per-
     sonality assessment and research.* New York: The Dry-
     den Press, 1957.   (*32*:464, 1958)

> SD is used in reference (1) to scale values of personality state-
> ments and (2) to the tendency of *S*s to attribute to themselves
> statements which are desirable and reject those which are unde-
> sirable. Topics developed are (1) comparability of social de-
> sirability scale values (SDSV) derived from different gps of
> judges; (2) probability of endorsement and SDSV; (3) the SD
> scale; (4) scale value items in MMPI; (5) SD and faking; (6)
> forced-choice inventory; (7) SD in Q-technique; and, (8) im-
> plications for personality assessment and research. Extensive
> bibliography.

305. Hogsett, S. G. A method to increase the vaidity of Inter-
     personal Check List "self" ratings. *D A I, 33*:1021A,

1973.

The ICL was compared with a modified form of the ICL (V-ICL) which included validity scales of the MMPI. ICL and V-ICL were admin to 2 diff gps of coll students, each gp taking the same test twice (interest interval unspecified). The V-ICL gp was then divided into valid and invalid gps. Test-retest reliability for "valid" V-ICL profiles were sig higher than for ICL profiles on the LOV dimension. "Valid" V-ICL DOM scores were no more reliable than the standard ICL DOM scores.

306. Karp, E. S., J. H. Jackson, and D. Lester. Ideal-self fulfillment in mate selection: A corollary to the complementary need theory of mate selection. *J of Marriage & the Family, 32:269-282, 1970.*

50 engaged fem undergraduates completed a 54-item abbreviation of the ICL to describe Self, Ideal-self, Fiancé and Fiancé's closest m friend. Agreement between Self and Fiancé descriptions was sig greater than would be expected by chance and was also sig greater than the agreement between Self and Fiancé's closest friend. Items endorsed differently on Self and Ideal-self ratings were more likely to be in agreement with the description of the Fiancé than expected by chance and than was the case for the description of the Fiance's closest m friend. A halo effect was ruled out as an explanation of the Ideal-self fulfillment effect by separate analyses on Ss that were high and low in their Self-Ideal-self discrepancy. Engaged females perceived their fiancés as being similar to themselves and as having those ideal qualities that they themselves lacked.

307. Kaye, J. D. Group interaction and interpersonal learning. *Small Group Behav, 4(4):424-448, 1973.*

Two coll student T-gps and 3 *C* gps were admin the Hill Interaction Matrix-B, FIRO-B and ICL before and after a 10-day, 18-session period and 8 months later. The ICL showed a complex pattern of changes.

308. Leff, H. S., R. V. Nydegger, and M. Buck. Effect of nurse's mode of dress on behavior of psychiatric patients differing in information-processing complexity.

J Consult Clin Psychol, 34(1):72-79, 1970.

19 m VAH pts were divided into 2 gps characterized by high or
low dependency on stereotypes (complexity of information-processing) and matched for race, age, education, duration of hosp,
diagnosis, ICL DOM and LOV scores and ICL Self-Ideal discrepancy. *S*s described "Nurses in general" on the ICL, engaged in
an experimental interaction with a nurse dressed either in street
clothes (SC) or uniform (UN), and then rated this nurse (Partner) on the ICL. The stereotypic nurse was described as sig
higher on DOM (64.7) than the mean standard score of 50.0.
The mean LOV score for the stereotypic nurse was 50.7. The
partner-nurse in SC was described as sig lower on both DOM and
LOV than was the same nurse in uniform. Discrepancy scores
between partner-nurse and stereotypic-nurse also revealed that
in the SC condition the partner-nurse was sig lower on DOM
than the stereotypic-nurse. Level of information complexity
did not appear to affect ICL descriptions. However, *S*s with
greater dependence on stereotypes tended to withdraw more
from the SC nurse than the UN nurse in the experimental interaction.

309. Leff, S., and N. Lamb. Experimental approach to defining
      the role of social desirability in personality assessment:
      Is there one response process or two? *J Consult Clin
      Psychol, 33*(3):287-291, 1969.

60 m undergraduates were divided into 4 equal gps defined by
high vs. low need for social approval (Crowne-Marlowe) and 2
instructions differing in their explanations of the *E*'s hypoth
about what characterizes good adjustment (high ideals and living
up to them vs. moderate ideals and recognizing ways in which
one fails to live up to them). Following these instructions, *S*s
completed ICL descriptions, in booklet form, of Self, Personal
Ideal and Social Ideal. High need for social approval was associated with higher scores on octants 7 and 8 for Self, on octants
6 and 7 for Personal Ideal and on LOV for both Self and Personal Ideal. Also, their Self tended to be more similar to their
Personal and Social Ideals (p < .10). Instructions that higher
ideals are hypoth to characterize better adjustment resulted
in higher octant scores on octants 4 and 5 (p < .05) and octants
1 and 2 (p < .10) for Personal Ideal and a greater diff between

Personal Ideal and Social Ideal (p $<$.05).

310. Liberman, R. A behavioral approach to group dynamics. I. Reinforcement and prompting of cohesiveness in group therapy. *Behav Ther, 1*:141-175, 1970.

(see Refs. No. 118 and 119)

311. —. A behavioral approach to group dynamics. II. Reinforcing and prompting hostility-to-the-therapist in group therapy. *Behav Ther, 1*:312-327, 1970.

Methodology and therapy gp composition (*Ss*) were identical to the Liberman study of cohesiveness in gp therapy (see Ref. No. 118). The diffs were that in this study the *E* gp was prompted and reinforced for hostility directed towards the therapist and changes in the DOM rather than the LOV dimension of the Leary IS were evaluated. Hostility-to-the-therapist was measured using the *Disagrees* and *Seems Negative* dimensions of Bales' Interaction Process Analysis. No relation was found between hostility-to-the-therapist and changes in DOM (Levels I-MMPI, I-Sociometric, II, III-TAT, and interlevel discrepancies) or changes in the Upward Downward dimension of the Bales' Three-Dimensional Personality System. Although the results supported the conception of psychotherapy as a learning process, the authors concluded that "As an area of group dynamics, hostility directed to the leader appears to be overrated in importance." Hostility-to-the-therapist comprised less than 1% of the verbal acts of pts and was unrelated to pts' symptomatic improvement.

312. Lorr, M., and D. M. McNair. An interpersonal behavior circle. *J Abnorm Soc Psychol, 67*(1):68-75, 1963.

A new inventory was developed using factor analysis. 13 scales resulted, 9 of which could be arranged in a circular order. As supporting evidence of the circular ordering, the authors presented new data on the ICL. An intercorrelation matrix of octant scores from a sample of 200 neurotic pts conformed "crudely to a circumplicial pattern." Three higher order factors were found (Dominance, Affiliativeness vs. Detachment, and Compliant Abasement) by higher order analysis of 3 intercorrelation matrices, one for the ICL, one for the Stern Activities Index and one for Campbell's Interpersonal Need Scales.

313. Malone, T. W. System simulation: Computer simulation of two-person interactions. *Behav Sci, 20*:260-267, 1975.

Describes a computer program to simulate two-person interactions based upon Leary's IS. As predicted, the simulated people developed reciprocal role patterns in the course of their interactions. Psychiatric abnormalities were also simulated. To validate the simulation model, the ICLs from real people were used to computer-simulate their interactions, and judges attempted to distinguish the simulated interactions from real interactions of these same people. The judges discriminated correctly with greater than chance frequency in only one out of the two interactions that were compared.

314. Nelson, C. M. The relationship between the Interpersonal Check List and a self report of roommate satisfaction in a women's residential hall. Master's thesis, University of Wyoming, 1970.

315. Rosen, A. C., and J. S. Golden. The encounter-sensitivity training group as an adjunct to medical education. *Int Rev Appl Psychol, 24*(1):61-70, 1975.

Three gps of beginning medical students were admin the Rosinski Medical Student Attitude Inventory (MSAI), Gordon Survey of Interpersonal Values, MMPI and ICL, before and after their first academic year. The 3 gps were a treatment gp, volunteer controls and non-volunteers. The most sig diffs appeared in the MSAI scores.

316. Taulbee, E. S., and H. W. Wright. A psychosocial-behavioral model for therapeutic intervention. In C. D. Spielberger (Ed.), *Current topics in clinical and community psychology (Vol. III)*. New York: Academic Press, 1971.

72 depressed psych pts were randomly assigned to 1 of 6 treatment subgroups: Kind Firmness (KF) only; KF with place-

bo; KF with antidepressant drugs; Active Friendliness (AF) only; AF with placebo; AF with antidepressant drugs. The combined KF and AF gps each contained 14 diagnosed schizophrenics, 18 anxiety reactions and 2 chronic brain syndrome diagnoses. *S*s completed the MMPI and ICL at admission, 2 weeks, 6 weeks and 6 months. The drug gps showed the same changes or less than the AF and KF attitudes alone, while the placebo gps showed no sig changes. Comparisons were made between interpersonal diagnoses of *1, 2, 7* or *8* and the "neurotic" diagnoses of *3, 4, 5,* or *6.* The KF gps showed sig more improvement (change in the direction of octants *1, 2, 7,* and *8*) than did the AF gps, at both Level I-MMPI and Level II-ICL. Prior to treatment, the KF and AF gps did not differ sig at either Level I or II, though they did manifest sig self-deception (Level I-Level II discrepancy). This self-deception also decreased sig following treatment.

317. Taylor, A. B. Role perception, empathy and marriage adjustment. *Sociol Soc Res, 52:*22-34, 1967.

50 couples entering marriage counseling and 50 couples from church-affiliated gps were selected on the basis of extreme low and high scores on the Wallace MSS. The ICL was used to measure each *S*'s self-perception, perception of spouse, prediction of spouse's self-perception and prediction of how spouse would perceive them. Empathy was defined as correct prediction of spouse's ICL responses. Marital adjustment was sig related to congruence between self-perception and how spouse perceived them, to 2 measures of empathy (husbands' self-perceptions versus wives' predictions of husbands' self-perceptions; wives' perceptions of husbands vs. husbands' predictions of how their wives perceived them) and to congruence in intra-individual perceptions (self-perception vs. prediction of how spouse perceives them; perception of spouse vs. prediction of spouse's self-perception). Implications for marital counseling are discussed.

318. Treppa, J. A., and L. Fricke. Effects of a marathon group experience. *J Counsel Psychol, 19*(5):466-467, 1972.

The study compared an *E* and a *C* gp consisting of 7 males and 4 females on the POI, MMPI and ICL immediately before a weekend marathon gp, 2 days after and 6 weeks after the gp.

On the ICL, the Ideal-Self DOM scores differentiated the 2 gps, showed sig changes over repeated test administrations. Overall, there was not a sig treatment effect.

319. Truckenmiller, J. L., and K. W. Schaie. Multilevel structural validation of Leary's Interpersonal Diagnosis System. *J Consult Clin Psychol,* 47(6):1030-1045, 1979.

(see Ref. No. 295)

320. Zimmerman R. L. Comparisons of psychiatric patient self-evaluation with evaluations made by members of their immediate family. *Catalog Select Documents Psychol,* 5:314, 1975.

Author Index

Subject Index

Self as others see you (cont'd)
of
Self-acceptance, as Self-Ideal-self
congruence: 5, 10, 14, 22, 40,
41, 51, 52, 55, 62, 70, 81, 90,
91, 120, 121, 127, 128, 135,
138, 145, 149, 158, 168, 199,
202, 205, 207, 215, 224, 235,
238, 243, 252, 259, 271, 273,
278, 306
Self-actualization: 135
Self-deception. *See* Self-Level I
congruence
Self-disclosure: 248
Self-Ideal-self congruence. *See*
Self-acceptance
Self-esteem: 67, 70, 79, 80, 81,
163
Self-Level I congruence: 151, 152,
224; *MMPI* 60, 62, 75, 101, 118,
160, 174, 244, 286, 299, 316;
sociometric 6, 36, 60, 118, 159,
167, 192, 256, 257, 285
Self-Level III congruence: 101, 118,
224, 249, 286, 293, 299
Self-Parent congruence. *See* Identification
Self-Peer congruence: 20, 30, 55, 56,
91, 118, 121, 194, 203, 280
Self-Spouse congruence, *see also* Empathy, *spouses:* 84, 86, 87, 126,
138, 221, 259, 281, 292, 306, 317
Self-Teacher congruence: 297
Semantic differential: 48
Sensitizers. *See* Repressors-sensi-
tizers
Sensory deprivation: 1, 29
Sentence Completion Test: 147,
291
Sex: *attitudes toward opposite* 248;
differences 9, 36, 42, 58, 120,
121, 129, 130, 136, 142, 145,

Sex (cont'd)
149, 154, 164, 168, 172, 210,
228, 250, 273, 288, 300; *disorders* 153; *of sibling* 188; *relationships* 284
Similarity. *See* Complementarity;
Attitude similarity
Similarity, assumed (ICL): 120
Sixteen-PF: 99
Social attraction. *See* Interpersonal choice, attraction, preference
Social class, socioeconomic level:
18, 58, 142, 145, 165, 288,
300
Social desirability: 21, 28, 30, 43,
44, 54, 79, 80, 81, 85, 87, 88,
92, 165, 180, 182, 211, 285,
293, 304, 309
Social perception, *see also* Empathy: 61, 118, 175, 207, 264,
274, 279
Social reinforcement: 25, 118,
119, 282
Sociometric ranking: 192
Spouse-Ideal-spouse congruence,
see also Mate-Ideal-mate congruence: 10, 202, 259, 268
Spouse-Parent congruence: 49,
127, 129, 160, 259, 291
Spouse ratings, *see also* Self-
Spouse congruence: 28, 42,
62, 82, 94, 133, 202, 217, 237,
253
S-R Inventories: 78
Stereotypes. *See* specific type and
roles
Strong Vocational Interest Blank:
246, 255
Subjects. *See* Adolescence; Alcoholics; Athletes; and other similar headings and topics

CHAPTER II

SHORT FORMS OF THE MINNESOTA MULTIPHASIC PERSONALITY INVENTORY

Introduction

The MMPI is a landmark test in the history of personality assessment techniques. Its use in both clinical practice and research is so common that it is frequently taken for granted as a mainstay in the psychological test battery. During the past four decades a mass of actuarial and statistical data has accumulated as a result of research and clinical use, as evidenced by the more than two thousand test references cited by Taulbee, Wright, and Stenmark,[1] and the more than three thousand references appearing since 1965. In spite of the test's extensive use, many individuals have felt that it is too long and requires too much time to administer. Therefore, since 1968, strong emphasis has been placed on devising short forms that can be depended upon to do essentially the same job as the longer MMPI.

The cost involved in shortening the MMPI is the potential for reduction in the reliability and validity of the resulting test profiles. Any time a test is shortened, there is a risk of reduced reliability that is not a mathematical necessity. The validity will be limited by the degree of reliability, and may also be affected by changing the sequence, and therefore the context, of the items. These objections to shortening the MMPI are empirical questions which are addressed by the research described in

---

[1] Taulbee, E. S., H. W. Wright, and D. E. Stenmark. The MMPI: Comprehensive, Annotated Bibliography (1940-1965). The Whitston Publishing Company, Troy, New York, 1977.

this bibliography.

Although a few attempts were made prior to 1968 to construct a satisfactory short form, none of the forms developed achieved much acceptance or very wide usage. Kincannon (1968) provided a new impetus to the development of abbreviated forms by extracting and rewording 71 items from the MMPI which resulted in the *Mini-Mult* (M-M). The Mini-Mult omits two of the ten MMPI clinical scales—the *Mf* and *Si* scales.

The next abbreviated form was developed by Hugo in 1971, and consisted of 173 items scored for all 13 standard MMPI scales.

Dean (1972) questioned the ability of the Mini-Mult to predict accurately standard MMPI scores when applied to a normal population and proceeded to change conversion equations and item-content for those scales that did not meet the specified criteria. This extended Mini-Mult (from 71 to 86 items) was called the *Midi-Mult*.

In 1973, Faschingbauer developed an abbreviated MMPI that did not attenuate the variance on each scale. Using the "substitution" model rather than regression equations to estimate MMPI scales scores, he produced the 166-item Faschingbauer Abbreviated MMPI (FAM).

The year 1974 was a very good year for MMPI short forms. Appearing that year were the *MMPI-168* (by Overall & Gomez-Mont), the *McLachlan Maxi-Mult* and the *Spera and Robertson Maxi-Mult* (Paper presented at the annual meeting of APA, New Orleans, 1974). Overall and Gomez-Mont developed a new scoring procedure utilizing conventional scoring keys on only the first 168 items of the standard MMPI. This is the only short form of the MMPI which does not change the context of the items. Spera and Robertson modified the Mini-Mult by adding Grayson's 38 Critical Items, which resulted in their 104-item Maxi-Mult. McLachlan's 94-item Maxi-Mult was an attempt to improve the test-retest stability of Kincannon's Mini-Mult and Dean's Midi-Mult.

This brief introduction brings to mind L. R. Goldberg's

comments in the Annual Review of Psychology, Vol. 25, 1974, concerning MMPI short forms. He stated, "Since the direction of this movement is evident, the future should see the MMPI reduced to bare bones, namely a few single-item scales. For detecting latent obesity, one needs only the lone item: 'I can't believe I ate the w-h-o-l-e thing.' The masculinity-femininity scale can be replaced by one true-false item: 'I am a male.' And the neurotic scales can all coalesce into the single item: 'I am a jerk.' " This trend probably will result in more studies being reported in the literature and this bibliography being lengthened.

Journal and Other References

(Hugo, FAM, Maxi-Mult, Midi-Mult, Mini-Mult, MMPI-168)

1. Adis-Castro, G., and M. Araya-Quesada. (Mini-Mult: A short form of the Minnesota Multiphasic Personality Inventory, MMPI). *Acta Psiquiátr Psicol de América Latina, 17*(1):12-18, 1971.

    MMPIs for hosp psych pts were rescored for the M-M and local regression equations employed to estimate the original MMPI scales. It was concluded that the M-M may be used instead of the MMPI if indicated because of time or educational limitations.

2. Armentrout, J. A. Correspondence of the MMPI and Mini-Mult in a college population. *J Clin Psychol, 26*(4): 493-495, 1970.

    Comparisons were made between the MMPI and tape-recorded M-M in terms of correspondence of scale pairs, profile validities, high point codes or general elevation of the related MMPI profile. The results indicate that the M-M profile permits few conclusions as to the validity, high points, or general elevation of its associated MMPI profile.

3. —, and D. L. Rouzer. Utility of the Mini-Mult with delinquents. *J Consult Clin Psychol, 34*(3):450, 1970.

Comparisons of the scores of individually admin M-Ms and MMPIs reveal good correspondence but the results of ind profile comparisons allow few conclusions about the validity, high points, or general elevation of the related MMPI profile.

4.   Bassett, J. E., G. C. Schellman, W. F. Gayton, and J. Tavormina. Efficacy of the Mini-Mult validity scales with prisoners. *J Clin Psychol, 33*(3):729-731, 1977.

Investigated the ability of the extracted M-M validity scales to detect invalid MMPI profiles when at least one of the original MMPI validity scales was invalid. The percentages of cases on which there was agreement of invalidity by the 2 forms using *L, F,* and *K* were 41%, 28% and 48%, respectively. The findings are very consistent with the results of previous studies questioning the adequacy of the M-M validity scales to detect invalid MMPI profiles.

5.   Berger, J., and J. Todorović. (MMPI Mini Mult evaluation of the effects produced by psychotherapy). *Anali Zavoda Za Mentalno Zdraolje,* 7(1):75-80, 1975.

Five hosp neurotic fem pts were admin the M-M before and after 2 months of encounter group therapy. Elevations on the clinical scales decreased on post-testing (greatest on *D, Hs,* and *Hy*). The "psychotic triad" scale decreases were not significant.

6.   Bolton, B. A brief instrument for assessing psychopathology in rehabilitation clients. *Arkansas Rehabilitation Research and Training Center Report,* University of Arkansas, 1975.

(see Ref. No. 7)

7.   —. A preliminary study of differential personality profiles of rehabilitation clients. *Rehabil Counsel Bull, 20*(1): 21-27, 1976.

The TSCS, M-M, and 16-PF were admin and demographic data collected. Factor analysis was done and the findings discussed in light of 4 issues related to the use of profile analysis as a taxonomic procedure.

8. —. Homogeneous subscales for the Mini-Mult. *J Consult Clin Psychol, 44*(4):684-685, 1976.

    Three M-M subscales—low morale, somatization, and psychotic distortion paranoia—were identified on the basis of data from rehab clients.

9. —. Client psychological adjustment associated with three counseling styles. *Rehabil Counsel Bull, 20*(4):247-253, 1977.

    Clients served by information providers, therapeutic counseling, and information exchanges completed 3 personality inventories at initiation of rehab services and again at time of case closure. Analyses of post-test scores demonstrated importance of multiple measures of outcome.

10. —. The relationship between two personality questionnaires: The Mini-Mult and the 16PF-E. *J Pers Assess, 43*(3):289-292, 1979.

    The M-M (in written form) and 16PF-E were admin to a heterogeneous sample of 216 clients at the time of acceptance for rehab services. Several multivariate analyses were computed. It was concluded that the 16PF-E provides a global estimate of the client's overall level of emotional adjustment, as well as information regarding a wide range of non-pathological traits. The M-M focuses on subtle aspects of maladjustment corresponding to traditional psych syndromes.

11. Butcher, J. N., P. C. Kendall, and N. Hoffman. The MMPI short forms: Caution. *J Consult Clin Psychol, 48*(2):275-278, 1980.

    The data from the Newmark et al. study (see Ref. No. 83) were reanalyzed to yield diff scores between the abbreviated MMPI (FAM and MMPI-168) and the standard MMPI for each *S* and the percentage of *S*s obtaining each diff score on the MMPI scales. The authors also performed the same analyses on data from 3 other published studies. They concluded that the optimistic conclusions of Newmark et al. about the validity of the 2 short forms are not warranted, that their sample was atypical and that their findings need to be replicated.

12. Calsyn, D. A., D. M. Spengler, and C. W. Freeman. Application of the somatization factor of the MMPI-168 with low back pain patients. *J Clin Psychol, 33*(4):1017-1020, 1977.

> Reported 2 studies on the usefulness of the Somatization factor with low back pain pts. Organic and mixed gps differed only on the Somatization factor of the 5 factors investigated. A second gp of low back pain pts was divided into mixed, organic and functional gps. The functional and mixed-pain gps differed from the organic and mixed-relief gps on the Somatization and Depression factors.

13. Coché, E., and A. A. Douglas. Therapeutic effects of problem-solving training and play-reading groups. *J Clin Psychol, 33*(3):820-827, 1977.

> Three gps of hosp psych pts—*E* gp, which met for 8 sessions in order to increase skills in interpers problem solving; *C* gp; and a "placebo" gp—were given a set of pre- and post-tests. In 5 of the 6 cases where sig was obtained on the M-M, both the *E* gp and the placebo gp made considerable gains, whereas the *C* gp did not.

14. Cohler, B. J., J. L. Weiss, and H. U. Grunebaum. "Short-form" content scales for the MMPI. *J Pers Assess, 38*(6):563-572, 1974.

> Used an abbreviated version of content scales and demonstrated both satisfactory long- short-form correls and promising internal consistency for the short-form scales.

15. Cooper, P. G., and S. E. Rubin. A short psychological adjustment screening instrument. *Psychosocial Rehabil J, 1*(3):21-28, 1977.

> Using data from a previous study (see Ref. No. 60), the authors attempted to develop a short psychological adjustment screening instrument. The M-M was analyzed through cluster analysis. Six subscales were defined and labeled: Poor Self-Concept, Ex-

cessive Health Concerns, Tendency Toward Reality Distortion and Paranoia, Undifferentiated Neuroticism, Cynicism, and Tendency Toward Social Acquiescence. The first 4 of these sub-scales are suggested as the basis of a conceptually consistent screening instrument.

16. Dean, E. F. A lengthened Mini: The Midi-Mult. *J Clin Psychol, 28*(1):68-71, 1972.

Investigated the ability of the extracted M-M to predict MMPI scores on a normal population. The short scales were modified so that they correl .80 or higher with the standard scales. Classification analysis concerning validity showed good correspondence between the Midi-Mults and MMPIs and normal-abnormal discriminations.

17. Devore, J. E., and J. L. Fryrear. Analysis of juvenile delinquents' hole drawing responses on the tree figure of the House-Tree-Person technique. *J Clin Psychol, 32*(3):731-736, 1976.

Study was concerned primarily with H-T-P drawings. *S*s whose tree drawings contained a hole were compared on 22 variables including the M-M, with *S*s whose drawings did not display the drawn hole. Only sig diffs were higher IQ and lower *Ma* for *S*s who drew a tree with a hole.

18. Duthie, R. B., and A. Borrero-Hernandez. Differentiating methadone outpatients from psychiatric outpatients and normals with the Mini-Mult. *J Clin Psychol, 35*(2):457-458, 1979.

A gp of each of outpt heroin addicts, psych outpts and non-random clinic staff were compared across the M-M scales. The pt gps did not differ sig. The addict gp scored sig higher than the normal gp on scales *L, F, Hs, D, Hy* and *Pd*.

19. Edinger, J. D., P. C. Kendall, J. F. Hooke, and J. B. Bogan. The predictive efficacy of three MMPI short forms. *J Pers Assess, 40*(3):259-265, 1976.

The FAM, Hugo and M-M short forms were extracted from the

MMPIs of inmates of a Drug Abuse Program and an OPC and their efficacy in approximating the standard MMPI profile compared. All 3 short forms were more accurate for the OP gp than the inmate gp. The FAM was superior to the other 2 forms across both gps.

20. Elsie, R. D., and J. F. C. McLachlan. Reliability of the Maxi-Mult and scale equivalence with the MMPI. *J Clin Psychol, 32*(1):67-70, 1976.

MMPIs and separately admin Maxi-Mults on a gp of alcohs were compared. Scores were not affected by order of presentation. Correls tended to be higher for the embedded Maxi-Mult. Test-retest correls of the Maxi-Mult and the short- vs standard scale were adequate.

21. Erickson, R. C., and C. Freeman. Using the MMPI 168 with medical inpatients. *J Clin Psychol, 32*(4):803-806, 1976.

MMPI-168 scored from the standard MMPI of a gp of orthopedic and neurological pts. The high average correls, satisfactory high-point codes and correspondence on Goldberg's rules suggest that the MMPI-168 can lead to conclusions and decisions similar to those made from the MMPI.

22. —, and M. O'Leary. Using the MMPI 168 with alcoholics. *J Clin Psychol, 33*(1):133-135, 1977.

MMPI-168 was scored from the MMPI. In general, the correls between scales of the 2 forms, conclusions about profile and validity, profile elevations, high point code correspondence, and high correls between ind profiles, are comparable in most cases.

23. Faschingbauer, T. R. A short written form of the group MMPI. *D A I, 34*(1-B):409, 1973.

Describes the development of the 166-item Faschingbauer Abbreviated MMPI (FAM) using cluster analysis and its comparison to other short forms.

24. —. A 166-item written short form of the group MMPI: The FAM. *J Consult Clin Psychol, 42*(5):645-655, 1974.

Describes the development of the FAM using coll *S*s and hosp pts. On code-type correspondence, configural classifications, profile validities, and scale elevations, the FAM compared favorably to a retest of the MMPI. It was concluded that the FAM is superior to the other short forms in most respects.

25. —. Substitution and regression models, base rates, and the clinical validity of the Mini-Mult. *J Clin Psychol, 32*(1): 70-74, 1976.

The hypoth that the M-M has shown lower standard deviations than corresponding MMPI scales due to regression toward the mean in estimating MMPI scale scores was supported in 2 studies using psych pts.

26. —. Some clinical considerations in selecting a short form of the MMPI. *Prof Psychol, 7*(2):167-176, 1976.

Describes and compares 4 short forms—Dean's, Hugo's, FAM, and M-M. Major diffs were found from test to test and from scale to scale within each short form. Perhaps a particular short form should be used in special situations.

27. —, D. T. Johnson, and C. S. Newmark. The interpretative validity of the FAM: Long-term psychotherapists' ratings of psychiatric inpatients. *J Pers Assess, 42*(1):74-75, 1978.

Replication of earlier study (see Ref. No. 70) using long-term psychotherapists as raters. Only sig diff was for 20 m psych inpts. It was concluded that the FAM yields interpretations as accurate as one would expect given its psychometric dissimilarity from the MMPI.

28. —, and C. S. Newmark. *Short forms of the MMPI.* Lexington, Massachusetts: D. C. Heath & Co., 1978.

Presents the history of short forms, the need for them, their development and relative utility. Forms discussed include the M-M, Midi-Mult, Hugo Short Form, FAM, MMPI-168, and the Maxi-Mults.

29. Fillenbaum, G. G., and E. Pfeiffer. The Mini-Mult: A cautionary note. *J Consult Clin Psychol, 44*(5):698-703, 1976.

An independent, orally admin M-M was included in a broad questionnaire used to gather data on a random sample of 997 noninstitutionalized black and white Ss ranging in age from 65 to 93 years. The results reveal sig sex and race-related diffs. The potential utility of the M-M is such that appropriate corrections for sex and race and standardization for the elderly should be seriously considered.

30. Finch, A. J., Jr., G. L. Edwards, and J. L. Griffin, Jr. Utility of Mini-Mult with parents of emotionally disturbed children. *J Pers Assess, 39*(2):146-150, 1975.

Comparisons were made between the standard MMPI and an extracted M-M and an ind admin M-M to determine potential usefulness of the M-M for screening purposes with this type population. It was concluded that it is not a good instrument for this purpose.

31. —, J. L. Griffin, Jr., and G. L. Edwards. Abbreviated Mf and Si scales: Efficacy with parents of emotionally disturbed children. *J Clin Psychol, 30*(1):80, 1974.

The accuracy with which the abbreviated *Mf* and *Si* scales would predict the standard scores with this type population was investigated. Serious doubts were raised about their use with this population. Further work with the abbreivated *Si* scale appears warranted.

32. —, P. C. Kendall, W. M. Nelson, and C. S. Newmark. Application of Faschingbauer's abbreviated MMPI to parents of emotionally disturbed children. *Psychol Rep, 37*(2):571-574, 1975.

The MMPIs were rescored for the FAM and the 2 forms compared. Many mean scores on the FAM were sig different from those on the MMPI. Modest correspondence on indexes of psychopathology, profile peaks, and validity criteria was found. It was concluded that use of the FAM is not justified with this population.

33. Freeman, C., D. Calsyn, and M. O'Leary. Application of Faschingbauer's abbreviated MMPI with medical patients. *J Consult Clin Psychol*, 45(4):706-707, 1977.

   The FAM was extracted from the MMPIs of 282 m VAH medical pts. The FAM and MMPI gp means were similar and highly correl. It was concluded that the FAM would be an adequate substitute when the full MMPI could not be used.

34. —, M. R. O'Leary, and D. Calsyn. Application of the Faschingbauer abbreviated MMPI with alcoholic patients. *J Clin Psychol*, 33(1):303-306, 1977.

   FAM was admin and *r*s computed between T-scores and those of MMPI, comparisons made on high-point codes, and number of scales with T-score above 70. It was suggested that when the admin of the MMPI is not feasible, the FAM is a valid substitute for alcoh populations.

35. Gaines, L. S., M. H. Abrams, P. Toel, and L. M. Miller. Comparison of the MMPI and the Mini-Mult with alcoholics. *J Consult Clin Psychol*, 42(4):619, 1974.

   The M-M was extracted from the MMPI and the comparative data studied. Gp results for 2 samples showed good scale correls but low M-M predictive accuracy with respect to invalid profiles, profile high points, and patterns of clinical scales with T scores > 70. Results indicate a need for cross-validation in using the M-M.

36. Gayton, W. F., J. S. Bishop, M. M. Citrin, and J. S. Bassett. An investigation of the Mini-Mult validity scales. *J Pers Assess*, 39(5):511-513, 1975.

   Examined the ability of the M-M validity scales to detect invalid MMPI profiles, using adult psych pts. The M-M was extracted from 34 invalid MMPI profiles. The M-M validity scales classified only 17 of the 34 as invalid.

37. —, M. E. Fogg, J. Tavormina, J. S. Bishop, M. M. Citrin,

and J. S. Bassett. Comparison of the MMPI and Mini-Mult with women who request abortion. *J Clin Psychol, 32*(3):648-650, 1976.

Although the correls between the MMPI and extracted M-M are highly sig, the M-M misclassified more than a quarter of the *S*s when it was used to predict profile elevation.

38.   —, K. L. Ozmon, and W. T. Wilson. Investigation of a written form of the Mini-Mult. *Psychol Rep, 30*(1):275-278, 1972.

Comparisons were made between an oral and written M-M and a standard MMPI, using coll *S*s. Sig correls were obtained between each of the M-M forms and the MMPI on all scales. Agreement in prediction of profile elevation was high. Scale pairs were sig diff only on *K* between the 2 M-M forms and the MMPI.

39.   —, and W. T. Wilson. Utility of the Mini-Mult in a child guidance clinic setting. *J Pers Assess, 35*(6):569-575, 1971.

Comparisons were made between the MMPI and the extracted M-M using a gp of CGC adolescents and a gp of CGC parents. There was a high degree of correspondence between the 2 forms but a decrease in correspondence when analyses of data were made from a practical point of view. Results of the 2 studies reported suggest that further investigations are warranted.

40.   Gilroy, F. D., and R. Steinbacher. Extension of the Midi-Mult to a college population. *J Pers Assess, 37*(3):263-266, 1973.

Investigated the use of both the "internal" and "external" Midi-Mult to predict the MMPI. The correls of the internal Midi-Mult with the standard MMPI were higher than those of the external Midi-Mult. The results question the adequacy of the regression equations when short forms are used with varying gps. The short form should be validated on the population with whom its use is considered. The Midi-Mult is recommended for use with "normal" populations when admin of the MMPI is prohibitive.

41 Graham, J. R., and H. E. Schroeder. Abbreviated Mf and Si scales for the MMPI. *J Pers Assess, 36*(5):436-439, 1972.

Abbreviated the *Mf* and *Si* scales by selecting 31 items representative of the factor dimens of the 2 scales and developing regression equations to predict standard scale scores—using psych pts. The addition of 20 items to the M-M allows for abbreviated *Mf* and *Si* scales.

42. Griffin, J. L., Jr., A. J. Finch, Jr., G. L. Edwards, and P. C. Kendall. MMPI/Midi-Mult correspondence with parents of emotionally disturbed children. *J Clin Psychol, 32*(1):54-56, 1976.

Comparisons were made between the MMPI and extracted Midi-Mult. The findings were consistent with those of previous studies on the M-M—that the correspondence is too low and variable to allow the short forms to be substituted for the MMPI with this population.

43. Harford, T., B. Lubetkin, and G. Alpert. Comparison of the standard MMPI and the Mini-Mult in a psychiatric outpatient clinic. *J Consult Clin Psychol, 39*(2):243-245, 1972.

Comparisons were made between the MMPI and the extracted M-M. The M-M was sensitive to the presence of psychopathology but underestimated extreme scores. It is not an accurate substitute for the MMPI in predicting clinical types.

44. Hartman, G., and M. Robertson. Comparison of the Mini-Mult and the MMPI in a community mental health agency. *Proc 80th Ann Conv Am Psychol Assoc, 7*(Pt. 1):33-34, 1972.

Comparisons were made between the standard MMPI and an extracted M-M and an individually admin M-M. There were sig diffs on 5 scales, although correls among the 3 forms were high. There was some disagreement on diagnoses based on profile interpretation. Caution in substituting the M-M for the MMPI is indicated.

45. Hedberg, A. G., L. M. Campbell, S. R. Weeks, and J. A. Powell.   The use of the MMPI (Mini-Mult) to predict alcoholics' response to a behavioral treatment program. *J Clin Psychol, 31*(2):271-274, 1975.

    Attempted to predict the *Ss*' response to behavior therapy and to assess M-M profile changes during the initial phase of treatment. Four scales discriminated between the successfully treated and the failures.   The successful gp had an overall profile of greater pathology at both the initial and the interim testing periods.

46. Hedlund, J. L., D. W. Cho, and B. J. Powell.   Use of the MMPI short forms with psychiatric patients.   *J Consult Clin Psychol, 43*(6):924, 1975.

    Comparisons were made between the standard MMPI and the extracted M-M and MMPI-168.   Estimated standard MMPI scores for both short forms showed very high relationships.   Degree of profile agreement for the 3 highest scales was quite high.

47. —, D. W. Cho,and J. B. Wood. MMPI-168 factor structure: A replication with public mental health patients. *J Consult Clin Psychol, 45*(4):711-712, 1977.

    Study replicates the factor-analytic approach of Overall, Hunter & Butcher (see Ref. No. 90) using the first 168 items of the MMPIs of a 2,116 unselected sample of inpts.   There was close correspondence with the 6 factors reported in the earlier study.

48. —, D. W. Cho, and J. B. Wood. Comparative validity of the MMPI-168 factors and clinical scales. *Multivariate Behav Res, 12*(3):327-330, 1977.

    Investigated relative merits of MMPI factor scores vs clinical scale scores using 2,116 public mental health pts.   Mental status exam findings and clinical diagnosis were used as criterion variables. Results failed to evidence any clear advantage for either the MMPI-168 factor scores, MMPI-168 estimated clinical scale scores, or the MMPI full scale clinical scores.

49. Hobbs, T. R.   Scale equivalence and profile similarity of the Mini-Mult and MMPI in an outpatient clinic. *J Clin Psy-*

chol, 30(3):349-350, 1974.

Comparisons were made between the standard MMPI and the extracted M-M using OPC pts. Results indicate an adequate degree of scale correspondence but poor profile similarity; and a respectable degree of profile agreement in assessing gross pathology. As a relevant description of the pathology became important, agreement between the forms deteriorated markedly.

50. —, and R. D. Fowler. Reliability and scale equivalence of the Mini-Mult and MMPI. *J Consult Clin Psychol, 42*(1):89-92, 1974.

Psych inpts were tested with the M-M and MMPI in 3 test-retest sequences. There was no sig effect on scale scores due to the order of presentation. Six of the 11 M-M scales (*F, K, D, Pa, Pt,* and *Sc*) appeared to measure consistently the same factors as the MMPI. Scales *L, Hs* and *Pd* had the most variation in correlation.

51. Hoffmann, N. G., and J. N. Butcher. Clinical limitations of three Minnesota Multiphasic Personality Inventory Short forms. *J Consult Clin Psychol, 43*(1):32-39, 1975.

Compared the M-M, FAM, and MMPI-168 using short- to standard-form correls. Correls for all 3 forms are generally high, but the success in accurately predicting the code type was quite low; an analysis of false positives and false negatives showed weakness in these short forms. Questions the use of these short forms for clinical interpretations based on the usual code-type analysis.

52. Hugo, J. Abbreviation of the MMPI through multiple regression. Unpublished doctoral dissertation, University of Alabama, 1971.

Discusses the development of an abbreviated form of the MMPI through multiple regression, using 176 college students.

53. Huisman, R. E. Correspondence between Mini-Mult and standard MMPI scale scores in patients with neurological disease. *J Consult Clin Psychol, 42*(1):149, 1974.

Comparisons were made between the standard MMPI and the extracted M-M using pts with verified brain damage. Close correspondence was found between mean M-M and MMPI scale scores for all scale scores except *Ma* (r=.579). The results suggested that the poor performance of the M-M for predicting useful information for the inds in spite of adequate gp prediction suggests weakness in the test rather than differences due to severity of illness.

54. Hunter, S., J. E. Overall, and J. N. Butcher. Factor structure of the MMPI in a psychiatric population. *Multivariate Behav Res, 9*:283-302, 1974.

Factor analyzed the 373-item MMPI short form. Results reveal 6 factors which are consistent with those previously identified by the authors for the first 168.

55. Jabara, R. F., and S. F. Curran. Comparison of the Minnesota Multiphasic Personality Inventory and Mini-Mult with drug users. *J Consult Clin Psychol, 42*(5):739-740, 1974.

Comparisons were made between the standard MMPI and the extracted M-M. There was good correspondence between scale pairs, but low accuracy with respect to clinical evaluation and high-point correspondence.

56. Justice, B., G. McBee, and R. Allen. Social dysfunction and anxiety. *J Psychol, 97*(1):37-42, 1977.

44 m and fem adult clinic outpts were admin the Denver Community MH Questionnaire on social functioning, the M-M, the Social Readjustment Rating Scale and the TMAS. The TMAS correl sig with the M-M scales of *Hs, D, Hy, Pd, Pa, Pt, Sc, F,* and *K*. Both the TMAS and the M-M are extractions from the MMPI.

57. Kincannon, J. C. An investigation of the feasibility of adopting a personality inventory for use in the mental status exam. *D A, 28*:2625B, 1967.

(see Ref. No. 58)

58. —. Prediction of the standard MMPI scale scores from 71 items: The Mini-Mult. *J Consult Clin Psychol, 32*(3): 319-325, 1968.

This article is based on the author's Ph.D. dissertation developing a short form of the MMPI by choosing a sample of items representative of the content clusters tapped by the 11 standard validity and clinical scales. The M-M was estimated to have suffered only a 9% loss in reliability and a 14% loss in correspondence in comparison with the readministration of the standard form. It was concluded that when the MMPI cannot be admin, the amount of error introduced by the M-M would be tolerable.

59. King, G. D., D. A. Gideon, C. D. Haynes, R. L. Dempscy, and C. W. Jenkins. Intellectual and personality changes associated with carotid endarterectomy. *J Clin Psychol, 33*(1):215-220, 1977.

M-M admin to 11 pts just prior to and 6 weeks after carotid endarterectomy, and to 8 *C* pts. The *C* gp did not change pre- to postsurgically the endarterectomy pts showed sig decreases on *Pa* and *Sc*.

60. Krauft, C., and B. Bolton. Client-reported psychological status and rehabilitation success. *Rehabil Counsel Bull, 19*(3):500-503, 1976.

The M-M, 16 PF and TSCS were admin to 148 rehab clients. Results did not predict rehab outcome (successful case closure).

61. Lacks, P. B. Further investigation of the Mini-Mult. *J Consult Clin Psychol, 35*(1):126-127, 1970.

Comparisons were made between the standard MMPI and the extracted M-M using hosp psych pts. The results essentially replicated those of Kincannon indicating the M-M predicts the MMPI with a higher degree of accuracy.

62. —, and B. J. Powell. The Mini-Mult as a personnel screening technique: A preliminary report. *Psychol Rep, 27*(3):909-910, 1970.

Comparisons were made between the standard MMPI and the extracted M-M using applicants for a psych attendant position. Four sig diffs were found. It was concluded that the M-M might be used to screen certain populations.

63. Lewandowski, D. G. The derivation and use of new conversions for the Mini-Mult for delinquents and college students. *D A I, 35*(1-B):513, 1974.

Two sets of new regression equations for predicting the MMPI from the M-M computed for a gp of juvenile delinquents and a gp of coll students. Equations were then applied to new gps and the resulting predictions compared with each other. Comparisons were made for both gp and ind data. It was concluded that the improvement was not substantial enough to warrant replacement of Kincannon's conversions. Also concluded that the M-M was adequate with delinquents and coll *S*s.

64. Lewis, J. L. Validation of MMPI, FAM and PSI with state hospital patients. *D A I, 39*(8-B):4043, 1979.

MMPI and FAM test results were interpreted blindly by raters. Two independent ratings were obtained for criterion (established from clinical records), MMPI, and FAM data collection, and mean ratings were used for experimental comparisons. Both the MMPI and FAM predicted level of depression and anxiety. FAM was able to predict chronicity and level of somatic concerns. Neither was able to provide sig accurate predictions concerning predicted length of stay, response to treatment, danger to others (by history), danger to others (within hospital), socialization difficulties (by history) evidence of thinking disturbance and defensiveness. The FAM was superior to the MMPI in predicting chronicity, and level of somatic concern. the MMPI was superior to the FAM in predicting length of stay.

65. McLachlan, J. F. C. Test-retest stability of long and short MMPI scales over two years. *J Clin Psychol, 30*(2):189-191, 1974.

Stability of the MMPI and M-M and Maxi-Mult was studied using readmitted alcohs. The retest *r*s were above .70 for M-M *D, Hy,* and *Pt* and the short-form of *Si. L* and *Mf* were found to be of questionable reliability, especially with females. In the Maxi-Mult, 11 scales were comparable to the MMPI in reliability.

66. Mlott, S. R. The Mini-Mult and its use with adolescents. *J Clin Psychol, 29*(3):376-377, 1973.

Comparisons were made between the standard MMPI and the extracted M-M using a gp of psych inpt adolescents. Concluded that the M-M is applicable to this type population if recognition is given to its tendency to under-estimate the *Pa* and *Ma,* and with m adolescents in particular its tendency to underestimate *Hs, Pa* and *Ma.*

67. —, and R. L. Mason. The practicability of using an abbreviated form of the MMPI with chronic renal dialysis patients. *J Clin Psychol, 31*(1):65-68, 1975.

Standard MMPI and ind admin Midi-Mult, FAM and M-M were compared. Average overall scores of the short forms and each diagnostic category were compared with the MMPI. The least discrepancy occurred between the MMPI and the Midi-Mult, with the FAM next and the M-M last. The conclusion was that the close correl between the 2 forms suggests the Midi-Mult can be used with this population.

68. Murray, L., J. Heritage, and W. Holmes. Black-white comparisons on the MMPI Mini-Mult. *South J Educ Res, 10*(2):105-114, 1976.

Compared M-M performance of a matched gp of white and Black m delinquents. No sig diff on any scale of the M-M between the gps.

69. Newmark, C. S., B. Boas, and T. Messervy. An abbreviated MMPI for use with college students. *Psychol Rep, 34*(2):631-634, 1974.

Comparisons were made between the standard MMPI and an extracted FAM in terms of correspondence of scale pairs, profile validities, high point codes and general elevation of the profiles. In general, the results revealed good correspondence.

70. —, A. J. Conger, and T. R. Faschingbauer. The interpretive validity and effective test length functioning of an abbreviated MMPI relative to the standard MMPI. *J Clin Psychol, 32*(1):27-32, 1976.

The comparative interpretive efficacy of the standard MMPI and an independently admin FAM was assessed for a gp of psych inpts. One of the authors interpreted each profile. Both FAM and MMPI interpretations were presented to the psych resident in charge of primary care for the pt. Each resident evaluated for each pt the accuracy of each interpretation on a 5-point scale. Sig higher mean ratings (greater accuracy) resulted for the MMPI. When data were collapsed across sexes, the quantity of loss was sig lower than expected. The authors concluded that the FAM functioned as an instrument 80% as long as the standard MMPI, although it contains only 30% of the items.

71. —, L. Cook, M. Clarke, and T. R. Faschingbauer. Application of Faschingbauer's abbreviated MMPI to psychiatric inpatients. *J Consult Clin Psychol, 41*(3):416-421, 1973.

Comparisons were made between the standard MMPI and the extracted FAM using hosp psych pts. Findings revealed that the 2 forms were markedly similar and highly correlated. It was concluded that the FAM should be given careful consideration for future use but as an independently admin form since the extracted form has no practical benefit.

72. —, L. Cook, and W. Greer. Application of the Midi-Mult to psychiatric inpatients. *J Clin Psychol, 29*(4) 481-484, 1973.

Standard MMPI and an extracted Midi-Mult were compared in terms of gp mean data and profile validities. Although there was good agreement, analysis of ind profile pairs revealed a lack of correspondence with respect to scale high point codes and general profile elevations. The results suggest limited applicability for the Midi-Mult with this type population.

73. —, R. Falk, and A. J. Finch, Jr. Interpretive accuracy of abbreviated MMPIs. *J Pers Assess, 40*(3):266-268, 1976.

Hosp psych pts were admin the standard MMPI and an independently admin FAM, Hugo or MMPI-168 short form in a counterbalanced order. Psych teams evaluated the accuracy of the interpretations on one short form and the standard MMPI for their pts. Only the interpretations of the MMPI-168 were comparable to that obtained from the MMPI.

74. —, and T. R. Faschingbauer. Bibliography of short forms of the MMPI. *J Pers Assess, 42*(5):496-502, 1978.

A bibliography is presented for the M-M, Midi-Mult, FAM, MMPI-168, Hugo Short Form, Maxi-Mult 104, Maxi-Mult 94, and Workshops and Symposia.

75. —, and A. J. Finch. Comparing the diagnostic validity of an abbreviated and standard MMPI. *J Pers Assess, 40*(1):10-12, 1976.

The MMPI-168 was scored from the standard MMPI and the 2 forms compared for diagnostic efficacy using hosp psych pts. With traditional psych measures and projective testing used for criterion diagnoses, no sig diffs were found between the MMPI and the MMPI-168.

76. —, R. Galen, and K. Gold. Efficacy of an abbreviated MMPI as a function of type of administration. *J Clin Psychol, 31*(4):639-642, 1975.

Comparisons were made between the standard MMPI and an extracted FAM and an independently admin FAM to investigate their relative accuracy in predicting the MMPI using hosp psych pts. The extracted FAM proved superior but the independent form showed potential for use when admin of the MMPI isn't practical.

77. —, and L. Glenn. Sensitivity of the Faschingbauer abbreviated MMPI to hospitalized adolescents. *J Abnorm Child Psychol, 2*(4):299-306, 1974.

Comparisons were made between the standard MMPI and an extracted FAM. The results showed close agreement. Additionally, several gross indices of psychopathology were successfully predicted by the FAM. The results were supported by a replication study. It was recommended that careful consideration be given to using the FAM as a preliminary screening device for adolescent psych inpts.

78. —, L. Newmark, and L. Cook. The MMPI-168 with psychiatric patients. *J Clin Psychol, 31*(1):61-64, 1975.

The MMPI-168 was scored from the standard MMPI and many correlational and clinically relevant comparisons made, including judges' diagnostic classifications and ratings as to degree of similarity of the 2 forms. The results demonstrated that the MMPI can be predicted from the short form with a high degree of accuracy.

79. —, L. Newmark, and T. R. Faschingbauer. Utility of three abbreviated MMPIs with psychiatric outpatients. *J Nerv Ment Dis, 159*(6):438-443, 1974.

Comparisons were made between the MMPI and the extracted FAM, Hugo and Midi-Mult short forms using OP psych pts. The gp profiles of the short forms correspond fairly accurately to the MMPI but there was a decrease in correspondence when analysis was made from a practical view. The FAM permitted the most accurate conclusions concerning the validity, high points, and general elevation of the corresponding MMPI.

80. —, M. Owen, L. Newmark, and T. R. Faschingbauer. Comparison of three abbreviated MMPIs for psychiatric patients and normals. *J Pers Assess, 39*(3):261-270, 1975.

Comparisons were made between the standard MMPI and the extracted FAM, Hugo and Midi-Mult short forms using a gp of hosp psych pts, and a gp of coll *S*s. For the pt gp the FAM gp means were markedly similar, highly correl, and seemed to be a fairly accurate substitute for the MMPI in predicting clinical types. Many deficiencies were evident with the Midi-Mult and Hugo forms. In contrast, results from the coll gp showed considerable correspondence regardless of the short form used. The need to validate the short form on the population with whom it's used is considered.

81. —, and D. Raft. Using an abbreviated MMPI as a screening device for medical patients. *Psychosomatics, 17*(1):45-48, 1976.

The MMPI-168 was scored from the standard MMPI and comparisons made between the 2 forms to assess their interchangeability in screening medical pts. The short form was found to predict the results of the standard MMPI with a high degree of accuracy.

82. —, G. G. Woody, D. R. Ziff, and A. J. Finch, Jr. MMPI short forms: A different perspective. *J Consult Clin Psychol, 48*(2):279-283, 1980.

The authors reply to the issues raised by Butcher et al. (see Ref. No. 11). The major areas of concern regarded the high congruence between the mean scale scores, the high correl coefficients for the corresponding scales, a restricted range of diff scores, and a high percentage of identical scores. Newmark et al. compared their data with other short form studies and concluded that with one exception the Butcher et al. concerns are not justified.

83. —, D. R. Ziff, A. J. Finch, Jr., and P. C. Kendall. Comparing the empirical validity of the standard form with two abbreviated MMPIs. *J Consult Clin Psychol, 46*(1): 53-61, 1978.

The standard form MMPI and ind admin MMPI-168 and FAM were compared with scores from the Brief Psychiatric Rating Scale (BPRS) for a large gp of m and fem pts admitted to a psych inpt facility. The findings suggest that the short forms are an accurate substitute for the MMPI in predicting objective measures of psychopathology.

84. Newton, J. R. A comparison of studies of the Mini-Mult. *J Clin Psychol, 27*(4):489-490, 1971.

An "external" and "internal" M-M were both compared with the standard MMPI. The order of presentation of the external M-M and MMPI to a gp of alcohs was varied. The internal M-M correl higher with the MMPI than did the external M-M, the latter not approximating the MMPI as closely as earlier findings suggested.   Data obtained on the 2nd admin (either the external M-M or full MMPI) were in the more socially desirable direction.

85.   Ogilvie, L. P., J. Kotin, and D. H. Stanley. Comparison of the MMPI and the Mini-Mult in a psychiatric outpatient clinic. *J Consult Clin Psychol, 44*(3):497-498, 1976.

Comparisons were made between the standard MMPI and an ind admin M-M, between a test-retest M-M, and between diagnoses obtained from the test data and an intake interview. Sig diffs were found between the MMPI and M-M on scales *F* and *Ma;* the 2 forms agreed on the 3 peak scales on about 66% of the *S*s; and on clinical diagnosis on about 62% of the cases.

86.   O'Leary, M. R., D. A. Calsyn, E. F. Chaney, and C. W. Freeman.   Predicting alcohol treatment program drop-outs. *Dis Nerv System, 38*(12):993-995, 1977.

MMPI-168 and Rotter's I-E were admin to 84 ATP inpts at the beginning of treatment. Pts who completed an 8-week inpt and a 1-year outpt program were compared to pts completing the inpt phase but who dropped out during the outpt phase. Two gps differed sig only on the I-E.

87.   Overall, J. E., J. N. Butcher, and S. Hunter. Validity of the MMPI-168 for psychiatric screening.   *Educ Psychol Measmt, 35*(2):393-400, 1975.

Compared the discriminant validity of the MMPI-168 with the standard 373-item short form, using hosp psych pts and coll *S*s. Revised equations for converting the MMPI-168 scores to equivalent MMPI clinical scale scores were provided.

88.   —, and F. Gomez-Mont.   The MMPI-168 for psychiatric screening. *Educ Psychol Measmt, 34*(2):315-319, 1974.

Described the development of a short form of the MMPI consisting of the first 168 items of the standard MMPI. Most of the reliable variance represented in the longer MMPI is adequately represented in this short form.

89.   —, W. Higgins, and A. deSchweinitz.   Comparison of dif-

ferential diagnostic discrimination for abbreviated and standard MMPI. *J Clin Psychol, 32*(2):237-245, 1976.

The MMPI-168 was scored from the standard MMPI and the results of the 2 forms compared using a gp of psych pts. The Ss divided into 10 major categories on the basis of final diagnosis. Multiple discriminant analysis was used to compare the discriminant validity of the forms. No loss of discrimination resulted from scoring based only on the first 168 items.

90. —, S. Hunter, and J. N. Butcher. Factor structure of the MMPI-168 in a psychiatric population. *J Consult Clin Psychol, 41*(2):284-286, 1973.

A factor analysis of items from the MMPI-168 of hosp and OPC pts suggested the presence of 6 independent factors—interpreted as Somatization, Low Morale, Psychotic Distortion, Depression, Acting Out and Feminine preferences. The results reveal considerable consistency both in number and nature of factors derived from factor analyses at the item level of the full MMPI.

91. Palmer, A. B. A comparison of the MMPI and Mini-Mult in a sample of state mental hospital patients. *J Clin Psychol, 29*(4):484-485, 1973.

The MMPI and M-M were admin in counter-balanced order and comparisons made between the 2 forms. Neither sex of the S nor the order of admin had any sig effect on the results. Scale pair correls were sig, although low, but correspondence between the 2 forms in terms of differential diagnosis or diagnostic impressions wasn't high. It was concluded that the data do not support the use of the M-M with state hosp pts.

92. Pando, J. R. Appraisal of various clinical scales of the Spanish version of the Mini-Mult with Spanish Americans. *D A I, 34*(11-B):5688, 1974.

Investigated the diagnostic predictability of the D, *Pa, Pt,* and *Sc* scales of the Spanish version of the M-M using Spanish American psych males. Results indicated that very few conclusions could be drawn from the M-M when North American interpretive standards were used. It was not shown to be an accurate predictor of type of psychopathology.

93. Pantano, L. T., and M. L. Schwartz. Differentiation of neurologic and pseudoneurologic patients with combined MMPI Mini-Mult and pseudoneurologic scale. *J Clin Psychol, 34*(1):56-60, 1978.

>   Study attempted to differentiate Pseudo-Neurologic and Neurologic pts using the M-M and the Shaw and Matthews Pseudo-Neurologic Scale. The diffs were statistically, but not clinically sig. An attempt to develop a new, more effective scale was disappointing.

94. Penk, W. E., and R. V. Kidd. Differences in word association commonality of schizophrenics: The self-editing-deficit model vs the partial-collapse-of-response-hierarchy hypothesis. *J Clin Psychol, 33*(1):32-39, 1977.

>   A comparison on the M-M of different psych and general medical and surgical gps. M-M was not a major part of the study.

95. —, and H. L. Charles. Psychological test comparison of day hospital and inpatient treatment. *J Clin Psychol, 35*(4): 837-839, 1979.

>   The effects of partial, day hosp treatment and full-time inpt care were compared, using pre- and post-treatment M-Ms, among other measures. All clinical scales were elevated with peaks on *D* and *Sc*. On the M-M post-tests the day hosp sample scored sig higher than inpts on *Hs*. Of the 3 best measures for gp separation one was the *D* scale. With-in-group comparisons revealed the day hosp sample decreased on *D* and *Pt* and the inpt sample increased on *K*.

96. Percell, L. P., and J. L. Delk. Relative usefulness of three forms of the Mini-Mult with college students. *J Consult Clin Psychol, 40*(3):487, 1973.

>   Comparisons were made between the standard MMPI and an independently admin M-M presented in oral question form, written question form and written statement form. While gp correls were somewhat higher for the written statement form, individual

analyses were mixed and not encouraging.

97. Platt, J. J., and W. C. Scura. Validity of the Mini-Mult with male reformatory inmates. *J Clin Psychol, 28*(4): 528-529, 1972.

Comparisons were made between the standard MMPI and the extracted M-M. Agreement between the 2 forms on a number of indices of clinical code types and indices of pathology was inadequate. The M-M was of limited usefulness in decision-making in individual cases.

98. Poythress, N. G., Jr. Selecting a short form of the MMPI: Addendum to Faschingbauer. *J Consult Clin Psychol, 46*(2):331-334, 1978.

This article offers an addendum, including a discussion of the MMPI-168, to Faschingbauer's review which presented guidelines for the clinician considering using an MMPI short form. It was concluded that the empirical evidence favors the FAM and the MMPI-168 over the other short forms.

99. —, and P. H. Blaney. The validity of MMPI interpretations based on the Mini-Mult and the FAM. *J Pers Assess, 42*(2):143-147, 1978.

29 clinicians did Q-sort descriptions for 36 pts' MMPI profiles prepared by using the standard MMPI, the FAM and M-M scales and norms. Interpretive similarity between the standard and short forms was investigated. It was concluded that the similarities between the interpretations based on the MMPI and the short forms suggest that the FAM but not the M-M could be considered an acceptable substitute for the full MMPI for purpose of clinical interpretation.

100. Pulvermacher, G. D., and W. G. Bringmann. The Mini-Mult used with French Canadian college students. *Psychol Rep, 29*(1):134, 1971.

Comparisons were made between the standard MMPI and the M-M. For m Ss, the correls were sig lower on 5 scale comparisons and for 4 on fem Ss. The need for standardization on this population is pointed out.

101. Rand, S. W.   Correspondence between psychological reports based on the Mini-Mult and the MMPI.   *J Pers Assess, 43*(2):160-163, 1979.

Assessed the utility of the M-M with counseling center clients. Four judges completed Q-item questionnaires based on MMPI and M-M profiles. Judges' reliability over time was calculated by repeated presentations of profiles. Results do not support the use of the M-M with a university counseling center clientele.

102. Rathus, S. A.   Factor structure of the MMPI-168 with and without regression weights.   *Psychol Rep, 42*(2):643-646, 1978.

MMPI-168 admin to 1669 adolescents to determine whether the scale factor structure was stable across sex and before and after using regression weights to predict full scale scores. Three factors accounting for 65-69% of the variance emerged—psychoticism and acting out, depression (or neuroticism), and defensiveness. It was concluded that the major response clusters appear to remain following use of regression equations.

103. Rusk, R., B. J. Hyerstay, D. A. Calsyn, and C. W. Freeman. Comparison of the utility of two abbreviated forms of the MMPI for psychiatric screening of the elderly. *J Clin Psychol, 35*(1):104-107, 1979.

Comparisons were made between the MMPI and the extracted FAM and MMPI-168. It was concluded that either of the short forms is useful with hosp older pts. The FAM was generally more in accordance with the MMPI than the MMPI-168.

104. Rybolt, G. A., and J. A. Lambert. Correspondence of the MMPI and Mini-Mult with psychiatric inpatients. *J Clin Psychol, 31*(2):279-281, 1975.

Comparisons were made between the standard MMPI and the extracted M-M. Although comparison generally yielded sig scale pair correls, gp means were sig different on 6 of 11 possible scales. There was also poor agreement on high points and profile elevation. The results don't support the M-M as a substitute for the MMPI with psych inpts.

105. Schaeve, N. R. Validation and possible utilization of the Mini-Mult with undergraduate college students. *D A I, 35*(4-A):2063, 1974.

> M-M and standard MMPI alternately admin with intervals of 0-2 days. Sig correls between corresponding scales except for *Hs.* It was concluded that the M-M has potential for use in research and counseling when the full MMPI would be a problem, yet indicates a need for further research with the instrument.

106. Scott, N. A., and M. G. Conn. Correspondence of the MMPI and MMPI—168 among incarcerated female felons. *J Pers Assess, 43*(5):473-478, 1979.

> The MMPI-168 was scored from the standard MMPI and the 2 forms compared for scale agreement, configural correspondence for validity scales, clinical scales and clinical scales above T-score of 70. It was concluded that the MMPI-168 would appear to be a useful short screening instrument for this population with respect to accurate assessment of profile validity, and configural and scale correspondence.

107. —, M. K. Mount, and S. A. Kosters. Correspondence of the MMPI and Mini-Mult among female reformatory inmates. *J Clin Psychol, 32*(4):792-794, 1976.

> Comparisons of the MMPI and internal M-M were made. Scale-by-scale correls were sig but gp means were different in 6 of the 11 scales. M-M was ineffective in detecting invalid profiles, showed poor agreement with MMPI on high points and degree of pathology as indicated by number of sig clinical scale elevations. Findings question the use of the M-M with this type population.

108. Simono, R. B. Comparison of the standard MMPI and the Mini-Mult in a university counseling center. *Educ Psychol Measmt, 35*(2):401-404, 1975.

> Comparisons were made between the standard MMPI and the

extracted M-M.   The correls, while sig, were not sufficiently
high to allow prediction of scale scores from the M-M to the
full MMPI.

109. Skovron, M. A. The Mini-Mult: Its reevaluation and im-
      provement as related to a profile analysis classifica-
      tion system. *D A I, 34*(4-B):1761, 1973.

      The M-M and standard MMPI were compared on 11 profile
      analysis classifications of Marks and Seeman. Correls failed to
      reach sig for any of the 11 criteria. Based on the results, a cor-
      rel factor was devised and added to the M-M. The revised test
      achieved statistical sig on only 2 of the 11 criteria. It was
      concluded that the results suggest that the revised M-M cannot
      be validly substituted for the MMPI, but it is a step in the right
      direction.

110. Spielberger, C. D., S. M. Auerbach, A. P. Wadsworth, T.
      M. Dunn, and E. S. Taulbee. Emotional reactions to
      surgery. *J Consult Clin Psychol, 40*(1):33-38, 1973.

      M-M was admin along with the STAI to 26 Ss 18-24 hours be-
      fore surgery and 3-9 days after surgery. Scores on the M-M
      were essentially unchanged by the stresses associated with sur-
      gery.

111. Streiner, D. L., J. T. Goodman, and A. McLean. Corre-
      spondence between the MMPI and the Midi-Mult. *Psy-
      chol Rep, 40*(2):551-554, 1977.

      Comparisons were made between the standard MMPI and an ex-
      tracted and an independently admin Midi-Mult using a range of
      pt psychopathology.   It was concluded that the Midi-Mult
      could not be used as an alternative to the MMPI for most clini-
      cal applications.

112. —, C. A. Woodward, J. T. Goodman, and A. McLean.
      Comparisons of the MMPI and Mini-Mult. *Canad J
      Beh Sci, 5*(1):76-82, 1973.

      Comparisons were made between the standard MMPI and an ex-
      tracted and an independently admin M-M, using psych pts. The

extracted form had a higher median correl with the MMPI; there was poor agreement on high point codes, especially for the independently admin M-M. The results don't support the use of the M-M as a reliable substitute for the MMPI.

113. Taulbee, E. S., and J. Samuelson. Mini-Mult vs MMPI. *J Pers Assess, 38(6):479, 1974.*

This was a brief note on a study comparing the results of a standard form R MMPI and an individually admin M-M, using Form R booklet (only the M-M and the abbreviated *Mf* and *Si* scale items being answered), and standard instructions. *S*s were general medical and surgical pts. The correls were highly sig— ranging from .45 for the *Mf* and *Ma* scales to .87 for *Hs*.

114. —, and H. W. Wright. Mini-Mult vs MMPI. *J Pers Assess, 36(6):590, 1972.*

This brief note reported on a study comparing the results of a standard MMPI and an individually admin M-M, using general medical and surgical pts. Scale pair correls between the 2 forms were all sig and ranged from .46 for *L* to .79 for *Hs*.

115. Thomas, M. R., and D. Lyttle. Development of a diagnostic checklist for low back pain patients. *J Clin Psychol, 32(1):125-129, 1976.*

Pts' medical diagnoses were correl with demographic and psychological variables. Detailed results of the M-M were not reported, but it was found that pts with recent lower back injuries tended to display lower average scores on some of their MMPI scales, whereas pts with long-term complaints of back pain scored higher on some MMPI scales. *D, Hy, Pd* and *Ma* were used in the checklist.

116. Thompson, R. J. Utility of the Faschingbauer Abbreviated MMPI as a function of patient group and sex. *J Clin Psychol, 35(3):546-553, 1979.*

Comparisons were made between the MMPI and the extracted FAM of pain and psych pts. All correls between mean T-scores on all scales were highly sig, but 54% of the means were sig different. The number and the nature of the diff in FAM and MMPI gp means and ind profile classifications varied as a function of pt subgroup and sex.

117. Thornton, L. S., A. J. Finch, and J. L. Griffin. The Mini-Mult with criminal psychiatric patients. *J Pers Assess, 39*(4):394-396, 1975.

Comparisons were made between the standard MMPI and the extracted M-M. Although the correls between scale pairs on the 2 forms were high, 8 of the 11 means were sig different.

118. Trybus, R. J., and C. W. Hewitt. The Mini-Mult in a nonpsychiatric population. *J Clin Psychol, 28*(3):371, 1972.

Comparisons were made between the standard MMPI and the extracted M-M using m and fem, black and white coll Ss. Racial diffs appeared to be minimal—the M-M predicted MMPI scores about equally well for both racial gps. Results suggest cautious use of the M-M as a substitute for the MMPI.

119. Tsushima, W. T. Relationship between the Mini-Mult and the MMPI with medical patients. *J Clin Psychol, 31*(4):673-675, 1975.

Comparisons were made between the standard MMPI and the extracted M-M. The 2 forms produced highly similar profiles. It was concluded that the M-M is a fairly accurate substitute for the MMPI as a screening device in a medical setting.

120. Turner, J., and G. McCreary. Short forms of the MMPI with back pain patients. *J Consult Clin Psychol, 46*(2):354-355, 1978.

Comparisons were made between the MMPI and the extracted Midi-Mult and the FAM, using a group of 186 m and fem outpts seen at a Back Clinic. Also, the 3 forms were compared to independent physician ratings of amount of functional component to pts' pain. Code-type agreement was higher between the MMPI and the FAM than between the MMPI and Midi-Mult. Both short forms were found to discriminate between "functional" and "organic" back pain pts.

121. Umansky, D. S. Another look at the Mini-Mult. Unpublished Master's thesis, Western Michigan University, 1972.

Using 100 psych outpts, compared the standard MMPI and M-M profile configurations. "Considerable instability" was found. The M-M appears to be able to make gross configural classifications.

122. Vincent, K. R. Validity of the MMPI-168 on private clinic subpopulations. *J Clin Psychol*, *34*(1):61-62, 1978.

Comparisons were made between the standard MMPI and the extracted MMPI-168 using 3 private psych subpopulations. The MMPI-168 was found to be a viable alternative to the MMPI on all 3 gps—adult and adolescent inpt samples and an outpt vocational rehab gp.

123. Vitalo, R. L. Teaching improved interpersonal functioning as a preferred mode of treatment. *J Clin Psychol*, *27*(2):166-171, 1971.

20 psych inpts were randomly assigned to 1 of 3 treatments: Training group, Group therapy control, and non-specific treatment control. Several outcome indices, including 2 indices from the M-M—the sum of the "T scores for all eight clinical scales" and the A.I.—were used to evaluate intrapersonal change. It was concluded that "group therapy did effect clinical changes on the MMPI" (M-M).

124. Walls, R. F., D. McGlynn, and D. H. Tingstrom III. An evaluation of three short forms extracted from the group form MMPI responses of incarcerated offenders. *J Clin Psychol*, *33*(2):431-435, 1977.

Comparisons were made between the standard MMPI and the extracted FAM, MMPI-168, and Hugo short forms in terms of correspondence of scale pairs, profile validities and high points. All scale pair correls were sig; there was little diff between the short forms in terms of accuracy with regard to validity; and the best short-form to MMPI clinical scale correspondence for the highest scale was only 63% (for the FAM). The FAM and MMPI-168 were more nearly equivalent. Results would question the use of these short forms as substitutes for the MMPI for this type of population.

125. Ward, L. C. Conversion equations for modified scoring of the MMPI-168. *J Pers Assess, 44*(6):644-646, 1980.

Using a sample of 300 pts who had been admin the MMPI, substitution equations for the MMPI-168 were calculated. These equations permit estimation of MMPI scores when the MMPI-168 is scored to incorporate those items normally excluded by Form R keys. Modified scoring was shown to improve predictability for *Pa* and *Sc*. Conversion equations were also computed for a new MMPI abbreviation, the Improved Readability Form, which was developed for use with verbally impaired persons. Correls of both short forms with the full MMPI were high and failed to indicate any advantage of one form over the other.

126. —, J. T. McDaniel, and R. B. Selby. A comparative study of the Mini-Mult and the MMPI-168. *J Clin Psychol, 36*(4):948-952, 1980.

The M-M was extracted from the MMPI and the 10 M-M items that are on the MMPI *Si* scale were scored to obtain a M-M *Si* score. Multiple regressions, permitting estimation of MMPI scores from the M-M, were derived from data on 165 pts. The equations thus derived were then applied to the data from the cross-validation samples, and comparisons were made between M-M and MMPI-168 estimates and between these estimates and the standard MMPI scores. The M-M performed at a level comparable to the MMPI-168 in terms of usual measures of correspondence to the full MMPI. Prediction of *Si* scores from the M-M was only marginally adequate.

127. —, H. W. Wright, and E. S. Taulbee. An improvement in the statistical validity of the MMPI-168 through modified scoring. *J Consult Clin Psychol, 47*(3):618-619, 1979.

Reported the results of rescoring the MMPI-168 to incorporate the normally excluded items when using the Standard Form R keys. The modified scoring procedure sig improved the correl between short-form and full-scale scores for *Pa* and *Sc* scales on 100 m alcohs. The importance of considering the repeated items in the MMPI in research with other short forms was pointed out.

Author Index

Subject Index

Faschingbauer Short Form (FAM)

Hugo Short Form

CHAPTER III

THE BLACKY PICTURES

Introduction

The Blacky Pictures test is a "modified projective technique" developed by Gerald S. Blum as a research tool for the systematic evaluation of psychoanalytic theory and for the clinical assessment of individual personalities within a psychoanalytic framework (Blum, 1949). The test is comprised of 12 cartoons which depict the adventures of a dog named Blacky; his/her parents, Mama and Papa; and Tippy, a sibling of unspecified sex and age—with a series of open-ended and structured questions about each cartoon. The cartoons show Blacky engaging in a variety of emotionally laden and psychoanalytically relevant activities, such as breast feeding, defecating, and dreaming. Each cartoon captures a particular area of psychosexual conflict. Scoring of the spontaneous stories given about each cartoon, the answers to a structured inquiry, cartoon preferences, and related comments occurring on other cartoons, yield conflict scores (Very Strong, Fairly Strong, or Weak or Absent) on each of 13 psychosexual dimensions: Oral Eroticism, Oral Sadism, Anal Expulsiveness, Anal Retentiveness, Oedipal Intensity, Masturbation Guilt, Castration Anxiety (males) or Penis Envy (females), Identification Process, Sibling Rivalry, Guilt Feelings, Ego Ideal, Narcissistic Love Object, and Anaclitic Love Object. A later alternative scoring system, based upon factor analysis, breaks these 13 dimensions into 30 factors. In developing the test, Blum began with the assumption that his 12 Blacky cartoons would actually measure the psychoanalytic dimensions which they are intended to measure, and proceeded to compare test results with postulates and inferences from psychoanalytic theory. Although the test was constructed on a totally rational and theoretical basis, the correspondence between test results and psychoanalytic theory was impressive.

Since Blum's original monograph was published, the Blacky Pictures test has been used to research the psychodynamics of various syndromes and the behavioral correlates of psychosexual conflicts. In accordance with psychoanalytic theory, BP indices have been related to the development of peptic ulcers and bronchial asthma, to stuttering, heavy smoking, sexual deviancy, conflicts about amputation, paranoia, area of specialization in college, verbal behavior in groups, ambivalence towards one's mother, the effectiveness of various reinforcers in operant conditioning paradigms, and a variety of other symptoms and behaviors.

A fairly popular addition to the BP test is the Defense Preference Inquiry (DPI). After each cartoon, the subject is presented with a list of five statements about what Blacky is doing. Each of the statements represents a particular defense. As with the BP test, the DP patterns have been related to a wide variety of behavioral and personality dimensions.

The Blacky Pictures have enjoyed considerable success for a test whose construction and interpretation have been so exclusively theoretical. In a Buros's review (1959), Beck concludes that "The test has the promise warranting its development." Nearly half of the references in this bibliography are dated between the year of that review and the present. So, the test has developed further and some of its promise has materialized. Despite this development, the test has been used much less in the past decade. Perhaps this is due to its foundation in psychoanalytic theory, which has also become less popular. Whatever the reason, the diminished use of the BP test was not a rational decision based upon the results of the latest empirical research. The authors, therefore, echo Beck's conclusion. The test continues to have the promise warranting its further development.

Journal and Other References

1. Adelson, J., and J. Redmond. Personality differences in the capacity for verbal recall. *J Abnorm Soc Psychol, 57*: 244-248, 1958.   (*33*:9771, 1959)

   Based upon an analysis of diffs in ego organization the hypoth was offered that "anal retentive" inds have a greater ability to recall verbal material than "anal expulsives." *S*s were 61 fem coll freshmen and the BT was the criterion of "anality." It was found that "anal retentives" recalled verbal material sig better than "expulsives"during both an immediate and a delayed recall test.

2. Ansbacher, H. L. "Can Blacky Blacken Testing?" *Am Psychol, 14*:654, 1959.

   This is a letter concerning a bill which was introduced in the Minnesota legislature to require parents' consent for a child to be psychologically tested.

3. Aronson, M. L. A study of the Freudian theory of paranoia by means of the Blacky Pictures. *J Proj Tech, 17*:3-19, 1953.   (*28*:2981, 1954)

   90 *S*s were categorized into 3 gps: Paranoid gp (psychotic pts), psychotic gp (non-paranoid pts), and normal gp (30 non-hosp inds). The BPT was admin individually to each of the 90 *S*s and comparisons were made among the 3 gps. "A large number of analytically-derived hypoths as to how the paranoids should differ from either of the *C* gps were tested and many supported by the results of this study. The paranoids, on a whole, tended to differ more markedly from the normals than from the psychotics."

4. Beck, S. J. Review of the Blacky Pictures. *J Consult Psychol, 20*(6):487-488, 1956.

   Beck concluded that the test has a potency for differentiating gps and has the projective instrument value of opening a window to latent character traits. He stated there is a major fallacy in the scoring procedure but that its agreement with clinical theory is logically sound. It was concluded that the test has the promise warranting its development.

5.   Berger, L.   Cross-validation of "primary" and "reactive"
      personality patterns with non-ulcer surgical patients.
      J Proj Tech, 23:8-11, 1959.

The extent to which Winter's Primary and Reactive scales (see
Ref. No. 122) are valid for non-ulcer pts.   Winter's cases were
compared with those 30 non-ulcer, surgical pts.   Predictions
were made about relationships between the scores of these pts on
B scales and corresponding Rorschach variables.   The Blacky-
Rorschach relationships were, in general, the same as those
found by Winter.   When Winter's original scoring system was
used, ulcer pts, as a group, scored higher than non-ulcer, surgical
controls in both the Primary and Reactive scales, though there
was some individual variability.   When the patterns were scored
according to the revised scoring system, no diffs were found between the 2 samples. Discrepancy in the findings of the 2 B scoring systems casts some doubt on the validity of at least one of
them.

6.   —.   Interrelationship between blood pressure responses to
      mecholyl and personality variables. *Psychophysiology,
      1*:115-118, 1964.

30 psych pts were admin the BPT and DPI.   Blood pressure was
then measured before and after intramuscular injection of
mecholyl.   Epinephrine-like responses to the mecholyl were associated with higher scores on Ana Lo Obj and General hostility,
lower scores on Disgruntled dependency, lower defense preference for Regression and Projection and a preference for the Reaction formation defense.   The reverse pattern chracterized the
norepinephrine-like response to mecholyl.

7.   —, and L. Everstine.   Test-retest reliability of the Blacky
      Pictures test. *J Proj Tech, 26*:225-226, 1962.
                                        (*37*:3185, 1963)

Analysis of BP test records of 50 m coll students revealed sig
test-retest correls on all 13 test dimensional scores and all 4
patterns of conflict.

8. Bernstein, L., and P. H. Chase. The discriminative ability of the Blacky Pictures with ulcer patients. *J Consult Psychol, 19*:377-380, 1955. (*30*:6202, 1956)

Three gps of hosp pts were studied with the BP: An ulcer gp; a psychosomatic, nonulcer gp; and a nonpsychosomatic gp. Sig diffs were found on 3 of 17 dimens for each inter-group comparison, but no differentiation was found on the basis of Ora Ero— the dimen the authors note was considered most important in a previous study by Blum and Kaufman. ***

9. Blatt, S. J. An attempt to define mental health. *J Consult Psychol, 28*:146-153, 1964. (*39*:2352, 1965)

Seven advanced graduate students in clinical psychology ranked, in an order most descriptive of optimal pers integration, 20 abbreviated paragraphs of Murray's "desires and effects of the 20 manifest needs." There was highly sig agreement between judges, and this pattern of needs is discussed as a conceptualization of mental health. 116 m research scientists, using the same paragraphs, described themselves. Deviation of self-descriptions from the ideal related sig to measures of creativity, ego strength, manifest anxiety, autonomy, and authoritarian values. Strong conflict on specific *B* scales was frequently associated with marked deviation of a need related to the particular psy-sex issue. ***

10. Block, W. E., and P. A. Ventur. A study of the psychoanalytic concept of castration anxiety in symbolically castrated amputees. *Psychiatr Q, 37*:518-526, 1963. (*39*:1932, 1965)

40 amputees were compared with normal controls on certain cas anx indices of the BP. Presumptive evidence validating the cas anx concept was found. Presumptive validity was also demonstrated for use of BP in investigating psy-ana concepts.

11. Blum, G. S. The Blacky Pictures: A technique for the exploration of personality dynamics. New York: Psychological Corporation, 1950.

The technique consists of 12 cartoons tailored to fit psy-ana theory and portrays the adventures of a dog named Blacky. The cartoons are designed to depict either a stage of psy-sex development or a type of object relationship within that development.

12. —. A study of the psychoanalytic theory of psychosexual development. *Genet Psychol Monogr, 39*:3-99, 1949.
(*23*:3650, 1949)

The "Blacky Test," a projective technique based on interpersonal relationships among 4 dogs, was developed with the specific aim of exploring psy-ana concepts. The 11 cartoons were admin to 119 m and 90 fem students in elementary psychology classes who were asked to make spontaneous recordings and to respond later to specific questions in the inquiry. "The protocols were scored in the form of analogues of psy-ana dimens of psy-sex development." Evidence was sought in the writings of Freud and Fenichel to determine whether or not the 31 statistically sig findings (sex diffs and dimen intercorrels) were consistent with psy-ana theory. Agreement between theory and experimental findings was noted in 14 of 15 areas where theory was specifically stated and in all 8 areas where theory could be inferred. In 8 areas psy-ana theory was too vague to permit valid inferences.

13. —. A reply to Seward's "Psychoanalysis, deductive methods, and the Blacky Test." *J Abnorm Soc Psychol, 45*:536-537, 1950.   (*25*:644, 1951)

In the opinion of the writer, Seward's results tend to confirm the original research. ***

14. —. An experimental reunion of psychoanalytic theory with perceptual vigilance and defense. *J Abnorm Soc Psychol, 49*:94-98, 1954.   (*28*:6928, 1954)

This experiment was designed to test, within the framework of perceptual behavior, two psy-ana hypoths: (a) The unconscious striving for expression of underlying psy-sex impulses (vigilance); and (b) the warding off of these threatening impulses as they begin to approach conscious awareness (defense). Using BP, the vigilance hypoth was supported in 11 of the 14 cases tested; the defense hypoth was supported in 12 of the 14 cases tested.

15. —. Perceptual defense revisited. *J Abnorm Soc Psychol,*

51:24-29, 1955.   (*30*:4179, 1956)

In the present study the following hypoth was submitted to experimental test: *S*s predisposed to use the mechanism of repression in conjunction with a given conflict will, when confronted
subliminally with a conflict-relevant stimulus, show defensive behavior to the perceptual process itself. . . . The results of this
study show that "with selective verbal report, familiarity, set and
antecedent conditions all controlled, an avoidance response directly traceable to the perceptual process was obtained."

16. —. Defense preferences in four countries. *J Proj Tech, 20*:
    33-41, 1956.   (*31*:3007, 1957)

The DPI for the BP was admin to m coll students in Italy, England, the Netherlands, and the United States. Analysis of mean
ranks assigned various defenses showed national diffs only with
respect to preferences for avoidance (regression-denial family),
with the Netherlands gp having the most preferences, followed by
England, Italy, and the U.S. No sig diffs were noted for reaction
formation, projection, regression and intellectualization. There
were widespread individual diffs in character structure in all 4
national gps, with some discernible diffs between countries in
regard to avoidance preferences.

17. —. "Reliability of the Blacky Test": A reply to Charen. *J
    Consult Psychol, 20*:406, 1956.   (*31*:7899, 1957)

This is a reply by Blum to Charen's article (see Ref. No. 34) in
which Charen raised some questions as to the reliability of the
Blacky Test; Charen, in his reply to Blum, comments upon the
criticisms offered by Blum on his paper.

18. —. An investigation of perceptual defense in Italy. *Psychol
    Rep, 3*:169-175, 1957.   (*32*:3646, 1958)

The present study, an outgrowth of 4 earlier researches linking
psy-ana theory to perceptual processes, attempted a cross-cultural
follow-up of Nelson's demonstration of perceptual defense. Results on 10 *S*s in a low accuracy gp confirmed the perceptual defense phenomenon: An individual who preferred the avoidance
alternative for a BP in the DPI reported perception of that

picture less frequently. Absence of this effect in a high accuracy gp provided empirical evidence for the necessity of investigating the effects of pers on perception throughout the continuum of awareness.

19. —. Blacky Pictures with children. In A. I. Rabin and M. R. Haworth (Eds.), *Projective techniques with children.* New York: Grune and Stratton, 1960, 95-104.

Among several apperceptive approaches covered, is the BPT by Blum.

20. —. Psychoanalytic behavior theory: A conceptual framework for research. In H. P. David and J. C. Brengelmann (Eds.), *Perspectives in personality research,* 1960, 107-138.

Academic psychology and psychoanalysis are both used in devising an electronic type model for behavior. The BT is used as an example.

21. —. *A model of the mind: Explored by hypnotically controlled experiments and examined for its psychodynamic implications.* New York: Wiley, 1961, 229.
(*36*:5II29B, 1962)

A purely conceptual model which "stresses those mental functions occurring between stimulus and response, and pursues them . . .techniques like hypnosis, GSR, and introspection. . . . It appraises some sig problems posed by psy-ana at the same time shaping a different theoretical base.

22. —. A guide for research use of the Blacky Pictures. *J Proj Tech, 26*:3-29, 1962.   (*37*:3188, 1963)

A factor analysis of *B* responses elicited from 210 m undergraduates produced 30 factors which are given dynamic interpretations. Sig relationships between factors along with their relationship to criterion variables are presented. This approach to evaluating *B* responses clarifies already existing scoring procedures and provides a guide for the systematic interpretation of test records.

23. —. Programming people to simulate machines. In Tomkins and Messick (Eds.), *Computer simulation of personality.* New York: John Wiley and Sons, 1963, 127-158.

A conference report on research described in *A model of the mind* focusing on problems of anxiety, geneal inhibition, and arousal. Hypnosis, dream reports, and the BP, are among the techniques used.

24. —. Defense preferences among university students in Denmark, France, Germany and Israel. *J Proj Tech Pers Assess, 28*:13-19, 1964.   (*39*:241, 1965)

An investigation of defense preferences among m university students in Denmark, France, Germany, and Israel was undertaken to follow up an earlier study conducted in England, Italy, the Netherlands, and the U.S. *** The findings are in close accord with the previous results, which also pointed to the hazards of indulging in the popular pasttime of invoking national stereotypes.

25. —. *Psychodynamics: The science of unconscious mental forces.* Belmont, California: The Wadsworth Publishing Company, 1966.

This small volume has sought to define and treat the content of psychodynamics in such a way as to bring it more into the mainstream of the academic discipline of psychology.

26. —, and J. R. Graef. The detection over time of subjects simulating hypnosis. *Int J Clin Exper Hypnosis, 19*(4): 211-224, 1971.

Explored feasibility of the use of simulator controls for long periods of time in a variety of hypnosis experiments as part of a 6 session training program.

27. —, and M. Green. The effects of mood upon imaginal thought. *J Pers Assess, 42*(3):227-232, 1978.

Explored the effects of mood upon imaginal thought using a highly trained female undergraduate who was hypnotically programmed to experience free-floating anxiety or pleasure just before exposure of combinations of 3 BP.

28. —, and H. F. Hunt. The validity of the Blacky Pictures. *Psychol Bull, 49*:238-250, 1952.   (*27*:2707, 1953)

The present article is intended to survey completed studies of the BP in a number of separate areas. Comparisons with theoretical predictions, validation by experimental techniques, prediction of behavior in a gp setting, and the clinician's judgment as a standard of comparison are discussed. It is concluded that the results, "encourage further exploration of the test and the personality theory it serves; they strongly suggest that 'there is something there,' but do not necessarily indicate 'what it is,' or 'where it is'."

29. —, and J. B. Kaufman. Two patterns of personality dynamics in male peptic ulcer patients as suggested by responses to the Blacky Pictures. *J Clin Psychol, 8*:273-278, 1952.   (*27*:6060, 1953)

The BP were admin to 14 m peptic ulcer pts. Exploration of the scored responses, in conjunction with those of 3 C gps, uncovered 2 opposite trends within the ulcer sample. *** The discrepancy between close-to-conscious expression of oral needs in the one-half, contrasted with obvious attempts at denial in the other, suggested the hypoth that there may be 2 very different patterns of ulcer dynamics.

30. —, and D. Miller. Exploring the psychoanalytic theory of the oral character. *J Pers, 20*:287-304, 1952.
(*27*:2353, 1953)

The purpose was to explore the feasibility of testing psy-ana theory by conventional methods. The Ss were third-grade children. Data on orality were secured from teachers' ratings, time sampling, sociometrics, and experiments. Resulting rank order *r*'s gave strong support for hypoths dealing with extreme interest in food, and social isolation, fair support for those dealing with need for approval, concern over giving and receiving, and boredom tolerance; and no support for those concerning need to be ingratiating, inability to divide loyalties, and depressive tendencies. Those (hypoths) remaining equivocal concerned dependency, and suggestibility.

31. Briggs, D. L., B. Lyon, H. B. Molish, and R. R. Deen. Selected sociocultural factors affecting interpersonal relations as revealed by the Blacky Pictures: discrimination between "unsuitable" and "normal" naval recruits. *USN Submarine Med Res Lab Rep, 12*:Rep 227, 1953. (*28*:4119, 1954)

1,847 recruits who successfully completed their recruit training are compared with 390 recruits who, because of their inability to make the transition from civilian to military life, were designated "unsuitable" for Naval service and were subsequently discharged from the Navy. ***

32. Carp, F. M. Psychosexual development of stutterers. *J Proj Tech, 26*:388-391, 1962. (*37*:6979, 1963)

Stutterers did not display any more anal retentiveness in the *B* than did nonstutterers. Higher scores in cas anx (males) and penis envy (females) were found as predicted among stutterers. In general, higher Ora Ero and Ora Sad scores were found among stutterers, and these results are consistent with psy-ana theory.

33. Cava, E. L., and H. L. Rausch. Identification and the adolescent boy's perception of his father. *J Abnorm Soc Psychol, 47*:855-856, 1952. (*27*:5020, 1953)

This paper reports a study of the relationship between conflict in ident with like-sex parent, as measured by a projective technique, and perceived communality of interests, activities, and traits.

34. Charen, S. Reliability of the Blacky Test. *J Consult Psychol, 20*:16, 1956.

Charen used *B* test in his dissertation (among Rorschach and 15 paper and pencil tests) with TB pts. Used only inquiry items. Used r_p to determine test-retest reliability (4-month interval). Scored by Blum's revised scoring system. From the other tests, no basic pers changes occurred in 4 months ". . .the highest r_p

obtained was .519 for Cas Anx with remaining cards low or negative." Charen suggests that equivocal results on *B* might be due to poor reliability.

35. —. Regressive behavior changes in the tuberculous patient. *J Psychol*, 41:273-289, 1956.   (*31*:5000, 1957)

It has been suggested that TB pts regress in pers in several ways due to enforced bedrest and hosp, with deprivation of normal social activities. An attempt is made to measure these changes, by means of pencil-and-paper tests, the Rorschach, and the *B* test. . . .

36. —. A reply to Blum. *J Consult Psychol*, 20:407, 1956.

Comments upon the criticisms offered by Blum on his paper.

37. Christiansen, B. Attitudes towards foreign affairs as a function of personality. Oslo, Norway: Oslo University Press, 1959, 283.   (*35*:3340, 1961)

. . .By means of attitude scales and such projective techniques as the Rosenzweig *P-F* Study and the *B* tests, several hypoths were tested on samples of applicants and students at the military naval academies in Oslo. Detailed analyses of results and the English versions of the scale are included. The relationships between attitudes toward foreign affairs and pers factors are found to be complex and to depend at least on manifest aggressiveness, latent aggressiveness, and nationalism.

38. Cohen, A. R. Experimental effects of ego-defense preference on interpersonal relations. *J Abnorm Soc Psychol*, 52:19-27, 1956.   (*31*:2539, 1957)

The hypoth that a connection exists between the pers defense of interacting inds and their attitudes toward and perceptions of their interaction is explored by assessing the defense mechanisms of a gp of *S*s to psy-sex stimuli, the BP, and evaluating their interaction when pairs of *S*s are engaged in a task which arouses a specific psy-sex disturbance. The results indicate that the interaction of 2 people who project the same psy-sex impulse is more negative than pairs of people who use other defenses. Dissimilar defenses do not seem to adversely affect the interaction; however, when both partners have high conflict, more negative interaction tends to result than when only one is disturbed. The relative hierarchies of defense mechanisms and psy-sex dimens, with regard to their effect on interpers relations are discussed.

39. Cohen, S. I., A. J. Silverman, W. Waddell, and G. D. Zuidema. Urinary catecholamine levels, gastric secretion and specific psychological factors in ulcer and non-ulcer patients. *J Psychosom Res, 5*:90-115, 1961.
(*36*:3JU90C, 1962)

Gastric secretory studies and urinary assays for catecholamines were carried out on 10 Ss with radiologically proven ulcers and 10 non-ulcer Ss. *** The Ss whose psychological measures were independently scored for high anxiety and low or disturbed expression of aggression were most likely to have a low noradrenaline output, and a duodenal ulcer.

40. Cooperman, M., and I. L Child. Differential effects of positive and negative reinforcement on two psychoanalytic character types. *J Consult Clin Psychol, 37*(1):57-59, 1971.

Study attempted to replicate the findings of Noblin, Timmons, and Kael (see Ref. No. 82) which related verbal conditioning to performance on the BP. Results indicate that acquisition and extinction procedures affected oral Ss in a direction opposite to their effect on anal Ss. The acquisition and extinction diffs between the 2 types were not obtained with either personal or mechanical reinforcement.

41. Corman, L. (The PN Test: Blackpaw). Paris, France: Presses Universitaires France, 1961.   (*37*:6464, 1963)

The PN Test is a children's projective technique which, like the CAT, uses the animal on which the child projects his attitudes, thoughts, and conflicts. ***

42. —. (The advantages of free projection in personality tests: The example of the P-N Test.) *Rev Psicol Appl, 11*:207-219, 1961.   (*36*:4HG07C, 1962)

The P-N Test (Test Patte Noire) inspired by the BT, consists of a series of plates involving a gp of unlabeled pigs, one of which has a black leg and haunch. ***

43. —, G. Corman, and F. Foulard. (A new technique for projective tests: The identification-preference method). *Rev Psicol Appl, 10*:25-37, 1960.   (*35*:4905, 1961)

This is a description of the BT and a discussion of its underlying theory. ***

44. Davids, A., and M. J. Lawton. Self-concept, mother concept, and food aversions in emotionally disturbed and normal children. *J Abnorm Soc Psychol, 62*:309-314, 1961.   (*36*:4FF09D, 1962)

Self-concept was measured via an adjective checklist and a self-rating task (child asked to compare himself to others on traits); mother child relationship was inferred from responses to specific cards of the BT and a story completion test; food aversion was measured from a food preference list. In general, the self-concept and mother-concept were related and there was an inverse relation between these and food aversion.

45. Dawson, J. G., E. O. Timmons, and C. D. Noblin. Dynamic and behavioral predictors of hypnotizability. *J Consult Psychol, 29*:76-78, 1965.   (*39*:8144, 1965)

16 fem psychology undergraduate students were drawn from a pool of 48 *S*s. 8 students having the highest "oral" scores and 8 having the highest "anal" scores were selected by means of the BT. One of the *E*s attempted a Taffel-type verbal-conditioning problem with each of the *S*s. In a separate phase the 2 remaining *E*s saw the 16 *S*s for a hypnotic induction experiment. A comparison of the 2 predictors of hypnotic susceptibility revealed that the oral-anal measure failed completely to predict satisfactory hypnotic *S*s while the verbal-conditioning test was successful at a highly sig level.

46. Dean, S. I. A note on female Blacky protocols. *J Proj Tech, 23*:417, 1959.

Evidence is presented that the ident of the name, Blacky, and of dogs is a characteristically male response.

47. DeLuca, J. N. Performance of overt male homosexuals and controls on the Blacky test. *J Clin Psychol, 23*:497, 1967.

20 homosexual and 40 nonhomosexual army inductees were admin the BP. The protocols were scored on 2 separate occasions for each of the 30 factors. The 2 gps differed only on one factor (which one is not indicated), which could have been due to chance.

48. —. Psychosexual conflict in adolescent enuretics. *J Psychol, 68*(1):145-149, 1968.

Enuretic and *C S*s were compared on the BP. Results suggest that enuretics are not defending against psy-sex conflicts that are any different from those of *C*s.

49. Dickson, S. An application of the Blacky Test to a study of the psychosexual development of stutterers. *Int J Soc Psychiatry, 20*(3-4):269-273, 1974.

The BPT was admin to 20 stutterers above the age of 9 and a matched *C* gp. The BP scores indicated sig stronger fixation at the anal state of development in the gp of stutterers. An overall score indicative of fixation suggested that stutterers manifested greater emotional disturbance than did non-stutterers.

50. Doidge, W. T., and W. H. Holtzman. Implications of homosexuality among Air Force trainees. *J Consult Psychol, 24*:9-13, 1960.   (*34*:8034, 1960)

Psychological tests were given to 80 airmen divided into 4 gps. Test records of the homsexual gp were different from the *C* gps. This suggests that homsexuals suffer from an emotional disorder which is pervasive, severe, and disqualifying for military service. The rest records of the partly homosexual gp were nearly similar to the 2 *C* gps. Severe psychopathology accompanies the "markedly homosexual individual."

51. Ellis, A.   The Blacky Test used with a psychoanalytic pa-
     tient. *J Clin Psychol, 9*:167-172, 1953.
                                          (*28*:2627, 1954)

     Comparisons were made between the ratings of 22 psychologists,
     the author of the test, a patient, and her therapist of the protocol
     of a BT. On the basis of data from this one case it is concluded
     that the test yields good inter-rater reliability but does not yield
     valid pers assessment.

52. —.   Review of the Blacky Pictures: A technique for the ex-
     ploration of personality dynamics.   In O. K. Buros
     (Ed.), *The fourth mental measurements yearbook.* New
     Brunswick, New Jersey: Rutgers University Press, 1953.

     The reviewer concluded that the BP makes an intriguing projec-
     tive technique of pers evaluation which appears to have some
     good possibilities of aiding in the *S*'s specific sexuo-amative prob-
     lems.

53. Fisher, D. F., and S. L. Keen.   Verbal recall as a function
     of personality characteristic.   *J Genet Psychol, 120*(1):
     83-92, 1972.

     Gps of anal retentive, anal neutral and anal expulsive army en-
     listed men were compared on verbal recall measures. Findings of
     previous studies showing anal retentives to be superior in verbal
     recall were not confirmed.

54. Freeman, R. W. A study of delinquent personality: A com-
     parison of certain aspects of the personality structures
     of delinquent and nondelinquent boys. Masters thesis,
     Wesleyan University, 1954.

55. Galinsky, M. D. Relationships among personality, defense,
     and academic failure.   *J Pers Assess, 35*(4):359-363,
     1971.

     A gp of 29 undergraduate academic failures and a gp of 27
     academically successful undergraduates were compared on the
     BP and the DPI to test out psy-ana hypoths about the relation-
     ships among defense, pregenital conflict, and school failure.

There were sig diffs on 7 *B* factors and on a DPI comparison. The findings support the hypoth that reliance on defensive processes that are considered to be inimical to intellectual functioning is related to poor academic work. The findings do not provide direct evidence that conflict associated with pregenital experience is universally characteristic of failing students.

56. Genn, M. M. Review of the Blacky Test. *Q J Child Behav,* 2:474-476, 1950.

The reviewer concluded that the validity of the BT has been established to some extent. However, the reliability, or the extent to which a protocol is actually representative of the *S*'s psysex development, has not as yet been demonstrated.

57. Granick, S., and N. A. Scheflen. Approaches to reliability of projective tests with special reference to the Blacky Pictures Test. *J Consult Psychol, 22*:137-141, 1958.
(*35*:3466, 1961)

In this study, the feasibility of developing reliability measures of projective tests based on the clinical aspects of the test material is considered. Using data obtained with the BP Test on 40 school-age children, several hypoths are explored related to judgment, temporal, and split-half reliabilities. . . . Evidence is derived which supports the test's stability to a modest degree. . . . This study indicates that integration of varied approaches to a test's consistency may serve as an appropriate alternative to an over-all coefficient of reliability.

58. Gross, S. J., M. Hirt, and W. Seeman. Psychosexual conflicts in asthmatic children. *J Psychosom Res, 11*(4): 315-317, 1968.

*S*s were 3 gps of 15 each (asthmatic, arthritic, and normal school children). BP test was used to determine if children with asthma would manifest greater conflict in selected areas of psy-sex development. Results reveal that the 3 gps did not differ sig on any one of the conflicts, although oral eroticism approached significance.

59. Harris, J. G. Some psychological differences between chil-

dren with well-aligned incisor teeth and those with spaced protrusive incisors as revealed by the "Blacky" projective test. Masters thesis, Wayne State University, 1964.

60. Josephthal, D. Investigation of the psychoanalytic theory of depression by use of the Blacky Pictures. Undergraduate thesis, Wesleyan University, 1956.

61. Kalish, H. I. The black box revisited. *Contemp Psychol, 8*:24-26, 1963.

    A review of Blum's *A model of the mind* (see Ref. No. 21).

62. Kimeldorf, C., and P. J. Geiwitz. Smoking and the Blacky orality factors. *J Proj Tech Pers Assess, 30*(2):167-168, 1966.

    A gp ot m coll students classified as heavy smokers and a gp of nonsmokers were compared on 6 orality factors of the BP test. Heavy smokers, compared with nonsmokers, scored sig higher on "oral craving" and exhibited more defensiveness in a situation involving hostility toward the mother. The results confirm the psy-ana hypoth of a relationship between orality and smoking.

63. King, F. W., and D. C. King. Projective assessment of the female's sexual identification, with special reference to the Blacky Pictures. *J Proj Tech Pers Assess, 28*:293-299, 1964.   (*39*:7900, 1965)

    The frontispiece of the BP was projected to gps of junior and senior HS students; stories were obtained from 72 males and 64 females. A comparable slide of "Whitey the cat" provided the stimulus for stories from an additional 71 m and 71 fem students. Ident responses were assumed to occur when a *S* referred to a sexually ambiguous cartoon character as being of the same sex as the *S*. When this operational definition of ident was employed, females did not identify more with "Whitey the cat" than with "Blacky the dog;" in fact over 95% of the fem *S*s referred to the main character as masculine regardless of which stimulus was presented. M and fem responses were essentially indistinguishable. There was no sig diff between M and fem *S*s in identifying the cartoon sibling as female. The results are interpreted in terms of linguistic and other socio-cultural determinants rather than in terms of psychodynamic factors. Caution is urged in the interpretation of alleged cross-sex ident responses in the verbal productions of females on projective techniques.

64. Klehr, H. An investigation of some personality factors in women with rheumatoid arthritis. *Am Psychol, 7*:344-345, 1952.

*S*s were all females—20 outpt arthritics, 20 outpts without muscle or bone involvement, and 20 normals. The TAT, A-V, and BP were used. There were no sig diffs among the 3 gps except for greater oral aggression for arthritics on one of the BP measures.

65. Kline, P., and A. Gale. An objective method of administering a projective test: The Blacky Pictures. *Br J Proj Psychol Pers Study, 14*(2):12-16, 1969.

An objective method of administering the BP in a language laboratory setting is presented.

66. Knapp, R. H. Demographic cultural and personality attributes of scientists. In C. W. Taylor (Ed.), *The 1955 University of Utah research conference on the identification of creative scientific talent.* Salt Lake City: University of Utah Press, 1956, pp. 204-212.

Students in the sciences, the social sciences and the humanities were admin a gp Rorschach, the BP, and the TAT. On the BP, the science students were almost universally the least disturbed on all variables.

67. Lasky, J. J., and L. Berger. Blacky Test scores before and after genitourinary surgery. *J Proj Tech, 23*:57-58, 1959.

*S*s were 30 m urological pts who were admin the BP before and after surgery. Pearson *r*'s between before/after scores indicated no sig change in patterns of conflict. Dimens sig affected by surgery were Mas Glt, Cas Anx Nar Lo Obj, Ana Ret, Sib Riv, Ego Id, and Ora Ero.

68. Lievens, S., and G. Mannekens. Dynamic psychology: Fundamental theory of the interpretation of projective techniques. *Revue Belge de Psychologie Et de Pedagogie, 32*(131):65-74, 1970.

   The authors use a Freudian basis and the relevance of certain projective tests to suggest that authorities have defined dynamic psychology as the fundamental theory in the interpretation of projective techniques.

69. Lindner, H. The Blacky Pictures test: A study of sexual and non-sexual offenders. *J Proj Tech, 17*:79-84, 1953.
   (*28*:2975, 1954)

   It has been found that the BPT is a valid indicator of psy-sex deviation in a selected population. It is sufficiently sensitive to discriminate between 2 gps of Ss; a sexually deviant gp and a non-sexually-deviant C gp. To the extent that this test represents psy-ana theory, these data may be considered to support such theory as a plausible rationale.

70. Machover, S., and F. S. Puzzo. Clinical and objective studies of personality variables in alcoholism: I. Clinical investigation of the "alcoholic personality." II. Clinical study of personality correlates of remission from active alcoholism. *Q J Stud Alcohol, 20*:505-527, 1959.
   (*34*:6253, 1960)

   Descriptive and statistical summaries of clinical psychological reports on 23 remitted and 23 unremitted alcohs suggest a schizoid isolation, with cognitive, affective, and conative ambivalence; with fuzziness of self-concept and confusion of level of masculinity and sex role, passivity, and hostility.

71. Magnussen, M. G. The Blacky Pictures as personality measures for undergraduate areas of specialization. *J Proj Tech, 23*:351-353, 1959.   (*35*:4931, 1961)

   Teevan found a correlation between pers, as measured by the BP, and vocation in the period of undergraduate specialization. The present study uses this instrument in a more orthodox manner to obtain similar results.

72. Margolis, M. The mother-child relationship in bronchial asthma. *J Abnorm Soc Psychol, 63*:360-367, 1961.
(*37*:1840, 1963)

> The responses to the BT and an objective test of attitudes re child rearing—Parental Attitude Research Instrument (PARI), Schaefer & Bell (1955)—of mothers of children with astham (A), were compared to those of children with rheumatic fever (RF), and a gp being seen in outpt clinic dealing with minor cuts and bruises (healthy controls, H). No diffs were found on the PARI, and sig was found on only 2 cards of the *B*. From these 2 cards, it was concluded that A mothers, as compared to others, had a greater intensity of oedipal conflict and were more inclined to be characterized as oral erotic.

73. Marquis, D. P., E. R. Sinnett, and W. D. Winter. A psychological study of peptic ulcer patients. *J Clin Psychol, 8*:266-272, 1952.
(*27*:6072, 1953)

> A battery of psychological tests was admin to 16 m adult pts with active peptic ulcer. On the basis of test results, 2 types of "ulcer personality" were distinguished, and designated the "Primary" ulcer type and the "Reactive" ulcer type. Both gps show in common marked oral fixations, sexual maladjustment secondary to strong dependency needs, feelings of inferiority, and "nervous" tensions. They are clearly differentiated, however, with regard to their acceptance or denial of their dependency needs.

74. McNeil, E. B., and G. S. Blum. Handwriting and psychosexual dimensions of personality. *J Proj Tech, 16*:476-484, 1952.
(*28*:2652, 1954)

> A survey of methodology in a number of previous experiments in the area of handwriting and pers is presented in tabular form. The analysis revealed a number of weaknesses in these experiments. "The present study, undertaken with these defects in mind, sought to relate scores of psy-sex dimens of pers, obtained from 119 undergraduate m BP protocols, to ratings on 16 classical graphology signs and an over-all sign of 'atypicality'. . . . The results provided a number of statistically sig relationships between B scores and handwriting variables."

75. Merchant, F. C. Psychosexual development in stutterers. *J Consult Psychol,* in press. (As listed in references of other articles. It seems to have appeared in print under the name of Carp—see Ref. No. 32.)

76. Michal-Smith, H., E. Hammer, and H. Spitz. Use of the Blacky Pictures with a child whose oedipal desires are close to consciousness. *J Clin Psychol,* 7:280-282, 1951.

    The use of the BP for projective material is illustrated by a case study.

77. Molish, H. B., B. Lyon, and D. L. Briggs. Character structure of adjusted and maladjusted naval recruits as measured by the Blacky Pictures. *Am J Orthopsychiatry,* 24:164-174, 1954.   (*29*:3141, 1955)

    Normative data are presented which were obtained from admin of the group *B* technique to a gp of 1,847 young men just entering the Naval Service. Comparing these results with those obtained from 390 recruits discharged from the Naval Service prior to completion of training because of their unsuitability, many sig diffs were found. The normals had many of the same feelings of dependency, oedipal intensity, etc., of the unsuitables, but the normals were able to channel these feelings and impulses, whereas those who were not able to make an adjustment to the Service did not have acceptable methods for handling them.

78. Nelson, S. Psychosexual conflicts and defenses in visual perception. *J Abnorm Soc Psychol,* 51:427-433, 1955.   (*31*:2280, 1957)

    Tachistoscopically presented stimulus material (BP) is used to study perceptual defense and vigilance in persons with different psy-sex conflict dimensions and ego-defense preferences. It is hypoth that when stimulus material is presented below the threshold of conscious recognition, perceptually vigilant behavior will be evoked under conditions where ego-defense mechanisms are not likely to operate, and perceptually defensive behavior will be evoked where ego defenses are likely to operate. The vigilance and defense hypoths are confirmed by the results.

79. Neuman, G. G., and J. C. Salvatore. Blacky Test and psychoanalytic theory: A factor-analytic approach to validity. *J Proj Tech, 22*:427-431, 1958.

(*34*:1405, 1960)

The purpose of the present study was to determine whether the dimensions underlying the BT were consistent with psy-ana theory. Blum's original published data for the test were factor analyzed and obliquely rotated. It was found that the factors underlying the test when admin to males corresponded reasonably well with the psy-ana oral, anal, phallic, oedipal, latency and genital areas. However, the data collected from fem Ss yielded contradictory factors when integrated according to psy-ana theory. As a consequence, it was concluded that the results yield partial confirmation for both test and theory when applied to m Ss only.

80. Newton, K. R. Review of the Blacky Pictures: A technique for the exploration of personality dynamics. In O. K. Buros (Ed.), *The fifth mental measurements yearbook.* New Brunswick, New Jersey: Rutgers University Press, 1959, pp. 214-216.

The reviewer stated that other than the clinician's own knowledge of psy-ana theory, there is little in the way of normative data. Also, that this technique would appear to be of little value to the practicing clinician; its value depending upon the psy-ana training of the administrator.

81. Noblin, C. D. Experimental analysis of psychoanalytic character types through the operant conditioning of verbal responses. *Am Psychol, 17*:306, 1962.

(see Ref. No. 143)

82. —, H. C. Kael, and E. O. Timmons. Differential effects of positive and negative verbal reinforcement on psychoanalytic character types. *Am Psychol, 18*:412, 1963.

Psy-ana theory depicts orals as dependent, compliant, and submissive to authority figures; anals are said to be negative, hostile, and resistant to authority figures. Consequently, we hypoth that orals would show conditioning to positive reinforcement and depression of the dependent variable with negative reinforcement, while anals should perform just the opposite. Strong oral and strong anal undergraduates were selected by the BT. Half of each gp was given affirmatory words and half mild criticism following the dependent variable in a simple verbal conditioning situation. The E was unaware of the character type of any S. All hypoths were supported.

83. —, and E. O. Timmons. Verbal behavior of orals and anals: Effects of schedules of reinforcement. *Am Psychol, 19*: 553, 1964.

It was predicted that anals acquire a conditioned verbal response more effectively under a rigid fixed-ratio schedule than under the less structured variable-ratio schedule. Orals were expected to perform better than anals under the VR schedules—an unstructured learning task was used. Both hypoths were supported.

84. Peak, H., B. Muney, and M. Clay. Opposite structures, defenses, and attitudes. *Psychol Monogr, 74*:(8, Whole No. 495), 1960.   (*36*:1HL25P, 1962)

Approximately 100 U. of Michigan undergraduates were Ss in this study of projection and reversal as defenses and as psychological structures, and of their role in attitude change. Ss were given a series of tests including: The BT, The Kent-Rosanoff word association test, the California F Scale, sorting 108 statements about Negroes, and rating 24 concepts on the Semantic Differential scales. Illustrative findings indicated that: (a) preferences for projection and for reaction formation were negatively correl, (b) tendency to opposite structuring was related to high preference for projection and low preference for reversal, and (c) preference for projection was positively associated with greater distance between ingroup and outgroup attitudes as well as to favorable ingroup attitudes in women and unfavorable outgroup attitudes in the males.

85. Pederson, F., and D. Marlowe. Capacity and motivational differences in verbal recall. *J Clin Psychol, 16*:219-222, 1960.   (*36*:2HJ19P, 1962)

An attempt was made to replicate previous findings of Adelson and Redmond (see Ref. No. 1) concerning anal retentive inds having a greater capacity for verbal recall than anal expulsive inds. ***** The findings suggest that expulsives tend to recall more disturbing material than the retentives, whereas the retentives tend to recall more insignificant material. "The findings constitute a failure to replicate the major results of Adelson and Redmond."

86. Perloe, S. I. Inhibition as a determinant of perceptual defense. *Percept Mot Skills, 11*:59-66, 1960.
(*35*:3509, 1961)

Recognition of BP presented tachistoscopically was consistent with an inhibition explanation of perceptual defense. *****

87. Pon, R. C. The psychoanalytic basis of religious, philosophical and moral beliefs. AB thesis, Princeton, 1955.

88. Porta, V., and N. Zangheri. (The Blacky Picture test of G. S. Blum: A projective test of psychoanalytic orientation). *Arch Psicol Neurol Psychiatry, 26*(4-5):426-440, 1965.

A critical evaluation of the BPT from the viewpoint of sexual, pathological, and cultural Italian-American diffs.

89. Rabin, A. I. Some psychosexual differences between Kibbutz and non-Kibbutz Israeli boys. *J Proj Tech, 22*: 328-332, 1958. (*33*:10180, 1959)

A gp of 27 ten-year-old boys from patriarchal-type families were compared with a gp of 27 boys who were reared in the Kibbutz (collective settlement) with respect to 3 psy-sex dimens: Oedipal intensity, positive ident, and sibling rivalry. The structured response items of the BT inquiry were used as a basis for comparison. Consistent with the stated hypoth, the *E* gp gave evidence of lesser oedipal intensity, more diffuse positive ident, and less intense sibling rivalry.

90. —, and M. R. Haworth (Eds.), *Projective techniques with children.* New York: Grune & Stratton, 1960, 392.

Apperceptive approaches covered include the Blacky.

91. Reinhold, B. A comparison of early conflicts in two different types of adolescent girls. BA thesis, Bennington College, 1962.

92. Robinson, S. A. The development of a female form of the Blacky Pictures. *J Proj Tech Pers Assess, 32*(1):74-80, 1968.

Because of the controversy about Ss' perception of the sex of the dog Blacky, a second form of the BPT was developed using a cat as the central figure. Ss were 53 14-year-old girls. A test-retest procedure was used. There was no sig change in numerical scores and preferences of "like" or "dislike" for the 11 cartoons whether the same or a different form was used in retesting. The scores of Ss receiving the cat form and those of Ss receiving the dog form at the first admin differed sig on 6 of the 30 scoring dimens.

93. Robinson, S. A., and V. L. Hendrix. The Blacky test and psychoanalytic theory: Another factor-analytic approach to validity. *J Proj Tech Pers Assess, 30*:597-603, 1966.

Blum's original data were subjected to principal component analysis and the resulting factors rotated using Kaiser's varimax criterion, a technique not generally available when Neuman & Salvatore (see Ref. No. 79) factor analyzed Blum's data. The results for males were similar to those of Neuman & Salvatore, although a separate factor of Guilt Feelings was found in this study. 4 levels of psy-sex development (oral, anal, phallic and genital) were found for females. It was suggested that psy-ana theory and the *B* may be more congruent with female psy-sex development than was thought in the past.

94. Rosen, E. Review of the Blacky Pictures. *J Proj Tech, 15*:109-111, 1951.

The reviewer concluded that the BP constitute a simple and ingenious device which promises to contribute to further clarification of systematic problems of pers and to take its place as a welcome addition to practical clinical instruments.

95. Rossi, A. M., and P. Solomon. A further note on female Blacky protocols. *J Proj Tech, 25*:339-340, 1961.

> These authors questioned the appropriateness of "Blacky" as a suitable name for pictures given to fem Ss; 60 fem coll students rated DOG, CAT, and BLACKY on semantic differential scale of 1 (masculine) to 7 (feminine). Results (medians): DOG, 2.16; CAT, 5.69; BLACKY, 1.85. Authors suggested use of CATS for figures and also to change central figures for females.

96. Ruble, D. W. Psychosexual development of 44 mentally retarded boys: A study. Masters thesis, Illinois State Normal University, 1952.

97. Sarnoff, I., and S. M. Corwin. Castration anxiety and the fear of death. *J Pers, 27*:374-385, 1959.
   (34:6264, 1960)

> ". . .the hypoth predicted that persons who have a high degree of castration anxiety (HCA) would show a greater increase in fear of death after the arousal of their sexual feelings than persons who have a low degree of castration anxiety (LCA). 56 undergraduates. . .were assigend to 2 E conditions in a 'before-after' design which permitted the manipulation of 2 levels of sexual arousal. Before being exposed to one or the other of these manipulations, Ss filled out booklets containing a scale designed to measure the fear of death (FDS), a questionnaire concerning moral standard of sexual behavior (MS), and a measure of castration anxiety (CA). . . . The results clearly confirmed the hypoth: HCA Ss showed a sig greater increase in fear of death than LCA Ss after being exposed to the sexually arousing stimuli of the HAS (high arousal of sexual feeling) condition."

98. Schaeffer, D. L. Addenda to an annotated bibliography of the Blacky Test (1949-1967). *J Proj Tech Pers Assess, 32*(6):550-555, 1968.

> Presents an addendum to the Taulbee & Stenmark (see Ref. No. 113) bibliography of the BPT.

99. —. Blacky the cat: I. Semantic differential ratings. *J Proj Tech Pers Assess, 32*:542-549, 1968. *(43*:9803, 1969)

   Two criteria for an alternate form of the BT, which would facilitate fem ident with *B*, are presented and semantic differential ratings of both the original *B* stimuli and a revised sexually neutral cat form indicated that an alternate version could meet both requirements.

100. Schill, T. Sex differences in identification of the castrating agent on the Blacky Test. *J Clin Psychol, 22*(3): 324-325, 1966.

   38 m and 60 fem coll Ss were given Blum's standard instructions and card 6 of the BT. There were sig sex diffs in ident of the castrating agent, with males preferring "Papa" and females preferring "Mama." This result was predicted from psy-ana theory. Also presented are reasons for the choice of the castrating agent (authority, improvement, discipline, custom, meanness, and miscellaneous). These reasons are discussed in terms of cultural influences and defenses.

101. Seiden, R. H. Onset age and psychosexual conflict in bronchial asthma. *Proc 73rd Annu Conv Am Psychol Assoc*, 267-268, 1965.

   45 m Ss who had developed asthma between birth and 7 yrs, were arranged into 3 gps according to age of onset (oral, anal, phallic) and were admin the BT. Results revealed that the gps differed sig in strength of conflict (anal, oral, phallic in descending order). Also, within each onset-age gp, the majority of Ss evidenced strongest conflicts in the psy-sex areas corresponding to their symptom onset.

102. Seward, J. P. Psychoanalysis, deductive method, and the Blacky Test. *J Abnorm Soc Psychol, 45*:529-535, 1950.

   Dr. Blum has contributed an original and stimulating piece of research. He has evaluated it conservatively with a clear eye for its limitations. Since others may not be so clear-eyed, I have underscored 2 characteristics of the method used to coordinate theory with data and indicated their effect on the interpretation of results. These characteristics are: (1) the exclusion of statistically insig but relevant data; (2) the likelihood that logical flaws in a theoretical structure may escape detection.

103. Shaffer, L. F. Review of the Blacky Pictures. *J Consult Psychol, 14*:332-333, 1950.

The author points out that the manual and the research monograph (see Ref. No. 12) suggest the purposes and uses of the test but make no attempt to provide full training for its interpretation. Also, that Blum wisely suggests that the BPT be used only by clinical psychologists with general competence in other projective tests and with a broad knowledge of psy-ana theory.

104. Smith, W., and E. K. Powell. Responses to projective material by pre- and post-menarcheal subjects. *Percept Mot Skills, 6*:155-158, 1956.

4 pictures from the BPT (I, IV, X, and XI) were admin to 138 tem *S*s from the 7th and 8th grade classes. Pre- and post-menarcheal gps were equated on the variables of age and SES. The 2 gps differed sig on 6 multiple choice questions (C IV-4 and 7, C X-2, and C XI-1, 4 & 5). On C XI, the post-menarcheal *S*s named their mother and showed interest in the mother more often.

105. Smock, C. D. Replication and comments: "An experimental reunion of psychoanalytic theory with perceptual vigilance and defense." *J Abnorm Soc Psychol, 53*:68-73, 1956.   (*32*:1166, 1958)

The results of an initial attempt to replicate the results of Blum's experiment indicated that stimulus similarity was an important determinant of errors of localization in the test of the perceptual defense hypoth. A second experiment was designed to test the defense hypoth under the specified conditions and at the same time yield information concerning the role of stimulus similarity on errors of recognition in the defense series. The results indicated similarity among the *E* and *C* stimuli was the primary determinant of the frequency of correct response. . . . Evidence was presented which tentatively suggests that systematic errors of localization might be due to an increased generalization gradient associated with anxiety arousal.

106. —, and G. G. Thompson.   An inferred relationship between early childhood conflicts and anxiety responses in adult life. *J Pers, 23*:88-98, 1954. (*29*:5325, 1955)

   BP were utilized to differentiate a gp of *S*s into hi and lo anxiety-intensity gps. "The. . .findings support the Freudian emphasis on experiences during the socialization process as prime influences on pers formation. The results are not inconsistent with the notion that these areas of conflict may be relatively discrete in so far as the content of the anxiety area is concerned.

107. Streitfield, H. S.   Specificity of peptic ulcer to intense oral conflicts.   *Psychosom Med, 16*:315-326, 1954. (*29*:4533, 1955)

   To test the hypoth that those with peptic ulcer could be differentiated from *S*s with non-gastrointestinal psychosomatic reactions in that the first would show intense conflict over oral-dependent needs or oral-aggressive wishes, the Rorschach and BT were admin to 20 cases in each class. Results from statistical analysis indicated that the oral-dependent need-conflict was not specific to the peptic ulcer cases and that conflict over oral-aggressive wishes tended to be more "common, intense, and chronic in the ulcer patients." ***

108. Stricker, G.   Stimulus properties of the Blacky Pictures Test. *J Proj Tech Pers Assess, 27*:244-247, 1963. (*38*:2727, 1964)

   The semantic differential technique was used with coll sophomores who rated the *B* cards. The author suggests that naive *S*s' tendency to respond to manifest content and to avoid underlying psy-sex themes may be reinforced by SD. Another problem posed is that of fem *S*s tending to identify with figures other than *B*.

109. —. Stimulus properties of the Blacky to a sample of pedophiles. *J Gen Psychol, 77*(1):35-39, 1967.

64 m pedophiles rated the BP on 21 scales of the semantic differential. Their response style indicated a guarded approach accompanied by an immature and feminine orientation with an indication that they experience problems in response to the cards attuned to orality.

110. Swanson, G. E. Some effects of member object-relationships on small groups. *Hum Relations, 4*:355-380, 1951.   (*26*:5486, 1952)

Two gps of 20 each were scored on object relations with the BPT. On the basis of these results and other information, semiblind analysis of each *S* was made. The *S*s were then observed in gp discussion and ratings were compared with the blind analyses. 4 predictions were sig at the .05 level and 1 at the .01 level. Three additional predictions were in the expected direction but did not meet the .05 criterion.

111. Taulbee, E. S., and D. E. Stenmark. The Blacky Pictures: Individual Scoring Blank—(Dimensional Scoring System). Ann Arbor, Michigan: Psychodynamic Instruments, 1967.

This individual scoring blank provides spaces for recording the Raw Scores, Corrected Scores and Overall Dimensional Scores for each Cartoon and a Psychogram reflecting the degree of involvement.

112. —, and D. E. Stenmark. The Blacky Pictures: Individual Scoring Blank—Factor Analytic Approach. Ann Arbor, Michigan: Psychodynamic Instruments, 1967.

This individual scoring blank provides spaces for recording scores of each of the 30 factors and for summarizing them on a psychogram.

113. —, and D. E. Stenmark. The Blacky Pictures Test: A comprehensive annotated and indexed bibliography (1949-1967). *J Proj Tech Pers Assess, 32*:105-137, 1968.

Lists 137 article abstracts for the BPT for personality assessment. A content index, author index, and a list of abbreviations are included to facilitate use in clinical practice and research.

114. Teevan, R. C. Personality correlates of undergraduate field of specialization. *J Consult Psychol, 18*:212-214, 1954. (*29*:3007, 1955)

> This study tried to discover whether pers factors were correl with choice of a major in undergraduate college. The BP were used for obtaining pers characteristics. Chief results obtained: (1) Majors in "literature" had higher disturbance scores on Ora Ero than the other 2 gps of majors. (2) "Social Sciences" gp had higher disturbance scores on Ora Sad, Oed Int, Glt Fee, and Ana Lo Obj. (3) The "Science"gp had the lowest disturbance scores on nearly all categories.

115. Thelen, M. H. Similarities of defense preferences within families and within sex groups. *J Proj Tech Pers Assess, 29*(4):461-464, 1965.

> (see Ref. No. 173)

116. —. The relationship of selected variables to intrafamily similarity of defense preferences. *J Proj Tech Pers Assess, 31*:23-37, 1967.

> (see Ref. No. 173)

117. Thompson, M. M. Motivational characteristics differentiating authoritarian and non-authoritarian personalities. Masters thesis, University of Oklahoma, 1957.

118. Timmons, E. O., and C. D. Noblin. The differential performance of orals and anals in a verbal conditioning paradigm. *J Consult Psychol, 27*:383-386, 1963. (*38*:3660, 1964)

> The oral character type is said to be dependent and suggestible; anals are said to be obstinate and resistant. Consequently, it was hypoth that orals would condition better than anals in a verbal conditioning experiment. 24 strong oral or anal undergraduate Ss were selected by the BT; E did not know the

character type of any *S*. A sig increase in the dependent variable was seen for the orals, while a pronounced drop was found for the anal *Ss*. The data support the prediction based on Freudian characterological theory.

119. Trent, R. D., and A. Amchin. An exploration of the relationships between manifest anxiety and selected psychosexual areas. *J Proj Tech, 21*:318-322, 1957.
(*33*:1333, 1959)

The relationship between manifest anxiety (CMAS) and specific areas of psy-sex conflict was investigated by giving white, Negro, and Puerto Rican delinquent boys the CMAS and the BPT. Whites, Negroes, and Puerto Ricans showed no diffs in psy-sex problems for the 13 areas studied by the BT. Mas Glt and Ana Lo Obj were the most frequent problem areas. *Ss* scoring high in Ora Ero, Ego Ide and Nar Lo Obj were more anxious than those scoring low on these variables. Ora Sad was negatively correl with anxiety. There were no sig correls with anxiety for the following variables: Ana Exp, Ana Ret, Oed Int, Mas Glt, Cas Anx, Pos Ide, Sib Riv, Glt Fee, and Nar Lo Obj. Freedom from psy-sex conflicts was not sig related to manifest anxiety.

120. Vernallis, F. F. Teeth-grinding: Some relationships to anxiety, hostility, and hyperactivity. *J Clin Psychol, 11*:389-391, 1955. (*30*:6129, 1956)

*** The *Ss* were 40 teeth-grinders and their controls.... Teeth-grinders were identified by means of a questionnaire and personal interview. Biserial correls with the Taylor and Ma scale of the MMPI were low but very sig above zero; with the Rorschach Content Test, very sig above zero with hostility, sig above zero with anxiety. The X^2 on Ora Sad from the BP was also sig greater than zero.

121. Weiss, L. R. Effects of subject, experimenter and task variables on compliance with the experimenter's expectation. *J Proj Tech Pers Assess, 33*(3):247-256, 1969.

A gp of "Oral" *Ss* and a gp of "anal" *Ss* estimated the number of dots flashed tachistoscopically under 3 different ambiguity conditions. Three expectation conditions (overestimation, underestimation, and no expectancies) were given under 2 involvement conditions. Fem orals were the compliant Ss and there was a trend for fem Ss to be more compliant than m Ss. Fem Es elicited more compliance than m Es and females complied with all Es whereas males complied with fem Es but not with m Es.

122. Winter, W. D. Two personality patterns in peptic ulcer patients. *J Proj Tech, 19*:332-344, 1955.
$$(30:5075, 1956)$$

A study of 68 peptic ulcer pts, using the Rorschach and BP to test hypoths about the pers dynamics of ulcer pts, led to the conclusion that "the 'typical' ulcer pers is not found in all peptic ulcer pts," and that "at least 2 different pers patterns are found in people with ulcers, and these can be validily measured by the B scales developed in this investigation."

123. Wolfson, W., and F. Wolff. Sexual connotations of the name Blacky. *J Proj Tech, 20*:347, 1956.
$$(31:6150, 1957)$$

"In this study it was shown that the dog name 'Blacky' by itself, was not sexually neutral as Blum implied but that 'Blacky' was predominantly male in connotation irrespective of the sex of the rater. This held for psych pts as well as normals. No attempt was made to see how much of a factor this was in the actual utilization of the BP."

124. Yabuki, S. Cognition and defense: III. On the dimension of inhibition-acceptance in mothers' attitudes towards children. *Jap J Psychol, 44*(1):10-16, 1973.

The BP were used as a basis for a series of photographs arranged in 14 stages from the vaguest to the clearest. Perceptual sensitivity and cognitive styles of boys and girls were measured by these photos. Ss with inhibitory mothers were more sensitive to those themes toned with "aggressiveness" and "fearfulness" than Ss with receptive mothers.

Doctoral Dissertation References

125. Berger, L. Interrelationships of autonomic and personality variables. *D A*, University of Michigan, 1958.
(Mic 58-3637)

> Using 30 m VA psych pts and 27 m coll *S*s, measures of autonomic functioning (skin resistance, heart rate, and respiration rate) at rest and under 3 stresses were linked to a battery of pers tests (BP, EPPS, DPI, and 16 PF). Factor analysis of phi coefficients was used. The findings indicate that certain personality patterns appear to be related to specific autonomic responses under all "stresses" whereas other characteristics correspond to specific responses under specific stresses.

126. Berlow, N. Psychosexual indicators on the Rorschach test. *D A*, University of Michigan, 1953.

> The Rorschach and BP were admin to 88 *S*s—paranoid psychotics, nonparanoid psychotics, and normals. Major results of the study were summarized as follows: (1) ratings of clinicians who judged extent of psy-sex disturbance from the Rorschach generally did not agree with BP scores; (2) clinicians did tend to agree sig with each other; (3) the empirical study did not reveal any consistent relationship between any Rorschach scoring categories or patterns of Rorschach scores and the BP scores.

127. Bernhardt, R. Personality conflict and the act of stuttering. *D A*, University of Michigan, 1954.
(No. 7605, Mic A54-1023)

> 44 m stutterers ages 11 to 22, were given the BP. Later, each *S* was presented with 2 sets of reading material for tape-recording. One set was *S*s' originally written stories to the BP. Second set, stories to BP of *S*s from another population. These "standard stories" were selected so that they all were of relatively uniform length, and so that they all demonstrated disturbance in the psy-sex dimens involved. The data were analyzed for relationships between: (a) measures in psy-sex areas of pers, and (b) amount of stuttering. Findings indicate that certain psy-sex dimens evoke sig more stuttering than do other dimens, and that *S*s with the highest over-all amount of conflict show the highest

over-all amount of stuttering. It was concluded that stuttering is related to pers difficulties of the stutterer and that certain environmental stimuli related to pers affect his stuttering.

128. Blumberg, A. A methodological study of two approaches to the validation of the Blacky test. Unpublished doctoral dissertation, Western Reserve University, 1955.

129. Boyd, R. D. Reading retardation as related to personality factors of children and their parents. *D A*, University of Michigan, 1953.   (Mic 53-1591)

Ss were 23 4th- and 5th-grade boys retarded in reading, who were matched with 23 not retarded. Ss were given the BP, Vineland, and WISC. Parents were admin the GZTS and interviewed. Specific predictions were made. The more salient findings were: (1) poor readers were not judged disturbed on a sig larger number of B dimens; (2) good readers were judged disturbed more often on Ora Ero but less (not sig) often on Ora Sad; (3) poor readers were judged disturbed more often on ident process; (4) poor readers did not show sig lower social maturity; (5) mothers of poor readers were more frequently relatively masculine while their husbands were relatively feminine.

130. Burnham, R. K. The relationship of personality to oral conditions in children: An evaluation by means of the Rorschach and the Blacky Test. *D A*, New York University, 1957.   (Mic 58-647)

The following hypoths were investigated: (1) sig pers diffs exist between children with disturbed dental conditions and those with little or no dental disease, (2) children with organic mouth disorders would manifest more orality fixation than children with normal dental conditions, and (3) children suffering from a high degree of dental disease would manifest more pers disturbance than children with healthy dental conditions. Two gps of 25 children each were equated in terms of age, sex, and I.Q. The E gp was comprised of children with a caries index of more than 20 on the D.F.M. scale, and the C gp with a score of less than 10. Methods used were case histories, questionnaires for parents, SB, judgments of overt test behavior, BP and the Rorschach. In all but one instance, where sig diffs are found, the

E gp shows signs of more pers disturbance than the controls.

131. Clapp, C. Two levels of unconscious awareness. *D A*, University of Michigan, 1951.   (Publication No. 3479)

Hypoth investigated: When "more" and "less" emotional stimuli are presented in pairs at two levels of unconscious awareness, there will be a relative shift in the judgment of perceptual clarity, from more emotional stimulus seen as clearer at the lower level toward less emotional stimulus seen as clearer at the higher. The pairs of "more" and "less" emotional stimuli were selected from the BP. The 2 levels of unconscious awareness were manipulated by tachistoscopic presentation of the pairs at fast and slow shutter speeds. College *S*s were only required to judge which picture within a given pair seemed the "clearer." The results were interpreted as specific support for the psy-ana concepts of ego defense and repressed strivings.

132. Cummings, C. P. Role of various psychological variables in children's nailbiting behavior. *D A*, Pennsylvania State University, 1954.

*S*s were 70 nailbiting children ranging in ages from 10 to 14 years. They were individually examined and ranked according to the degree of nailbiting using the index devised by Malone and Massler. A positive relationship was hypoth between nailbiting and Ora Ero, Ora Sad, Oed Int, Mas Glt, and Glt Fee. It was concluded that on the basis of the findings the hypoths were upheld.

133. Eastman, D. F. An exploratory investigation of the psychoanalytic theory of stuttering by means of the Blacky Pictures test. *D A*, University of Nebraska, 1960.   (Mic 60-4500)

The possibility of a relationship between severity of stuttering and disturbance in psy-sex development was investigated empirically. Of the several hypoths tested, the following was considered to be the most crucial: More stutterers will show disturbance on the dimens of Ana Sad and Glt Fee than on any other of the 12 dimens, and few stutterers will show disturbance on Sib Riv than on any other dimension. *S*s were 2 gps of m stutterers, an adult gp and a children's gp. The BPT was individually admin to each *S* and all *S*s were rated on a 5-point scale for degree of severity of stuttering. The Over-all Dimen Score and an index of psy-sex disturbance were utilized for the statistical analysis. The hypoths was confirmed at a high level of confidence for both gps. It was pointed out that the relationship between stuttering and disturbance on the dimens of Ana Sad and Glt Fee need not be a causal relationship, and other possible interpretations of the results were given.

134. Field, L. W. Personality correlates of college achievement and major areas of study. *D A*, University of Houston, 1953.   (No. 9229)

An attempt to demonstrate that high achievers and low achievers in college and successful physical and social science majors can be differentiated on a series of pers measures. Testing techniques included 5 pers measures, a perceptual task, an attitude scale, and 7 measures of ident with the father figure. A modification of the SVIB and the BP were used to measure two levels of ident. Results for the BP were: (1) HA made sig higher scores on the following. Intercorrelations between all the measures were carried out within the high-low gp, within the physical science gp, and within the social science gp. Among the intercorrels which showed consistent relationships were (BP results only): *** (b) A negative relationship between the F-Scale and disturbance in ident on the *B*. The greater the disturbance in ident, the more authoritarian in all 3 gps. *** (d) In the social science gp, there were positive relationships between disturbances in ident on the *B* and Emotional Control and Inquiring Intellect. There was a negative relationship between Conformity and disturbance in Ident on the B. (e) In the physical science gp, there were negative relationships between disturbance in ident on the *B* and Emotional Control and Inquiring Intellect.

135. Figetakis, N. Process-reactive schizophrenia: Ego-strength and selected psychosexual dimensions. Unpublished doctoral dissertation, Michigan State University, 1964.

136. Frankel, E. An experimental study of psychoanalytic theories of humor. *D A*, University of Michigan,

1952. (No. 5671)

Three hypothetical relationships between humor and personality were formulated. The BP and a humor test of 30 cartoons were admin. *S*s were divided into gps on the basis of objective scores indicating degree of disturbance in each *B* dimen, and their enjoyment responses to the relevant cartoons were compared by means of chi-square tests. The finding that people with relatively more pers disturbance along a specific psy-sex dimen show a greater tendency than people with relatively less disturbance to dislike cartoons depicting the specific area of disturbance was discussed in terms of its implications for pers theory and for future research.

137. Gibson, R. M. An exploratory study of the effects of surgery and hospitalization in early infancy on personality development. *D A*, University of Michigan, 1959.
(L. C. Card No. Mic 59-2119)

Investigated the effect of both constitutional-physiological and the experiential-environmental influences on pers development. *S*s were 3 gps of children born with congenital anomalies and 29 *C S*s, who were admin a battery of tests. Their mothers completed 4 attitude and trait inventories. Results reveal that children who had experienced surgery and hosp for anomalies within the first 4 months of life differed from those who had remained well. The results bore out the findings of previous studies which have highlighted the adverse effects of traumatization in infancy on pers development.

138. Ginsparg, S. Post-partum psychosis. *D A*, Washington University, 1956. (No. 20,753)

The study investigated the pers dynamics and underlying psychogenic patterns involved in post-partum psychosis. It was assumed that women with post-partum psychosis had rejected feminine goals and had instead established a masculine ident. Women with post-partum psychosis, when compared with normal post-partum women, indicated a greater tendency toward unresolved oedipal needs, masculine ident, lack of positive ego ideal, and choice of narcissistic love object. There were no sig diffs in the psychodynamic conflicts manifested by the two psychotic gps. Post-partum psychosis seems to occur in women who have failed to resolve adequately their unconscious emotional involvement with the parent of the opposite sex and have therefore been unable to fully accept their own sexual role, with its biological as well as social implications.

139. Goldstein, R. H. Behavioral effects of psychological stress. *D A,* University of Michigan, 1959.
(L. C. Card No. Mic 59-2123)

The effects of a particular type of stress situation on a variety of behaviors were explored. Stress was induced by having *S*s think about and later discuss their adjustment in the psy-sex problem areas depicted by the BP. It was found that the stress situation impaired word length judgment of words associated to loaded stimulus words, caused *S*s to make more errors on a hand steadiness task, and led to poorer performance on the BAT. These results were obtained only for the m sample, fem *S*s showing no such impairment.

140. Goldstein, S. A projective study of psychoanalytic mechanisms of defense. *D A,* 12:218, 1952.

Coll *S*s were admin a modified BPT and DPI for 8 cartoons. The DPI required *S*s to rank 4 statements, corresponding to the defense mechanisms of repression, regression, reaction formation and projection, according to the statements' agreement with their own spontaneous story. Analyses revealed a small subgroup of *S*s who tended to employ the same defenses for each cartoon. This gp manifested fewer areas of strong conflict than the *S*s who employed more varied defenses. These data also supported the theoretical notion that reaction formation is an extension of repression.

141. Grayden, C. The relationship between neurotic hypochondriasis and three personality variables: Feeling of being unloved, narcissism, and guilt feelings. *D A,* New York University, 1958.   (L. C. Card No. Mic 58-2127)

30 *S*s, divided into 2 gps: Gp I (*Hs* gp), 15 hypochondriacal neurotics, Gp II (*NHs* gp) 6 non-hypochondriacal neurotics and 9 "normals." *S*s were assigned to *E* gp on the basis of clinical

evaluation and MMPI *Hs* scores. The BP data supported Alexander's theory to the extent of confirming the relationship between Hs and the variables Narcissism and Guilt Feelings, and
indicated that hypochondriacs exhibit a greater degree of the
feeling of being unloved as compared to non-hypochondriacs.

142. Hart, R. An evaluation of the psychoanalytic theory of
male homosexuality by means of the Blacky Pictures.
Unpublished doctoral dissertation, Northwestern University, 1953.

143. Hilgeman, L. M. Developmental and sex variations in the
Blacky Test. Unpublished doctoral dissertation, Ohio
State University, 1951.

144. Hogan, V. The reliability of the Blacky Pictures with institutionalized senile psychotics. Unpublished doctoral
dissertation, Western Reserve University, 1954.

145. Housman, H. A psychological study of menstruation.
D A, University of Michigan, 1955.   (No. 11,298)

*S*s were 39 schizophrenic women divided into gps of 19 regular
and 20 irregular menstruators. Sources of data were: a Menstrual Questionnaire, a Rorschach and a *B.* Major results: (1)
All showed a marked decrease in sexual confusion during menstruation and seemed to have increasing need for affection and
approval, and were more sensitive to interpersonal slights. During this time there was an increased defensiveness in the more
direct expression of sibling rivalry. (2) The irregular, in contrast
to the regular, were characteristically anal expulsive. They pro-
fessed more unconcerned acceptance of their sexual role but
gave less evidence of a genuine feminine ident than did the
regulars. The irregulars showed less concern with conformity.
Lastly, they appeared less involved with sibling rivalry and instead gave more direct expression to feelings of frustration and
rejection by their parents. (3) The regular menstruators exerted
much more effective control in coping with their impulses and
external reality. The irregulars showed a marked abandonment
of ego constraints. Menstruation was accompanied by an exac-
erbation of the masturbatory conflict among the irregulars and
a contrasting alleviation of the same conflict for the regulars.

146. Irwin, T. C. A contribution to the construct validity of
the oral scale of the Blacky Pictures Test. *D A,* University of Rochester, 1963.   (No. 63-7769)

The Ora Ero and Ora Sad scales were the focus of the research.
It was predicted that 38 Ss between the ages of 10 and 14, hosp
for severe functional emotional disturbance, would show sig
more disturbance on the oral scales than a matched C gp. Conclusions: (1) The Ora Ero scale showed more disturbance in the
E gp as predicted. (2) Ora Ero scores were shown to be associated with patterns of perception of the test figures which
would be consistent with the psy-ana theory of oral eroticism.
(3) The Ora Sad scale showed more disturbance in the E gp as
predicted. (4) Perceptions of the test figures found to be related to Ora Sad scores were considered consistent with psy-ana
postulates about the nature of oral sadism. (5) Of the 6 new
oral scoring dimens, one sig differentiated the 2 gps and one
tended to differentiate them.

147. Jacobs, M. O. A validation study of the oral erotic scale of
the Blacky Pictures Test. *D A,* University of Oklahoma, 1957.   (No. 21,974)

A correl study of the relationship between scores on the Ora
Ero scale and scores on 2 separate criteria of orality, a self-rating
scale and a perceptual test. The perceptual test involved tachistoscopic presentations of 12 pictures of everyday objects, 6 of
which represented "oral cues" and 6 of which were non-oral in
symbolic value. Ss were 48 HS and 47 coll students. Results
revealed no sig relationship between scores on the Ora Ero scale
and scores on the self-rating scale. An analysis of relationship
between the Ora Ero scale and the perceptual test revealed
several sig correls. When the Ss were broken down into separate
gps on the basis of sex and age, sig correls were found. It was
concluded that the Ora Ero scale appears to be a valid test of
orality only for some gps of inds, and may be influenced by
such factors as age, sex, test sophistication and perhaps pers
factors unknown from the data at hand.

148. Kahane, T. An experimental investigation of a conditioning treatment and a preliminary study of psychoanalytic theory of the etiology of nocturnal enuresis. Un-

published doctoral dissertation, UCLA, 1954.

149. Klehr, H. An investigation of some personality factors in women with rheumatoid arthritis. Unpublished doctoral dissertation, Northwestern University, 1950.

150. Leichty, M. M. The absence of the father during early childhood and its effect upon the oedipal situation as reflected in young adults. *D A*, Michigan State University, 1958. (L. C. Card No. Mic 58-7103)

> The purpose of the study was to examine the effect of absence of the father on the resolution of the Oedipal conflict. Ss were 62 m coll freshmen. Fathers of the E Ss were overseas during WW-II and the fathers of the C Ss were not overseas, when the boys were between the ages of 3 and 5. Support was obtained for 3 of 4 hypoths. (1) There was some evidence to indicate that Oed Int is greater in those Ss who were separated from their fathers. (2) The hypoth that fewer of the E Ss, as compared to the C Ss, will show strong ident with the father, and ident of the E Ss will be more diffuse than will be the case with the C Ss received the most consistent support. (3) The hypoth that fewer of the E Ss will choose their fathers as the type of figure adapted for their ego-ideal was somewhat supported by the data. (4) The hypoth that fewer of the E Ss will show strong castration anxiety was not supported by the data.

151. Maes, J. L. Identification of male college students with their fathers and some related indices of affect expression and psychosexual adjustment. *D A*, Michigan State University, 1963. (No. 63-6158)

> It was predicted that successful adult male identifiers would demonstrate less psy-sex conflict, less defensiveness, and greater affective complexity when placed in a situation reminiscent of relationship with parental figures. Ss were m coll students, 62 successful identifiers and 62 unsuccessful identifiers based on their scores on the Block Adjective Check List. The BP, TAT, and DPI were admin. Results: (1) The prediction regarding greater psy-sex conflict for the unsuccessful identifiers was supported by the data. (2) There were no measurable diffs between the DPI scores for the 2 gps. (3) The Affective Com-

plexity scores were in the opposite direction to that predicted. Psy-ana theory appeared to receive some support from the B responses for the 2 gps. It appeared that Ss who had not been able to identify successfully with their fathers did manifest greater psy-sex conflict than those who had been able to identify successfully, and that this conflict was most evident at the psy-sex stages of development where it might be expected on the basis of theory.

152. Marcus, M. M. The relation of personality structure to the capacity for memory retention. *D A, 26*(3):1779, 1965.

In an attempt to replicate the work of Adelson & Redmond (see Ref. No. 1), 16 anal retentives, 36 anal expulsives and 12 neutral *C* Ss were selected from 152 fem undergraduates who were admin the BP. Ss were given a paired-associate learning task and 3 retention tasks. Stimulus words were either hostile or neutral; response choices were either verbal ('Turkish words) or nonverbal (Chinese idiographs). Expulsives were inferior to retentives and controls when the correct responses to both hostile and neutral stimulus words were combined. During acquisition, the expulsives and controls committed sig more errors to hostile than to neutral stimulus words. Diffs in intelligence, acquisition rate, or motivation apparently did not contribute to the inferior memory capacity of the expulsives.

153. Martin, J. O. A psychological investigation of convicted incest offenders by means of two projective techniques. *D A,* Michigan State University, 1958.
                    (L. C. Card No. Mic 60-2375)

An investigation of certain pers factors and their relationship to the crime of father-daughter incest. Pers traits descriptive of the "Phallic Character" were presented as hypoths to be confirmed. Three hypoths suggested the continued presence of disturbances in the following psy-sex areas: Ora Ero, Oed Int, and Cas Anx. Three more hypoths were concerned with current behavioral reactions associated with the dynamics to be found in the Phallic Character; i.e., the presence of aggressive drives, resentment toward authority, and a contempt and hostility toward women. The final 4 hypoths contained predictions concerning perceptions expected from this type of individual. These included perception of the wife as unavailable sexually, a self-percept of inability to compete successfully with others, perception of the environment as hostile, and perception of young adolescent females as being interested in heterosexual activity. Ss were 30 Incest Offenders and 41 other prisoners. Instruments used were the BP, 6 TAT cards, and one card from the Michigan Picture Test. Findings indicated that the Incest Offender gp had a sig greater frequency of the proposed reactions on 3 of the 10 hypoths. These diffs were in the areas of Ora Ero, Cas Anx, and Oed Int, supporting the 3 hypoths. The Incest gp had a sig higher number of Ss who were judged as generally disturbed in the psy-sex areas.

154. Maruyama, Y. The sense of competence in middle adolescent boys. *D A I, 30*(5-B):2405-2406, 1969.

Ss were 80 boys, ages 14 or 15. 40 boys had been separated from their parents during the age period of 2 to 6 (*E* gp); 40 boys were still living with their parents (*C* gp). The *E* gp scored lower on 3 CPI subscales: Self-acceptance, Achievement via Independence, and Responsibility. From the BP, only the Oed Int Picture differentiated the 2 gps. The results were interpreted as supporting the theory that constant object relations in early childhood are important for achieving a sense of competence.

155. Minkowich, A. Correlates of superego functions. *D A,* University of Michigan, 1958.
                              (L. C. Card No. Mic 59-2156)

Purpose of the study was to test the generality of superego (SE) functioning across several behavioral areas and to examine relationships among psy-sex conflicts, attitudes towards parents, reported childhood experiences, and SE functions, using 29 m and 37 fem coll students. The dependent variables—behavioral fantasy and accompanying affect—were derived from structured situations represented by 6 *B* pictures involving sex and aggression. It was concluded that the evidence suggests that family background, type of parental control, and parent-child relationships all contribute to superego development and functioning in clearly specifiable ways.

156. Nelson, S. Psychosexual conflicts and defenses in visual perception. Unpublished doctoral dissertation, University of Michigan, 1955.

> (see Ref. No. 70)

157. Noblin, C. D. Experimental analysis of psychoanalytic character types through the operant conditioning of verbal responses. *D A, 23*:1076-1077, 1962.

> The BP served as one of 3 criteria used to identify 60 hosp m psych pts as either oral or anal characters. In addition to the *B* scores, there were behavioral and diagnostic criteria. A verbal operant conditioning paradigm was established with gumballs and pennies serving as the oral and anal reinforcers, respectively. The hypoth, that oral character types would respond more readily to oral reinforcement and that anal character types would respond more readily to anal reinforcement, were clearly supported.

158. Normington, C. J. Some aspects of psychosexual development in process-reactive schizophrenia. *D A, 26*:5387-5388, 1965.

> 45 schizophrenics, classified as process or reactive according to their scores on the Abbreviated Becker-Elgin Scale, and 15 normal VA pts were studied. BP narcissism was higher for schizophrenics than for normals, but this was confounded by a correl between narcissism and duration of hosp. Process schizophrenics scored higher on BP narcissism than did reactive schizophrenics, again with the same confounding of hosp stay. Process schizophrenics identified more often with the mother than did reactive Ss. The reactive gp did not differ from normal gp in preferred ident object, overtly positive perceptions of self and father, overtly negative perceptions of self and father, or heterosexual fantasy. There was a marked tendency for process Ss to exceed reactive Ss on test indices of oral rejection.

159. Orbach, C. H. Perceptual defense and somatization: A comparison of the perceptual threshholds of obese and peptic ulcer patients. *D A,* University of Southern California, 1956.   (L. C. Card No. Mic. 60-1314)

Psy-ana theory maintains that obese and peptic ulcer pts are both fixated at an oral level of psy-sex development. It further maintains that the repressed impulses associated with such fixation are constantly striving for expression. Whereas the obese ind gives in to his oral impulse by eating, the peptic ulcer ind develops a counteractive defense. This study was designed to tap both the impulse striving and the defensive aspect by measuring, on two different levels of awareness, the perceptual responses of ulcer and obese *S*s to the tachistoscopic presentation of an oral stimulus. *S*s were 65 m pts of VA medical facilities (25 ulcer pts, 15 obese pts and 25 controls). Conclusions: The hypoths relating to perceptual vigilance and defence were not supported. However, obese and ulcer pts were shown to be more typically oral in their interests and attitudes. It was speculated that oral character traits represent successful repression of oral conflict.

160. Perloe, S. I. An experimental test of two theories of perceptual defense. *D A,* University of Michigan, 1959.
(L. C. Card No. Mic 59-2164)

Designed to test explanations of perceptual defense proposed by hypothesis theorists on the one hand and inhibition theorists on the other. The former assert that perceptual defense occurs as a result of the frequent, inappropriate confirmation of relatively strong hypoths which are similar to the relatively weak hypoths against which the defense occurs. The latter hold that the phenomenon is due to an inhibitory process which interferes directly with the activation of a threatening perceptual response. *S*s were 31 m and 31 fem coll students. Two sets of predictions were tested, one derived from each theory. The tentative conclusion suggested by this study was that the conditions specified by each theory are sufficient for the production of perceptual defense.

161. Pollie, D. M. Conflict and defense in three psychosomatic syndromes. *D A,* University of Michigan, 1957.
(L. C. Card No. Mic 58-974)

Study explored some of the psychological characteristics of hosp m veterans who manifested the symptoms of either of 3 psychosomatic syndromes. *S*s were: duodenal ulcer pts (N=61), nonulcerated gastrointestinal pts (N=52), bronchial asthma pts (N=46), and a gp of 20 hosp pts afflicted with nonpsychosomatic illnesses. The test battery included a Personal Information Questionnaire, the BP, and the DPI. The following characteristics typified the *ulcer pts.* They attempted to conceal signs of psychological disturbance in almost all areas of psychological conflict. They avoided expression of hostile feelings, feelings of inadequacy, and feelings of fear of punishment. They emphasized the approving and tolerant attitudes of the parents and their own masculine adequacy. They were involved in an inner struggle to control expression of attitudes and needs unacceptable to their self-imposed demands for exemplary behavior. Tension and anxiety accompanied these attempts at control. The *asthmatics* were less defensive than the ulcer Ss. They indicated a greater preference for avoidance and a lower preference for reaction formation as defenses. Over attachment to the mother was the focus of their psychological disturbance. She was, for them, the object of attitudes of both intense love and hate, and was regarded as the decisive disciplinarian. The asthmatics were intensely hostile toward other members of the family who threatened to come between them and the mother. In their love relationships, they preferred a mother-like love object. Neither the nonulcerated gastrointestinal pts nor the nonpsychosomatic pts were very clearly distinguished from the others. However, the former gp as well as the ulcer and asthma pts, were psychologically more disturbed than the nonpsychosomatic Ss. It was concluded that specific pers features are exhibited by the inds who manifest the symptoms of these 3 psychosomatic syndromes. These features are most similar to those cited by Alexander and his coworkers as etiologically significant for these illnesses.

162.   Pryor, D. B. Regression in the service of the ego: Psychosexual development and ego functions. *D A*, Michigan State University, 1962.   (No. 63-1750)

The BP and 3 cards of the Rorschach were admin to 60 m coll students. Rorschach responses were scored by the Holt system, yielding measures of primary process, secondary process, control and defense, and an estimated psychic level. The correls relating to the hypoths were in the expected direction, but few of them reached sig. It was suggested that both the progressive and regressive ego functions may be related to early development and that the mode of reaction must be considered in this relationship as well as the point of organ fixation. It was also suggested that the same ind probably has both adaptive and unadaptive ego movements and that the relationship of each of these to development may be quite different.

163. Reed, W. W. Parent-child relationships reflected by the Blacky Pictures test. *D A,* University of Nebraska, 1955. (No. 14,352)

Study was designed to test a number of specific hypoths concerning parent-child relationships as reflected by the BP. As a secondary phase of the investigation husband-wife relationships, and the relation of marriage adjustment to over-all psy-sex disturbance were investigated. Ss used consisted of 30 families, composed of one child in kindergarten and at least one other child. The children included 16 five-year-olds and 14 six-year-olds, and within this gp there were 14 boys and 16 girls. BP were admin to the mother, father, and the child, and the Marriage Adjustment Form to the mother and father. The data provided support for 3 of the 10 hypoths. Ora Ero, Ana Ret, and Ego Id disturbances in parents were sig related to the same disturbances in their children. In the parent-child comparisons 8 sig relations were obtained, and only 2 would be expected by chance. Marriage adjustment was not sig related to the over-all psy-sex disturbance of either parent or the child. Certain hypoths regarding parent-child relationships received strong support from the data obtained with the BP.

164. Robinson, S. A. A comparison of expressed acceptance of self and of others and responses on the Blacky Pictures of two adolescent groups. *D A I, 28*(4-A):1311, 1967.

21 delinquent and 21 non-delinquent females completed the Berger Questionnaire measure of acceptance of self and others and 2 forms of the BP, one of which used cats as the central figures. Delinquents expressed less self-acceptance than the non-delinquents. The gps did not differ on any of the 30 BP scoring dimens. The cat and dog BP forms differed sig on the dimen of Sugar Coating, Disguised Oedipal Involvement, Over-

whelming Castration Conflict and Evasion of Identification Issues.

165.　Rosen, I. C.　A comparison of a group of rapists and controls on certain selected variables.　Unpublished doctoral dissertation, University of Pittsburgh, 1952.

166.　Segal, A.　Prediction of expressed attitudes toward the mother. *D A,* University of Michigan, 1954.

(No. 8407)

An attempt to predict actual behavior by knowing an individual's underlying drives and by knowing his characteristic mode of defending himself against unacceptable drives.　A model situation was designed to test the accuracy of predictions made on this basis.　This was the feelings toward the mother that would be expressed in an interview by girls who had similar strengths of hostility or dependency drives toward the mother, but who utilized different defense mechanisms.　The BP, selected TAT cards and the DPI were admin to 61 fem coll students.　It was concluded that defense is a crucial variable which must be taken into consideration when attempting to understand and predict behavior, and that the strength of the drive also must be taken into account.

167.　Sharma, S. L.　The genesis of the authoritarian personality. *D A,* University of Michigan, 1957.

(L. C. Card No. Mic 58-989)

Investigated the genesis and some of the behavioral correlates of the authoritarian pers as described by Frenkel-Brunswik.　*S*s were 32 m and 32 fem undergraduates.　They were admin the California Predisposition to Fascism (F) Scale, BP, DPI, scales from the CPI measuring Tolerance, Flexibility and Self-Acceptance, a Negro Attitude scale, and the Einstellung Arithmetic test.　The major contributions were (a) experimental confirmation of Frenkel-Brunswik's speculations concerning the role of anal and oedipal conflict in authoritarianism, (b) suggestive evidence concerning the importance of masturbation guilt in authoritarianism, and a suggestion concerning the role of oral conflict, (c) the suggestion that authoritarianism, itself, may serve as a defense against dependency needs, and (d) the establishment of certain important behavioral correlates of, and sex diffs in, the genesis and manifestation of authoritarianism.

168. Shellow, R. S. Perceptual distortion in the spatial localization of emotionally meaningful stimuli. *D A,* University of Michigan, 1956. (No. 18,649)

The basic hypoth was that disturbing stimuli would differ from nondisturbing stimuli, when the *S*'s task was to estimate the size of stimulus objects and their distance from him. The BP and DPI were admin to 28 coll women and 30 men. The results supported a simple avoidance notion of defense. No relationship was found to exist between distance, size, or visual angle settings of threatening stimuli and defenses manifest on the DPI. Almost all *S*s made threatening stimuli take up less visual space than neutral simuli.

169. Shire, A. Personality correlates of defense preferences. *D A,* University of Michigan, 1954. (No. 7724)

Study explored: (1) the relationship presumed to exist between an inflexible defense structure and the pers dimens of rigidity and maladjustment; (2) pers correlates of preferences among psy-ana defense mechanisms. The DPI, Group Rorschach and the *I* and *N* factors of the G-M were used. *S*s were 135 coll students; one gp of 90 specific defenders and another gp of 45 general defenders. Two general hypoths were tested: (1) the general defenders are more disturbed psychologically than the specific defenders, and (2) with the exception of the gp selecting regression as the preferred defense, are more inflexible in their perceptions, attitudes, and values than the specific defenders. The first hypoth was confirmed. The second hypoth was not confirmed.

170. Sinnett, E. R. An experimental investigation of the Defense Preference Inquiry for the Blacky Pictures. *D A, 13*:442, 1953.

DPI rankings were studied in 117 coll males for 3 areas of conflict: Ora Sad, Oed Int, and Sib Riv. Projection and reaction formation were associated with diffs in the conflict areas of Ora Sad, and reaction formation was likewise related to sibling rivalry conflict. Recall of story content was also measured and was related to defense preference. The author suggested that the defensive process alters the conflict material through selective perception and selective forgetting, thereby influencing story recall. The DPI was considered a promising defense measure.

171. Sirota, L. M. A factor analysis of selected personality domains. *D A,* University of Michigan, 1957.
(L. C. Card No. Mic 58-1462)

A test of the general theoretical assumption that there is a coherent structure underlying pers which manifests itself in widely different behaviors. Scores on 136 variables were available for 44 m coll Ss. A master matrix showed that 75 of the 136 variables were sig interrelated.

172. Taylor, K. E. A comparison of a group of pedophiliacs and controls on certain psychological variables. Unpublished doctoral dissertation, University of Pittsburgh, 1952.

173. Thelen, M. H. Similarities of defense preferences within families, within sex groups, and their relationship to parental identification in adolescent males. *D A,* Michigan State University, 1964.

50 m HS students and both of their parents completed the DPI and the Block Adjective Check List. Similarities between check list descriptions were used as indices of ident. The adolescents were more similar to their fathers in defense preference (DP) than to unrelated adult males, though this similarity was itself not related to paternal ident. The adolescents showed no more similarity to their mothers in DP than to unrelated adult females, and DP similarity was again unrelated to maternal ident. The mothers and fathers did not differ in DP, though the fathers were sig more heterogeneous than the mothers in DP. The adolescents' DP were no more similar to their father than to their mother.

174. Thomas, R. W. An investigation of the psychoanalytic theory of homosexuality. *D A,* University of Kentucky, 1951.   (L. C. Card No. Mic 60-112)

The *E* gp consisted of 40 overtly homosexual m veterans of WW-II. They were divided into active and passive homosexual gps on the basis of their preference for the active or passive role in intercourse. The *C* gp consisted of 20 hosp veterans. These men showed no homosexual content on their Rorschach Tests. The MMPI and BP were admin. Results of the BP: (1) Theory states that all homosexuals have regressed to the early oral stage of psy-sex development. This was not supported. (2) Active homosexuals showed a marked disturbance at the Ora Sad level. (3) No hypoth made concerning Ana Exp. (4) Theory states that passive homosexuals are fixated at the anal stage. Since the aim of Ana Ret is more passive than in Ana Exp, it was hypoth that they would show disturbance at the Ana Ret phase. The hypoth was supported. (5) One of the important causes of homosexuality is an inadequately resolved Oed complex, which persists as oed intensity. Theory supported. (6) Active homosexuals would show masturbation guilt. Hypoth was not supported. (7) Cas Anx is a very important consideration in the etiology of homosexuality. It is the castration anxiety which causes a homosexual man to choose another man for a love object. Not supported. (8) They have a feminine instead of a masculine ident. Theory supported. (9) Psy-ana theorizes a special type of homosexuality caused by intense sibling rivalry. Hatred toward the older sibling is over-compensated into love and results in homosexuality. Evaluation of the results of this investigation with theory is not possible. (10) Inferred that homosexuals would show disturbance in the area of Pos Ego Id. This inference was made because homosexuals show difficulty in the resolution of the oedipal complex and in positive ident. Inference supported. (11) Active homosexuals choose a Narcissistic Love Object. Study shows that active homosexuals choose more Narcissistic Love Objects than did the passive homosexuals. (12) Passive homosexuals choose Anaclytic Love Object. Theory supported. (13) Passive homosexuals act and feel like women. Therefore, they should reveal marked feminine interests on the Mf scale of the MMPI. Theory supported. (14) Active homosexuals are men in every respect and there is nothing effeminate about them. Theory not supported.

175. Tober, L. H.   An investigation of the personality dynamics and behavior patterns of older people in a

mental hospital as measured by the Blacky Pictures and a Q-rating scale of behavior. Unpublished doctoral dissertation, Western Reserve University, 1953.

176. Vroom, A. L. W. A validation study of the Blacky Analogies Test. *D A,* University of Michigan, 1959.
(L. C. Card No. Mic 60-2582)

It was hypoth that the BP would arouse anxiety which would tend to affect test performance. The BAT, intellectual measures, and an anxiety measure were admin to 187 fem and 114 m freshmen. Results: (1) Factor analysis of the BAT items for the males revealed only one clear factor, identified as Letter Manipulation. (2) Eight orthogonal factors were extracted from the test battery intercorrels. (3) The BAT loaded most highly on Verbal Flexibility for the fem *S*s. (4) It was found that the entire common variance of the BAT was neary equal to its reliable variance. (5) The correl between the BAT and GPA was .43 and .34 for the m and fem samples respectively. (6) The BAT was found to be a better predictor of GPA than high school percentile rank for the females, and to improve the prediction of GPA of men when included in a multiple correl with HS percentile rank. (7) Prediction of grades from the BAT fell roughly in the same range as predictions from subtests of the ACE Psychological Examination and the ACE Cooperative English Test, C_2: Reading Comprehension.

177. Watson, D. J. Some social-psychological correlates of personality. Unpublished doctoral dissertation, University of Michigan, 1953.

*S*s were 100 NTL gp members. The BPT was studied in relation to selected demographic and behavioral variables, including the AVSV, response to induction from authorities and from a peer gp, perceptions about one's role in the gp, and sociometric popularity ratings. A pers typology, based upon the BPT, was found to be consistent with psy-ana theory.

178. Weingarten, L. Correlates of ambivalence toward parental figures. *D A,* University of Michigan, 1962.
(No. 63-5030)

The BP, DPI, Minkowich ambivalence test, a measure devised to
tap evaluations of parental behavior, and biographical questionnaire were admin to 62 coll males. *B* factor correlates suggested
that *S*s who were ambivalent toward mother have unresolved
oedipal attachments. They appear simultaneously attracted and
repelled by the maternal figure and express feelings of oral crav-
ing and resentment over oral deprivation. They revealed aggressive oral and anal impulses. *S*s with ambivalent attitudes toward
father manifested anal hostility and disturbances in masculine
ident. They also seemed threatened by a love object exhibiting
maternal characteristics. With respect to defense mechanisms,
ambivalence toward mother was associated with the choice of
projection and regression items, as well as a general preference
for the expression of emotional conflict. Ambivalence toward
father was not as clearly related to specific defense patterns but
high-scoring *S*s revealed rigid defense choices across psy-sex
areas. The family attitudes questionnaire showed both perceived paternal rejection and maternal dominance in childrearing to be associated with higher ambivalence scores toward
mother. No major relationships were found with ambivalence
toward father. Many of the results in previous studies linking
ambivalence and biographical data were replicated in the present
research. Severe, especially corporal, discipline was more often
noted by ambivalent *S*s in the case of mother and father. Those
less ambivalent reported more frequent reward and infrequent
punishment. Maternal noninvolvement and inconsistent discipline appeared related to ambivalent reactions, especially toward mother. Ambivalent *S*s generally rejected the importance
of inculcating moral standards and preferred less parental control in childrearing. The specific disciplinary techniques associated with lower ambivalence were reasoning or explaining the
child's mistakes and withholding privileges. Conversely, sham-
ing or making the child feel guilty, and spanking or slapping,
were linked with higher ambivalence scores, especially toward
mother. Also, there was a marked tendency for Catholic sons
to be ambivalent toward mother. Other positive correlates were
sibling death and the presence of many brothers and sisters. In
conclusion, the salient empirical findings were elaborated in
terms of their contribution to a potentially sound theory of the
causes and concomitants of ambivalence toward parental
figures.

179. Weiss, J.   An experimental study of the psychodynamics
      of humor. *D A,* Univesrity of Michigan, 1955.
                                                    (No. 11,371)

The relationships between 2 major pers variables and 3 aspects
of humor behavior were explored using 45 members of a social
fraternity. The BP and a new auxiliary measure (Picture Problem Ranks) were used to evaluate the intensity of conflict related to 5 dimens of early psy-sex development: Ora Ero, Ana
Exp, Oed Int, and Cas Anx. The DPI and several supplementary
indices were utilized for the assessment of preferences among
the following 5 defenses: avoidance (including repression and
denial), reaction formation, projection, regression and intellectualization. The aspects of humor behavior studied were: (1)
enjoyment, (2) recall or repression, and (3) the use of humor
in daily interpersonal relationships. The following conclusions
were drawn concerning the role of pers in the response to psy-
chosexually meaningful humor: (1) the repression of humor is
related to (a) preference for the defense of avoidance and (b)
the presence of strong conflict; (2) the enjoyment of humor
is related to (a) preference for the defense of regression, (b) the
absence of conflict in the dimen of Ora Sad, and (c) the presence of conflict in the dimen of Ana Exp.

180. White, J. L.   Attitudes toward child rearing as related to
      some psychodynamic factors in mothers. *D A,* Michi-
      gan State University, 1961.   (No. 62-1694)

Major purpose was to examine the relationship between extreme
patterns of mothering and maternal pers dynamics as formulated by psy-ana theory. *S*s were 72 mothers, primarily wives of
coll students. Instruments used were the BP, DPI, and a version
of the Parental Attitude Survey Instrument. The findings offered partial support for the general prediction that mothers designated as extreme in their child rearing attitudes would show
stronger evidence of emotional disturbance than mothers not
classified as extreme.

181. Winter, L. M.   Development of a scoring system for the
      children's form of the Blacky Pictures. *D A,* Univer-
      sity of Michigan, 1956.   (No. 19,728)

Major objective was to explore the possibility of developing an objective scoring system for research use of the BP. The study made used 2 gps of school children in the 3rd and 4th grades. First gp was 30 boys and 30 girls. A cross-validation gp of 40 children was used. The source of criterion data were a number of diverse measures. In conclusion, it appeared that routine school measures of the type employed in the study can be used to derive behavioral criteria for research on psy-ana theory.

182. Winter, W. D. The prediction of life history data and personality characteristics of ulcer patients from responses to the Blacky Pictures. *D A,* University of Michigan, 1954.   (No. 7767)

On the basis of earlier findings, the BP were examined and those responses most characteristic of each pers pattern in pts with peptic ulcers were selected. The items were than combined into 2 scales, designated as "Primary" (P) and "Reactive" (R). Briefly, the P scale describes an ind who is overtly dependent, demanding, disgruntled, and immature. The R scale measures the pattern more typically thought to be characteristic of ulcer pts: overt self-sufficient, high drive to achieve, and little ability to tolerate their own passive-dependent needs. Ss were 68 m veterans with duodenal ulcers. Of the 43 predictions made, 20 were sig at the .10 level or better. Two general conclusions can be drawn from the study. (1) The "typical" ulcer pers is not found in all peptic ulcer pts. (2) At least 2 different pers patterns are found in people with ulcers, and these can be validly measured by the B scales developed in the investigation.

183. Wirls, C. Personality and breast feeding. Unpublished doctoral dissertation, Western Reserve University, 1957.

The BPT was used to determine if there were pers diffs between mothers who breastfed, planned to breastfeed but did not, did not plan to breastfeed. Out of 78 comparisons, 6 were statistically significant. Four of the sig diffs supported the hypoths and the other two, although not predicted, were consonant with the other results and the theory.

Author Index

Subject Index

Physiological correlates (cont'd)
104, 125, 145
Positive Identification. *See* Identi-
fication
Primary scale (BPT): 5
Prisoners: 153
Projection: 6, 16, 38, 84, 155,
167, 170, 178, 180
Psychoanalytic theory: 12, 14, 20,
25, 30, 68, 79, 87, 93, 102
Psychologists, ratings: 51
Psychosis, post-partum: 138
Psychosomatics. *See* Subjects,
psychosomatics

Reaction Formation: 6, 16, 84,
86, 140, 155, 167, 168, 170,
179
Reactive scale (BPT): 5
Reading retardation: 129
References: *bibliographies* 98,
113; *books and manuals* 11,
21, 25; *book chapters* 19, 20,
23; *reviews* 4, 52, 56, 61, 94,
102, 103
Regression: 6, 16, 35, 155, 162,
169, 178, 179
Reliability: 7, 17, 34, 36, 51, 56,
57, 144
Religion: 87, 89
Repression: 15, 86, 140, 159,
168, 179
Rheumatic fever: 72
Rheumatoid arthritis: 58, 64, 149

Scoring. *See* Administration and
Scoring
Screening, adjustment: 31, 77
Self-concept: 44, 70
Sex differences: 12, 46, 79, 84,

Sex differences (cont'd)
93, 95, 100, 108, 139, 143, 147,
155, 167, 176
Sex role: 70
Sexual arousal: 97
Sexually deviant. *See* Subjects,
sexual offenders
Sibling Rivalry: 67, 89, 106, 119,
133, 145, 170, 174
Smoking: 62
Social desirability: 108
Stress: 139
Stuttering: 32, 49, 75, 127, 132
Subjects, *see also* particular diagnostic groups: *adolescents* 48,
54, 63, 91, 92, 104, 127, 147,
154, 163, 164, 173; *children* 19,
30, 41, 42, 44, 54, 57, 58, 59,
72, 76, 89, 96, 124, 127, 129,
130, 132, 133, 137, 146, 163,
181; *college students* 1, 7, 12,
16, 24, 45, 55, 62, 71, 74, 82,
84, 85, 99, 100, 114, 118, 120,
125, 131, 147, 151, 155, 160,
162, 166, 168, 169, 170, 171,
176, 178; *military personnel* 31,
37, 47, 50; *normal* 3, 8, 9, 10,
29, 31, 50, 77, 123, 126, 129,
133, 138, 141, 158, 159, 163;
prisoners 153; *psychoneurotics*
51, 123, 141; *psychosomatic
patients, see also* Ulcer patients
8, 58, 107, 141, 161; *Schizophrenics (psychiatirc patients
and other psychotics)* 3, 6, 125,
126, 144, 145, 157, 158, 175;
sexual offenders 69, 109, 153,
165, 172
Superego: 155
Surgical patients: 5, 67, 137

APPENDIX A

Abbreviations

ACE	American College Entrance Examination
admin	administered
AGCT	Army General Classification Test
alcoh(s)	alcoholic(s)
AMA	Against Medical Advice
Ana Lo Obj	Anaclitic Love Object dimension, Blacky Test
Ana Exp	Anal Expulsive dimension, BT
Ana Ret	Anal Retentive dimension, BT
Ana Sad	Anal Sadistic dimension, BT
A-V (AVSV)	Allport-Vernon Study of Values
B, BP, BPT	Blacky, Blacky Pictures, Blacky Pictures Test
BAT	Blacky Analogies Test
C	control subject(s) or group(s)
Cas Anx	Castration Anxiety dimension, BT
CAT	Children's Apperception Test
CMAS	Children's Manifest Anxiety Scale
CMI	Cornell Medical Index
coll	college
correl(s)	correlation(s), correlated
CPI	California Psychological Inventory
D	Depression Scale, MMPI (Scale 2)
DA (I)	Dissertation Abstracts (International)
DAP	Draw-A-Person Test
diff(s)	difference(s)

dimen(s)	dimension(s)
DOM, dom	Dominance-Submission Axis of the ICL; dominance
DP, DPI	Defense Preference; Defense Preference Inquiry

E	experimental subject(s) or group(s)
Ego Id	Ego Ideal dimension, BT
EPPS	Edwards Personal Preference Schedule
Es	Ego Strength Scale, MMPI

F	Validity Scale, MMPI
Fe	Femininity Scale (Gough), MMPI
fem	female
FIRO-B	Fundamental Interpersonal Relations Orientation—Behavior

Glt Fee	Guilt Feelings dimension, BT
G-M	Guilford-Martin
gp(s)	group(s)
GPA	Grade Point Average
GSR	galvanic skin response
GZTS	Guilford-Zimmerman Temperament Survey

HS	high school
Hs	Hypochondriasis Scale, MMPI (Scale *1*)
hosp	hospital, hospitalized
Hy	Hysteria scale, MMPI (Scale *3*)
HyD	Denial of Hysteria Scale, MMPI
hypoth(s)	hypothesis, hypotheses, hypothesized

IAV	Index of Adjustment & Values (Bills)
ICL	Interpersonal Check List
ident	identification
I-E	Internal-External Locus of Control Scale (Rotter)
ind(s)	individual(s)

inpt(s)	inpatient(s)
interpers	interpersonal
IPAS	Institute of Personality Assessment
IPAT	Institute for Personality and Ability Testing
IS	Interpersonal System (Leary)
ISB	Incomplete Sentence Blank
K	Correction Scale, MMPI
L	Lie Scale, MMPI
Level I	Public behavior, Interpersonal System (MMPI)
Level II	Conscious descriptions, Interpersonal System (ICL)
Level III	Pre-conscious, Interpersonal System (Level III-TAT or III-MMPI)
Lo Obj	Love Object, BT
LOV	Love-Hate Axis of the ICL
m	male
Ma	Manic Scale, MMPI (Scale *9*)
MAS (TMAS)	Manifest Anxiety Scale, Taylor
MAS (Locke)	Marital Adjustment Scale (Locke)
Mas Glt	Masturbation Guilt dimension, BT
Mf	Masculinity-femininity Scale, MMPI (Scale *5*)
MCH(s)	Mental Hygiene Clinic(s)
MMPI	Minnesota Multiphasic Personality Inventory
MSS	Marital Success Scale (Wallace)
MTAT	Minnesota Teacher Aptitude Test
Nar Lo Obj	Narcissistic Love Object dimension, BT
Octant(s)	
1	Managerial—Autocratic
2	Competitive—Narcissistic
3	Aggressive—Sadistic

Octant(s) (cont'd)

4	Rebellious—Distrustful
5	Self-effacing—Masochistic
6	Docile-Dependent
7	Cooperative—Over-controlled
8	Responsible—Hypernormal
Oed Int	Oedipal Intensity dimension, BT
OMI	Opinion about Mental Illness Scale
Ora Ero	Oral Eroticism dimension, BT
Ora Sad	Oral Sadism dimension, BT
outpt(s)	outpatient(s)

Pa	Paranoia Scale, MMPI (Scale *6*)
Pd	Psychopathic Deviate Scale, MMPI (Scale *4*)
Pen Env	Penis Envy dimension, BT
pers	personality
P-F Study	Picture-Frustration Study (Rosenzweig)
PgR	Barron's Ego Strength Scale, MMPI
Pos Ide	Positive Identification dimension, BT
psy-ana	psychoanalytic, psychoanalysis
psych	psychiatry, psychiatric
psy-sex	psycho-sexual
Pt	Psychasthenia Scale, MMPI (Scale 7)
pt(s)	patient(s)

rehab	rehabilitation
R-S	Repression-Sensitization Scale, MMPI

S(s)	subject(s)
SAT	Scholastic Aptitude Test
S-B	Stanford-Binet
Sc	Schizophrenia Scale, MMPI (Scale *8*)
SD	social desirability
SDQ	Self-Disclosure Questionnaire (Jourard)
SDSV	Social Desirability Scale Values
SES	Socioeconomic status
Si	Social Introversion Scale, MMPI (Scale *0*)
Sib Riv	Sibling Rivalry dimension, BT
sig	significance, significant, significantly

| STAI | State-Trait Anxiety Inventory (Spielberger) |
| SVIB | Strong Vocational Interest Blank |

TAT	Thematic Apperception Test
TB	tuberculosis, tuberculous
TSCS	Tennessee Self-Concept Scale

WA	Word Association test
WAIS	Wechsler Adult Intelligence Scale
WISC	Wechsler Intelligence Scale for Children

| 16PF | Sixteen Personality Factor Questionnaire |

| ? | Cannot Say Scale, MMPI |

APPENDIX B

Journal References and Abbreviations

Acta Psiquiátrica y Psicológica de América Latina (*Acta Psiquiatry Psicol America Latina*)

Alberta Journal of Educational Research (*Alberta J Educ Res*)

American Journal of Obstetrics & Gynecology (*Am J Obstet Gynecol*)

American Journal of Orthopsychiatry (*Am J Orthopsychiatry*)

American Journal of Psychiatry (*Am J Psychiatry*)

American Psychologist (*Am Psychol*)

American Review of Respiratory Disease (*Am Rev Respir Dis*)

Archives of General Psychiatry (*Arch Gen Psychiatry*)

Archives of Neurology & Psychiatry (*Arch Neurol Psychiatry*)

Archives of Sexual Behavior (*Arch Sex Behav*)

British Journal of Projective Psychology & Personality Study (*Br J Proj Psychol Pers Study*)

British Journal of Social & Clinical Psychology (*Br J Soc Clin Psychol*)

Bulletin of the Menninger Clinic (*Bull Menninger Clin*)

Canadian Journal of Behavioural Science (*Can J Behav Sci*)

Catalog of Selected Documents in Psychology (*Catalog Select Documents Psychol*)

Ceskoslovenská Psychiatrie (*Ceskosl Psychiatrie*)

Contemporary Psychology (*Contemp Psychol*)

Counselor Education & Supervision (*Counselor Educ Supv*)

Diseases of the Nervous System (*Dis Nerv Syst*)

Educational & Psychological Measurement (*Educ Psychol Measmt*)

Engineering Industrial Psychology (*Engng Industr Psychol*)

Genetic Psychology Monographs (*Genet Psychol Monogr*)

Group Psychotherapy (*Gp Psychother*)

Human Relations (*Hum Relations*)

International Journal of the Addictions (*Int J Addict*)

International Journal of Aging & Human Development (*Int J Aging Human Dev*)

International Journal of Neuropsychiatry   (*Int J Neuropsychiatry*)

International Journal of Social Psychiatry (*Int J Soc Psychiatry*)

International Review of Applied Psychology (*Int Rev Appl Psychol*)

Journal of Abnormal & Child Psychology (*J Abnorm Child Psychol*)

Journal of Abnormal & Social Psychology (*J Abnorm Soc Psychol*)

Journal of Clinical Psychology (*J Clin Psychol*)

Journal of Consulting Psychology (*J Consult Psychol*)

Journal of Consulting & Clinical Psychology (*J Consult Clin Psychol*)

Journal of Counseling Psychology (*J Counsel Psychol*)

Journal of Drug Issues (*J Drug Issues*)

Journal of Educational Research (*J Educ Res*)

Journal of Experimental Research in Personality (*J Exper Res Pers*)

Journal of General Psychology (*J Gen Psychol*)

Journal of Genetic Psychology (*J Genet Psychol*)

Journal of Marriage & the Family (*J of Marriage and the Family*)

Journal of Nervous & Mental Disease (*J Nerv Ment Dis*)

Journal of Personality (*J Pers*)

Journal of Personality Assessment (*J Pers Assess*)

Journal of Personality & Social Psychology (*J Pers Soc Psychol*)

Journal of Projective Techniques (*J Proj Tech*)
Journal of Projective Techniques & Personality Assessment (*J Proj Tech Pers Assess*)
Journal of Psychology (*J Psychol*)
Journal of Psychosomatic Research (*J Psychosom Res*)
Journal of Research in Personality (*J Res Pers*)
Journal of Social Psychology (*J Soc Psychol*)
Journal of Teacher Education (*J Teacher Educ*)

Multivariate Behavioral Research (*Multivariate Behav Res*)

Nursing Research (*Nurs Res*)

Perceptual & Motor Skills (*Percept Mot Skills*)
Personality (*Personality*)
Personnel & Guidance Journal (*Personnel Guid J*)
Proceedings of the 73rd Annual Convention of the American Psychological Association (*Proc 73rd Annu Conv Am Psychol Assoc*)
Professional Psychology (*Prof Psychol*)
Przeglad Psychologiczny (*Przeglad Psychologiczny*)
Psychiatric Quarterly (*Psychiatr Q*)
Psychiatric Research (*Psychiatr Res*)
Psychiatry (*Psychiatry*)
Psychological Bulletin (*Psychol Bull*)
Psychological Record (*Psychol Rec*)
Psychological Report (*Psychol Rep*)
Psychological Review (*Psychol Rev*)
Psychology in the Schools (*Psychology in the Schools*)
Psychology Newsletter (*Psychol Newsltr*)
Psychosocial Rehabilitation Journal (*Psychosoc Rehabil J*)
Psychophysiology (*Psychophysiology*)
Psychosomatic Medicine (*Psychosom Med*)
Psychosomatics (*Psychosomatics*)
Psychotherapy & Psychosomatics (*Psychother Psychosom*)

Quarterly Journal of Child Behavior (*Q J Child Behav*)
Quarterly Journal of Studies on Alcohol (*Q J Stud Alcohol*)

Rehabilitation Counseling Bulletin (*Rehabil Counsel Bull*)
Revue de Psychologie Appliquee (*Rev Psicol Appl*)

Small Group Behavior (*Small Group Behavior*)
Sociology & Social Research (*Sociol Soc Res*)
Sociometry (*Sociometry)*
Southern Journal of Educational Research (*South J Educ Res*)
Southern Medical Journal (*South Med J*)
SPATE

Weight Control (*Weight Control*)
Western Psychologist (*West Psychol*)